In accordance with neo-liberal doctrine, a free market in ideas, information, finance, goods and services gradually pervaded our lives from the 1970s. However, free market doctrine is notably absent in international migration policies. Here three major social actors are in play:

- Employers who often want to increase the supply of imported labourers, either because they cannot find suitable local workers or because they wish to reduce their labour costs.
- Migrants who are often stopped, but sometimes bypass border control illegally, through being trafficked or at their own initiative.
- Politicians who are under pressure, often from local workers and sometimes from extreme xenophobic elements, to restrict immigration.

In this book, Robin Cohen shows how the preferences, interests and actions of global capital, migrant labour and national politicians intersect and often contradict each other. Does capital require subordinated labour? Is it possible for capital to move to labour rather than labour to capital? Can trade substitute for migration? Cohen explores how nation-states segment the 'insiders' from the 'outsiders' and how politically powerless migrants relate to more privileged migrants and the national citizenry, discussing the functions and effects of social exclusion and deportations. He asks whether politicians can effectively control national borders even if they wish to do so.

These important questions are addressed in a wide-ranging, lucid and accessible narrative, offering readers a compelling account of the historical origins and contemporary dynamics of global migration.

Robin Cohen is ESRC Professional Research Fellow and Professor of Sociology at the University of Warwick. He served as Dean of Humanities at the University of Cape Town in 2001-3, and directed the nationally designated UK Centre for Research in Ethnic Relations from 1985-9. He has also held academic positions in Nigeria, the Caribbean, the USA and Canada. His many books include *The New Helots: Migrants in the International Division of Labour* (1988); *The Cambridge Survey of World Migration* (edited, 1995); *Global Diasporas: An Introduction* (1997) and *Global Sociology* (co-authored with Paul Kennedy, 2000). His work has been translated into Danish, French, German, Greek, Italian, Japanese, Mandarin, Portuguese and Spanish.

Research in Migration and Ethnic Relations Series

Series Editor:
Maykel Verkuyten, ERCOMER
Utrecht University

The Research in Migration and Ethnic Relations series has been at the forefront of research in the field for ten years. The series has built an international reputation for cutting edge theoretical work, for comparative research especially on Europe and for nationally-based studies with broader relevance to international issues. Published in association with the European Research Centre on Migration and Ethnic Relations (ERCOMER), Utrecht University, it draws contributions from the best international scholars in the field, offering an interdisciplinary perspective on some of the key issues of the contemporary world.

Other titles in the series

International Migration Research: Constructions, Omissions and the Promises of Interdisciplinarity
Edited by Michael Bommes and Ewa Morawska
ISBN 0 7546 4219 4

East to West Migration: Russian Migrants in Western Europe
Helen Kopnina
ISBN 0 7546 4170 8

**EUROPEAN RESEARCH CENTRE
ON MIGRATION & ETHNIC RELATIONS**

Migration and its Enemies

Global Capital, Migrant Labour and the Nation-State

ROBIN COHEN
University of Warwick, UK

ASHGATE

© Robin Cohen 2006

Published by
Ashgate Publishing Limited
Gower House
Croft Road
Aldershot
Hampshire GU11 3HR
England

Ashgate Publishing Company
Suite 420
101 Cherry Street
Burlington, VT 05401-4405
USA

Ashgate website: http://www.ashgate.com

British Library Cataloguing in Publication Data
Cohen, Robin, 1944-
   Migration and its enemies : global capital, migrant labour
   and the nation-state. - (Research in migration and ethnic
   relations series)
   1.Alien labor 2.Emigration and immigration - Economic
   aspects 3.Emigration and immigration - Government policy
   4.Alien labor - Great Britain 5.Great Britain - Emigration
   and immigration - Economic aspects 6.Great Britain -
   Emigration and immigration - Government policy
   I.Title
   331.6'2

Library of Congress Control Number: 2005933809

ISBN 0 7546 4657 2 (Hbk)
ISBN 0 7546 4658 0 (Pbk)

Typeset by Oxford Publishing Services.
Printed and bound in Great Britain by TJ International Ltd, Padstow, Cornwall.

Contents

Acknowledgements

The author and publishers would like to make the following acknowledgements:

The principal title of this book was found in the title of one of the subsections of an edited book by Leo Lucassen and Jan Lucassen (eds) *Migration, migration history, history, old paradigms and new perspectives* (Bern: Peter Lang AG Europäishcher Verlag der Wissenschaften, 1997, p. 223).

While a number of the chapters are drawn from earlier work, several are from recent essays. They all have been thoroughly revised for this publication in the hope that the book as a whole will contribute to the intellectual, political and ethical understanding of migration and its enemies. Some of the argument in the Introduction was rehearsed in a contribution to *Index on Censorship* (32 (2), May 2003, 60–9). Material in Chapter 1 is drawn from Robin Cohen, *The new helots* (Aldershot: Gower 1987, 1–30). Chapter 2 is based on a paper given to the World Forum on Workers' Movements and the Working Class organized by the Braudel Center, NY, the Maison des Sciences de l'Homme, Paris, and the Institute for Labour Studies, Moscow (19–21 June 1991). A section of the paper was published as 'East–West and European Migration in a Global Context' (*New Community*, 18 (1) October 1991, 9–26). Chapter 3 was first published in Leo Lucassen and Jan Lucassen (eds) *Migration, migration history, history, old paradigms and new perspectives* (Bern: Peter Lang AG Europäishcher Verlag der Wissenschaften, 1997, 351–73). Chapter 4 was presented as a paper for a conference on *Immigrazione sterotipi pregiudizi* organized by the Università di Roma 'La Sapienza' and the Consiglio nazionale delle ricerche (Rome, 5–7 April 1995) and is revised here for publication in English. Chapter 5 is drawn from a previously unpublished report (1995) and is revised here for publication. Chapter 6 was first published in the *Hitotsubashi Journal of Social Studies* (21 (1) August 1989, 153–65) and subsequently in Robin Cohen, *Contested domains: debates in international labour studies* (London: Zed Books, 1991, 151–80). Chapter 7 was first published in Malcolm Cross (ed.) *Ethnic minorities and industrial change in Europe and North America* (Cambridge: Cambridge University Press, 1991, 19–35). Chapter 8 was given as a paper to a conference on 'International Migration and Globalization' convened by the Portuguese Social Science Council, *Casa de Mateus* (Portugal, 4–5 October 2002) and was revised for publication in English in a forthcoming issue of *Labour, Capital and Society*. Chapter 9 was presented at the first joint ESRC/SSRC colloquium on Money and Migration, St Hugh's College, University of Oxford (25–28 March 2004) and was posted on the web at www.csgr.org.

For comments on Chapter 3 I would like to thank Jan and Leo Lucassen. For help in securing the data for Chapter 5 my thanks go to Anne Shaw at the Resources Centre, Centre for Research in Ethnic Relations, Warwick University; Diana Zinnerman, at the Center for Migration Studies, Staten Island, New York; the Librarians at the Refugee Studies Programme, Oxford University and Sharon Molteno for using her youthful eyesight to summarize the contents of an indistinct micro-film. Chapter 8 includes some text from joint publications with Paul Kennedy and Steven Vertovec. Although I recall the text concerned as my own draft inevitably there is some 'crossover' in joint writing and I am grateful for their permission to use these passages. Stan Cohen provided a vignette, also in Chapter 8. I wish to thank Eleni Tsingou and Sian Sullivan for comments on Chapter 9 and Martin Ruhs for giving me his joint paper with Ha-Joon Chang, which has been used here.

For the book as a whole, I wish to thank Selina Cohen warmly for her editorial and production help and Jason Cohen for redrawing the graphs. I also proffer my thanks to Maykel Verkuyten, the academic editor of this series, who facilitated publication of this volume. Caroline Wintersgill and Mary Savigar were creative and supportive editors at Ashgate. Richard Higgott was instrumental in arranging a part-time attachment to the Centre for the Study of Globalisation and Regionalisation at Warwick University, which gave me valuable research and writing time. My thanks go to him and to the co-director of the Centre, Jan Aart Scholte.

Robin Cohen

Acronyms and abbreviations

9/11	11 September 2001 when terrorists bombed the World Trade Center in New York and the Pentagon in Washington
911	terrorist attack in Madrid that occurred 911 days after 11 September 2001
CAP	Common Agricultural Policy
CERPOD	Centre d'Etudes et de Recherche sur la Population pour le Développement (Centre for the Study of Population and Development, Mali)
DP	displaced person
EC	European Community
ESRC	Economic and Social Research Council (UK)
EU	European Union
FAO	Food and Agricultural Organization
Frelimo	Frente de Libertação de Moçambique (Mozambique Liberation Front)
GATT	General Agreement on Tariffs and Trade
GCIM	Global Commission on International Migration
GDP	gross domestic product
GDR	German Democratic Republic (East Germany)
GM	genetically modified
GNP	gross national product
Gulag	Glavnoye Upravleniye Lagerei (Soviet prison and labour camp system)
ICIHI	Independent Commission on International Humanitarian Issues
ID	identity
IGO	international governmental organization
ILO	International Labour Organization/Office
INGO	international non-governmental organization
Interpol	International Criminal Police Organization

IOM	International Organization for Migration
IPEC	International Programme on the Elimination of Child Labour
IT	information technology
LCHMT	Lords Commissioner of His Majesty's Treasurer under the direction of the Master of the Rolls
NAFTA	North American Free Trade Agreement
NGO	non-governmental organization
NIC	newly industrializing country
NIDL	new international division of labour
NRI	non-resident Indian
OECD	Organization for Economic Cooperation and Development
OPEC	Organization of Petroleum-Exporting Countries
PRC	People's Republic of China
PRD	Pearl River Delta
PRI	Partido Revolucionario Instituional (Institiutional Revolutionary Party, Mexico)
RSPCA	Royal Society for the Prevention of Cruelty to Animals
SS	Schutzstaffel (German protection squad/Nazi paramilitary organization)
SSRC	Social Science Research Council (USA)
TNC	transnational corporation
UNHCR	United Nations High Commissioner for Refugees
US-VISIT	Depart of Homeland security programme to enhance the USA's entry and exit system
USCSIMCED	United States Commission for the Study of International Migration and Cooperative Economic Development
WTO	World Trade Organization

Detail of *BORDER DYNAMICS*, 2000-2003, by Alberto Morackis and Guadalupe Serrano, courtesy of the Collection of The University of Arizona, Tucson, Public Art Collection.

Introduction

It is always a disturbing moment when something that is buried deep in our history and our consciousness suddenly surfaces. Such a moment happened on 5 February 2004, when those tuned to the *BBC News* heard that 19 Chinese cockle-pickers had died on the sands of Morecambe Bay in northwest England. They had been caught by the dangerous tides. The workers had been recruited illegally and risked their lives to collect the cockles for £7.00 an hour. Father of two children, Guo Binglong, used his mobile phone to reach his family in China: 'The water is up to my chest. The bosses got the time wrong. I can't get back in time.' Could they pray for him? He was from Fujian province, the source for so many Chinese wandering around the world in search of work (Pieke et al. 2004). Mr Guo had paid a large fee to a 'snakehead' (an illegal labour recruiter) to find him work and had already managed to send £2000 to his family in Fujian province.

Mr Guo's situation highlights three principal themes of this book. First, many migrant workers are still locked into forms of labour exploitation that marked the birth of global capitalism. Second, employer demand for cheap, often illegal, labour has not abated despite the spread of an evangelical form of neo-liberal capitalism proclaiming that opportunity and fairness are available to all. Whether manufacturing is exported to low-wage areas or migrants are imported to work in metropolitan service sectors, the distinctions between established workers, privileged foreigners and helot labourers have remained and may even have deepened (see Chapter 6). Third, politicians in migrant importing states have been zealous in trying to police their national frontiers, whether in the name of security or to prevent economic migrants 'masquerading' as political refugees. As I will show later in the book, measures to 'manage' migration have been of enormous ideological and political importance, but they are rarely successful in actually stopping migration when wider social, environmental and economic forces continue to fuel the movement of peoples.

Migrant workers in the twenty-first century

Let us return, for the moment, to Morecambe Bay. Gangmasters, illegal entrants, hair-raising working conditions, workers living in sleazy hostels: surely this must be the nineteenth century, not a pleasant British seaside resort in the new millennium? As I show in Chapters 1 and 2 in this book, after 1834 British recruiters had fixed on indentured Asian workers as a means of replacing African plantation slaves. But indenture has long been discredited as 'a new system of slavery' and had been abolished in the British colonies in 1920. Surely it was not back again in the twenty-first century? Only the poignant phone call to Fujian province reminded us that this is the age of corporate globalization with its triumphalist message proclaiming that connectivity, if not affluence, is in nearly everybody's reach. Somehow, this seemed to make it all worse. That his family shared Mr Guo's anguish in real time made the contrast between their opportunities and those who enjoy the affluence of the West all the more graphic.

The Fujianese are by no means the poorest migrants in global terms – that honour would probably currently be reserved for the refugees from devastated areas like Darfur in the Sudan. Being able to contemplate international migration as a means of social mobility is a sign of relative success in the international labour market, and a way, however imperfect, of closing the gap between rich and poor. While recruiters, smugglers and travel agents facilitate international mobility, demand for their labour comes from a host of employers, particularly in the catering trade (in the case of Chinese workers). In the wake of the Morecambe Bay tragedy, it transpired that restaurants in London's Chinatown alone (not to mention the thousands of 'takeaways' nationally) were partly staffed by hundreds of illegal workers. Jun Chen of the Luxuriance restaurant in London openly admitted that he hired illegal workers from Fujian and the northeast of China. 'They're hardworking and easy to train. And it was easy to communicate with them as we speak the same language' (*Guardian*, 2 June 2004).

Two social actors in the triangular drama played out in the pages of this book have now been identified – workers (labour) and employers (capital). The third party to the triangle, namely bureaucrats and politicians (the functionaries of the state), is in a more ideologically contested corner. For the assistant chief constable of Morecambe Bay, Julia

Hodson, there was no mincing of words. Asked what she thought of those who profited from the labour of illegal workers like the Chinese cocklers, she said: 'I think they would be criminals of the worst possible kind, that are prepared to exploit those who are the most vulnerable in our communities' (*BBC News*, 6 February 2004: http://news.bbc.co.uk). Home Office officials were more circumspect, but quietly drafted a circular to employers stating that they faced heavy fines and up to two years in prison if they hired workers without proper documentation. In contrast to their normal verbosity, the politicians stayed tellingly silent, as they did again in August 2004 following suicides in an asylum-seekers' detention centre in Britain. It was embarrassing to admit that the rigid methods of scrutinizing asylum claims designed to placate the dominant population had resulted in such distress.

This mixed response from those who staff the state apparatus or give it direction is explicable if not justifiable. Politicians of all parties have simultaneously to yield to the majority of public opinion and the media (both pressing for immigration restrictions), respect international treaties and human rights, and ensure that there is an adequate labour supply to sustain economic growth and balance the demographic overload towards older locally-born dependants. The lobby groups that speak on behalf of migrant workers (churches, some migrant groups and human rights activists) as well as those demanding more restrictions and detentions in the wake of the increased threat of terrorism provide additional complications. Often, as we shall see, these contradictory pressures are resolved by a great show of immigration control, which, in practice, often debouches into forms of ideological and social exclusion rather than effective prevention of entry or facilitation of exit.

Immigration control, then and now

I start my discussion of contemporary immigration control with a story of a prosaic return trip from the USA, which has stuck in my mind. My wife and I funnelled out of a flight from New York towards the immigration desks at Heathrow. At the time, the channels were labelled 'UK and Commonwealth', 'European Union' and 'Other'. 'But where should I go?' demanded a perfectly groomed American woman with expensive hand luggage. 'Other', replied my wife, rather tartly. The woman jerked back, astounded at the thought of being so categorized.

While the American's reaction was openly and innocently indignant, we all experience a sense of quiet unease or anxiety as we approach an immigration officer in an unfamiliar country. Many officers are no doubt perfectly charming people who don their slippers and stroke their cats when they get home from work. Others behave like cardboard Hitlers. Often underpaid and working unsocial hours, immigration officers derive their occupational power from being the 'frontier guards' of national identities. The turnstiles they protect are symbolic gateways to belonging and acceptance. If the light is green we are wanted and feel relieved. By contrast, being stopped or deported can be interpreted as what Lévi-Strauss called 'anthropemy', the ejection of dangerous individuals from the social body.

The passport we carry is normally the key to determining a 'stop' or 'go' at a frontier. William the Conqueror is said to have invented the document in the wake of his successful invasion of southern England (see Chapter 3). Concluding that it was all too easy for someone to emulate him, William nominated five exclusive ports of entry. The process of passing through these points gave birth to the word 'passport'. Though eleventh century in their origin, passports were not widespread until 1914, when they became one way of separating out the combatants in the confused circumstances of war-torn continental Europe.

Nationalists have always needed strong frontier controls and stony-faced sentinels because identities are much more fragmented and overlapping than their fantasies or historical reconstructions allow. For the pure nationalist a process of ethno-genesis has taken place (often in the prehistorical past and with divine or biblical sanction). In this reconstruction, a particular 'race' is meant to inhabit a particular space, to the exclusion of all others. Even the most naïve cursory appreciation of the history of migration (reinforced now by the evidence of the Human Genome Project) demonstrates a more plausible alternative proposition. A single human race has a common origin in Africa and intermingling, plurality and segmentation based on non-biological markers characterize its subsequent dispersion and settlement patterns.

The idea that nations are socially, not somatically, constructed reached its apogee in Benedict Anderson's oft-cited book *Imagined communities* (1983). In fact Anderson, or perhaps more precisely the epigones who casually referred to his book, rather over-egged the constructionist custard. Incommensurate languages, religions, histories, political institutions and, as Anderson stressed, appeals to a common culture through the medium of print, *have* created distinct societies. Often, too, there are phenotypical differences. One does not have to be a Nazi to observe that most Finns look different from most Malians. By recognizing the weight of ethno-nationalism and the heritage of ethnocentricity, we are better able to gauge the strength of cultural, economic and linguistic hegemony exercised in the name of the more powerful nation-states. By contrast, we can also better describe the major bearers of the new pluralism, namely migrants who generate an enhanced social diversity and complexity and who provide major challenges to the national identities of all societies, particularly Western industrialized ones.

Despite more guards, more laws and more restrictions, the symbolic and real boundaries that divide societies are eroding. This is a result of ideas, images, money, music, electronic messages, sport, fashion and religions that can move without people, or without many people – forms, if you like, of virtual migration. But nothing is as disturbing to national societies as the movement of people. It is perhaps useful to think here about population mobility in general, including tourists – though tourists are not normally considered as migrants. From 1950 to 1990 the volume of tourist arrivals across the world increased by 17 times. There was a modest fall in 2001 following the terrorist attacks in New York on 11 September 2001, but 'arrivals' soon went up again, reaching an estimated 764 million in 2004 (see Chapter 8). It is difficult to conceive the sheer size of the movement: it is as if every member of the entire population of Britain each had 12 holidays a year. But as salient as the numbers is the increasing penetration of tourism to hitherto remote parts of the world, which leads to major cultural and social effects. Well-intentioned but mulish visitors demand familiar goods, services and forms of entertainment, stipulations that serve to cover isolated societies like a cultural oil slick. Few societies can remain unaffected by the scale and intensity of such cultural contacts.

We should also not forget other kinds of mobility, such as people on religious pilgrimages (millions go to Mecca, the Ganges and Lourdes each year) or the movement of troops during war, or the prelude to war (think of current US military deployments). The impact of such forms of mobility is often overlooked because the predominant focus of political sensitivity and social unease is, without question, migrants who are thought to be potential settlers. Despite the disquiet surrounding such migrants, numbers alone do not provide irrefutable evidence of a necessarily major impact. Take the example of the USA. While the proportion of the foreign-born population attained a 90-year high in 2000 at 10 per cent (26.4 million people), it was considerably short of the 14.7 per cent record achieved in 1910; the low was 4.3 per cent in 1970.

However, any assessment of the impact of migrants needs to be set in the context of a fundamental qualitative change in the reception of immigrants in the twenty-first century. A century ago the USA was committed to an ideology and often a practice of Americanization. This can be symbolized by the opening nearly a century ago, in 1908, of Israel Zangwill's Broadway hit musical, *The melting pot*, which played to packed houses. The pogrom orphan of the play declaimed:

> America is God's Crucible, the great Melting Pot where all the races of Europe are melting and re-forming! Here you stand, good folk, think I, when I see them at Ellis Island, here you stand in your fifty groups with your fifty languages and histories, and your hatreds and rivalries, but you won't be long like that, brothers, for these are the fires of God you've come to – these are the fires of God. A fig for your feuds and vendettas! Germans and Frenchmen, Irishmen and Englishmen, Jews and Russians – into the Crucible with you all. God is making the American.

The melting pot never entirely worked, but even Zangwill's rhetoric now looks hopelessly dated. Governments have all but abandoned policies of assimilation in favour of 'integration', or more nebulous goals such as 'multiculturalism', 'pluralism' or 'rainbow nationhood'. They have abandoned assimilation partly because key local actors are xenophobes or outright racists. Many who have been citizens for a long while and, sometimes more fiercely, many who have recently acquired a secure legal status determinedly pull up the ladder behind them. With increased global inequalities, violent political conflict and often the complete collapse of livelihoods, attaining work and residential rights in favoured societies can be a matter of life and death. Consequently, illegal and refugee migrants advance their claims with similar determination.

The stage is thus set for ethnic tension between the self-declared indigenes and the desperate newcomers. To be sure, the popular media exaggerate the number of undocumented and irregular migrants, which is rarely comparable with the number of tourists and other migrants who are allowed entry because of family links or common descent, or who come in on permits, visas or work programmes. However, the unpredictability of illegal migrant flows and the sense that governments and frontier guards are losing control of the borders fuel nativist fears. To the more familiar taunts that outsiders take jobs, houses and women away are now added the charges that they bring crime, terrorism, alien cultures and contagious disease with them.

The collapse of programmes and policies that imply cultural absorption also stems from a general scepticism towards all forms of social policy. Many political elites have largely abandoned social interventions in the cynical belief that the poor will always be with us, criminal conduct and corruption are (to a degree) acceptable, certain minority groups are uneducable and immigrants are not dissolvable – either in melting pots or any other receptacles. For such elites, social relations have been reduced to reified commodities – to be bought and sold, like everything else, in the marketplace. Poor locals and marginalized outsiders, who are the victims of the state's evacuation from its sites of social responsibility, will have a long wait for relief from their poverty and isolation. Although a few social democratic regimes show small signs of positive movement, it will still take some time before naïve neo-Thatcherites and American 'neo-cons' recognize the utter futility of relying on the marketplace to solve every social, political and cultural problem.

The transnational turn in migration

Despite my foregoing argument, we must not assume that migrants do not 'fit in' only because they are not allowed to by angry racists or indifferent ruling classes. Retaining an old identity in a new setting, or creating a syncretic compromise between old and new, is often a matter of choice. Migrants are more likely to develop complex affiliations, meaningful attachments and dual or multiple allegiances to issues, people, places and traditions that lie beyond the boundaries of the resident nation-state. This holds true especially of members of ethnic diasporas and other transnational communities, including faith communities. For diasporas in the traditional sense of that word this is not at all surprising. Groups such as the Jews, Armenians, Africans, Irish and Palestinians were 'victim diasporas' dispersed by force. They ended up where they were more by accident than intent. The traumatic events that triggered their movement were so encompassing that such populations remained psychologically unsettled. They characteristically looked backwards, or manifested a dual loyalty to their places of settlement and also to their places, often creatively fabulated, of origin. Indeed, this propensity to link 'home' and 'away' often got them into hot water at the hands of monochromatic nationalists.

What has changed is that many more groups than the traditional diasporas are now attracted to a diasporic consciousness and cosmopolitan lifestyle (see Chapter 8). People move to trade, to study, to travel, for family visits, to practise a skill or profession, to earn hard currency, to experience an alternative culture and way of life and for other reasons too. They are not permitted or do not intend to settle permanently, adopt an exclusive citizenship, abandon their own language, culture or religion, or cut off the possibility of returning to a familiar place. In short, they are transnational by intent, adaptation or compulsion. From time to time social researchers have questioned the extent of the migrants' transnationalism. Leading sociologists in the USA have found that new migrants are accomplished at 'switching' between a transnational mode when they are with their families and 'home' communities, and standard US idiom when they are seeking jobs, university admission or the social acceptance of neighbours from dissimilar backgrounds (see, for example, Rumbaut 1997).

While accepting that many social actors display versatility in managing their various affinities, this does not obviate the profound legal and political changes consequent on moving from a singular to a complex identity. Take the litmus test of dual citizenship. From under 10 per cent, the proportion of countries that legally accepted dual citizenship had risen to 50 per cent by 1998. In that year, Mexico (notably) permitted its citizens in the USA, then comprising from four to five million people, to retain both US and Mexican nationalities. They were encouraged, for example, to vote in Mexican elections and, it is clear, they affected the outcome of the last election. By the same token, the USA, which had historically been highly negative about such arrangements, tacitly accepted dual nationality and, perhaps even more crucially, abandoned its hitherto unshakable monolingual stance by recognizing Spanish as a quasi-official language in a number of key states. The outcome of such a shift away from the goal of cultural absorption can be stated in a more exaggerated form. If full loyalty to a state cannot be assumed, the recruitment of a citizen army, one of the key elements of nation-state power that dates from the French Revolution, has to be abandoned. Increasingly, states are modifying and abandoning conscript armies because citizens are likely to include members of the enemy's country or their descendants. It is thus no coincidence that, with rare exceptions, states will more and more come to rely on technologically driven warfare and a professional, paid, army.

As the Mexican example also illustrates, the attitudes of those governments that export migrants have also shifted radically. In the nineteenth century, Europeans recruited indentured workers from India, Japan and China to work in tropical plantations. This period is often regarded in those countries with shame, as demonstrating their weakness in the face of European power. Now the descendants of such communities (in Brazil, Peru, the USA and elsewhere), together with new emigrants, are celebrated and lionized in their countries of origin. The NRIs (non-resident Indians) provide an excellent example. They are a conduit for Indian goods and influence flowing out and a source of remittances and investment income flowing back. In 1970, remittance income to India was US$ 80 million. In 1993 the sum had increased to US$ three billion; by 2002/3 it had rocketed to US$ 14.8 billion (Kundu 2004). Investments placed by returnees and NRIs have developed the burgeoning and successful Indian software industry. Rather than trying to stop emigration, the government of India has made large-scale investments in training Indian IT professionals for work abroad. What was decried as 'brain drain' in the 1970s and 1980s is now constructed as 'brain gain', as skilled exported professionals place contracts at home with Indian companies and close the virtuous circle.

Some rich and wonderfully unexpected cultural products also arise from this new acceptance in the originating countries of their communities abroad. One case concerns two Scottish Pakistanis who developed a TV soap called *Des Padres* (*Foreign Homeland*), filmed in Britain, but aimed at audiences of two to three billion viewers in the

Indian subcontinent and beyond.[1] While cultural flows are often depressingly uniform and are still overwhelmingly sourced from a limited number of rich countries, as the TV soap example illustrates, flows can go both ways, indeed in multiple directions. As diversity is enhanced, social actors become self-aware that they are transgressing national frontiers and identities become broader. Such developments illustrate the benign effects of transationalism or cosmopolitanism. We could advance the argument that if old-fashioned nation-states, based either on the idea of racial uniformity or cultural absorption, are failing, so what? The benefits of enhanced trade, the return flow of income, the movement of fertile ideas and the enhancement of cultural choices and opportunities may greatly outweigh the benefits of retaining an undisturbed national heritage. Better a chapatti and a curry than a cold chop in a cold climate.

It may be helpful to introduce here a distinction between globalization on the one hand and transnationalism and cosmopolitanism on the other. The distinction is not generally accepted. However, I use it to argue that powerful nation-states and big corporations often lead the much advertised forms of economic globalization, while cosmopolitanism implies a more subtle form of intervention by a multitude of social actors, notably migrants. Such actors, who have no grand scheme in mind, may nonetheless, through their choices, conduct and movements, effect profound long-term changes. As Vertovec and Cohen (2002: 1–22) maintain, one reason why cosmopolitanism has acquired fresh appeal is because the term

- transcends the nation-state model based either on uniformity or cultural absorption;
- is able to mediate actions and ideals oriented both to the universal and the particular, the global and the local;
- is culturally anti-essentialist; and
- is capable of representing variously complex repertoires of allegiance, identity and interest.

In these ways, cosmopolitanism seems to offer a mode of managing cultural and political multiplicity and now extends far beyond its historical reference to rootless, disengaged members of the leisured classes, literati or 'bohemian' outsiders. Through the agency of travellers and migrants, transnationalism or cosmopolitanism may presage our post-national future.

Conclusion

I have suggested that there is much continuity in the evolution of global migration flows, particularly when we observe that large numbers of subordinated workers continue to meet the demand for low-cost production and service provision. However, the shift to a more globalized and interconnected world has somewhat improved the bargaining power of a section of migrants, namely the fraction that is economically and culturally able to enter the global labour market and acquire some level of everyday cosmopolitan consciousness. Neither their enhanced mobility nor their claims to relative cultural autonomy have been passively accepted by existing dominant populations and political classes. Enhanced levels of cosmopolitanism are also by no means universally welcomed. Reactions to these developments have had a major impact on migration.

For the primordial nationalists who have emerged from the ruins of the Soviet empire and the Yugoslavian federation the appeals to ethnogenesis are as enticing as ever, whether in the Caucasus, the Balkans or the Baltic. 'Georgia for the Georgians', 'Bosnia for the Bosnians' and never mind the ethnic and religious minorities who have been living there for centuries. Historically, the emergence of nationalism was usually linked organically to the growth of liberalism and democracy. This notion has been seriously challenged by the sight of the thuggish conjurors of Balkan nationalism with their fake army uniforms, bulging bellies and menacing handguns? Such nationalism produces long lines of refugees, orphanages, camps, the burning of neighbours' houses, and that chilling practice, ethnic cleansing.

A second reaction to an embryonic cosmopolitanism can be found in that increasingly clumsy, bloated and dangerous Gulliver, the USA. Enter '9/11' or, as we Lilliputians say, 11 September 2001. It is a poor argument and definitely one I do not make, that what happened in the USA was not a horrific and morally indefensible act of terrorism. However, when we see armies mobilized, Afghanistan pounded, the deaths of 100,000 Iraqis (*Guardian*, 29 October 2004) and a perilous war

against terrorism unleashed it is difficult to find any sense of pro-
portionality or justice. The fatuous evocations of biblical eyes and teeth,
the tone of moral righteousness by President Bush (and his ally Prime
Minister Blair) the diminished civil rights for travellers to, or residents
in, the USA – all this invites comparisons with the reactionary regimes of
the 1930s or the McCarthyist period in the USA. The conservative Sikh
community, resident in California since 1907, was compelled to pay for
TV and newspaper advertisements showing Sikhs and Afghans with their
differing turbans. This is a good guy; this is a bad one, pointed out the
red arrows. Perhaps the very Orwellian name of a department for homeland security says it all – shoes off at the airports, surveillance and
interrogation of the enemy within, and an apparent war without end
abroad.

As I show in this book, expressions of extreme nationalism and the
mobilization of nativist sentiments by cynical or deluded politicians have
been with us for a long time. Migrants are always convenient targets for
hate and fear. Like the biblical scapegoat or Jung's 'shadow' in psycho-
analysis they become bearers of all the morally reprehensible feelings
and sentiments that the dominant populations want to offload. What
makes the negative projections more complex (as in Jung's shadow) is
that migrants also often exhibit exemplary values – showing initiative,
sobriety, hard work, dedication to family values, modesty and courtesy.
The dilemmas and dynamics of immigrant control and integration thus
become mediated in complex ways. As we will see later in this book,
migrants are used and abused, hated and admired. They show a mirror
to the dominant populations who do not always want to peer too hard at
the looking glass.

Note

1. My thanks go to Steven Vertovec for this example.

Chapter 1
Unfree labourers and modern capitalism

C an a wage labourer be described as 'free'? The very concept of
'labour' implies at least some degree of compulsion. As Womack
(1979: 739) pointed out, for about 2500 years Western cultures
distinguished between 'labour' and 'work'. The Greeks separated *ponein*
from *ergazesthai*, the Romans distinguished *laborare* from *facere* while
the Germans contrasted *arbeiten* with *werken*. In every European
language, he writes: 'labour meant pain, effort, pangs, penalty, strain,
drudgery, struggle, battle, suffering, grief, distress, poverty, loneliness,
abandonment, ordeal, adversity, trouble. Work meant making, building,
providing, causing, accomplishment, completion, satisfaction.' The
secular distinction was paralleled by a religious viewpoint. For the Bene-
dictines, 'labour' was not seen as noble or rewarding, but as a penance
designed to avoid the spiritual dangers of idleness.

To understand the concept of a 'free' labourer under capitalism, we
need to start with Marx's central idea that the working class is formed as
the agricultural producer, the peasant, becomes detached from the soil.
In these moments, 'great masses of men are suddenly and forcibly torn
from their means of subsistence, and hurled onto the labour-market as
free, unprotected and rightless proletarians' (Marx 1976: 876). In earlier
translations the expression *vogelfrei* was rendered as 'unattached' rather
than 'rightless', which perhaps better captures Marx's meaning. For him,
the freedom of wage labourers comprises two elements. First, labourers
are no longer part of the means of production themselves, as would be
the case with a slave or a serf; they are, therefore, free of any direct proprietorial rights exercised over them. Second, they no longer own their
own means of production and subsistence and therefore are unencum-
bered by their own tools or land. They are free, but of necessity required,
to sell their remaining possession, their labour, in the market.

In his formulation, Marx indubitably captures the central aspect of the transition from European feudalism to capitalism, the first major reorganization of the division of labour for hundreds of years. However, what is far more uncertain is whether it is part of the intrinsic and necessary definition of a capitalist mode of production that it relies exclusively on free wage labourers (in the senses Marx indicated). In general, Marx does hold this view and it is one that I shall contest – advancing indeed a contrary thesis that capitalism has always survived, and even thrived, by deploying substantial numbers of unfree or semi-free labourers.

This mixture of workers of different statuses is sometimes concealed by a national definition of the boundaries of the political economy (ignoring, therefore, imperial and colonial relations), or is sometimes all too evident, as when quasi-free workers from the countryside or peripheral zones of the political economy are driven or sucked into the vortex of capitalist production. Though there are hints of my counter proposition in Marx's references to New World slavery and in his limiting reference to the classical case of England, Marx (1976: 452) flatly and unequivocally states that 'the capitalist form presupposes from the outset the free wage-labourer who sells his labour power to capital'. By contrast, I seek to demonstrate that capitalism has historically coexisted with a combination of labour regimes. I propose to do so by citing examples from a wide range of countries and periods – an exercise that is more than random but less than comprehensive: 'less than' because I seek to illustrate my argument rather than write a complete history of capitalist labour regimes.

Slavery in the New World

The history of unfree labour of course predates capitalism and many early societies operated a combination of compelled and free labour. For example, Finley's powerful writings (1980; 1981) on Ancient Greece provide ample documentation of the mix of slave and free labourers and the intermediate forms of dependent labour between the two polarities. Bearing in mind the helots and slaves, if women are also excluded (they did not count as citizens), Hegel's observation that the Greeks only knew that some men were free, is even more powerfully understood nowadays than he intended. A number of other precapitalist societies deployed vast armies of compelled labourers to erect the pyramids, religious monuments, irrigation systems and public works – from China, Burma, Mexico, Peru, Egypt, Mesopotamia, Persia to Rome, workers were coerced by military force and closely supervised by taskmasters.

Despite these intriguing early cases from which no doubt some continuity can be established, my primary examples must begin as European capitalism expanded into what Wallerstein (1974) calls 'the modern world system' during the late fifteenth and early sixteenth centuries. The first and most obvious discontinuity is that slavery in the modern period was set in a wholly different context from classical slavery. Vast numbers were commercially transhipped from the labour reserve of western Africa as European supplies decreased and as the indigenous populations of the New World declined under the impact of European diseases, from food shortages triggered by depredations of imported animals, or as a result of being worked to death. The figures of population decline are every bit as staggering as the number of slaves shipped. In New Spain (Mexico) the population fell from 11 million in 1519 to about 1.5 million in about 1650. Similar steep falls are recorded for Brazil and Peru (Wallerstein 1974: 88, 89).

The different context of New World slavery integrated the phenomenon into a capitalist world economy in a number of concrete ways. The slave was a commodity – a unit of labour power *par excellence*: the only concern for a slave's welfare was whether handling or shipping conditions affected the price received. From being a family retainer, a domestic servant, or a small farm labourer often working alongside their masters, most New World slaves became field hands working on large plantations, normally under the supervision of an overseer. Next, the product (usually sugar, coffee, cotton or tobacco) was directly integrated into the capitalist world market and followed the rhythms of market demand, such as that established by the triangular trade between Europe, Africa and the Americas. In polemicizing against the popularizer of dependency theory, A. G. Frank, Laclau (1971) legitimately argued that integration into a world market is quite a different thing from capitalist 'relations of production'. So it is, but it is implausible to imagine that the first does not affect the second. The supervision of work tasks, the division of labour, the deskilling of the labour force, the production rhythms, together with the overtly capitalist relations of production in the processing plants (like the sugar mills, rum distilleries and cotton ginneries) all show the influence of the world market on the forms and relations of plantation production.

If these relations are not capitalist, they are a passably fair imitation thereof. But where, Laclau would object, is the wage? Even here, the formal appearance of slavery concealed a 'hidden wage'. Payments 'in kind' were often in commodities that could be traded, or were, like tobacco, used directly as currency. Paternalist favouritism and sources of income and subsistence from provision plots were both ways for the plantation owner to subsidize his reproduction costs and a means of accumulating some modest savings by plantation workers. The hiring of slave workers for cash has also been reported (Fraginals 1976: 131–53). Had such possibilities for acquiring income not existed it is impossible otherwise to explain why so many slaves were able to purchase their freedom when that became legally possible or why 'freedmen' constituted from 30 per cent of the total population in pre-emancipation slave societies like Curaçao, Minas Gerais (Brazil) or Puerto Rico (Cohen and Greene 1972: 4).

Those who hold that slavery in the New World constituted a separate mode of production, also take no account of the real (as opposed to formal) boundaries of the contemporary political economy. Instead, anachronistic notions of geographical and political sovereignty are projected back to a period when such national distinctions did not exist. As John Stuart Mill (cited in Fraser 1981: 320) says of the West Indies in the nineteenth century:

> [Our West Indian colonies] are hardly to be looked upon as countries carrying on an exchange of commodities with other countries, but more properly as outlying agricultural or manufacturing establishments belonging to a larger community. … If Manchester, instead of being where it is, were on a rock in the North Sea (its present industry nonetheless continuing); it would still be but a town of England, not a country trading with England; it would be merely, as now, a place where England finds it convenient to carry on her cotton manufacture. The West Indies, in like manner, are the places where England finds it convenient to carry on the production of sugar, coffee and a few tropical commodities.

This idea of a 'class of trading and exporting communities' (as Mill called them) firmly integrated into a core economy can give rise to the situation where different forms of labour regime can coexist within this larger unit. As Wallerstein (1974: 127) has it, 'Free labour is the form of labour control used for skilled work in core countries, whereas coerced labour is used for less skilled work in peripheral areas. The combination thereof is the essence of capitalism.' This is a compelling generalization, though the geographical demarcations Wallerstein suggested are too rigid to encompass the variety of labour forms in the central and outer zones. Wallerstein's argument also takes little account of the more detailed controversy Nieboer (1910) started at the turn of the century as to whether the introduction of slavery as an industrial system (as Nieboer terms it) is a variant pattern related to land scarcity, or whether, as Kloosterboer (1960) argues, such a labour regime can be explained by more general factors.

Whatever the specific causes for utilizing slave labourers in particular areas, the general point is clear. If capitalism is compatible with slavery, it is likely to be compatible with other forms of coerced or involuntary labour. These can range as widely as *repartimiento* or *cuatequil* labour (Mexico), *mita* (Peru), serfdom, debt bondage, apprentice labour, child labour, indentured or contract labour, penal labour, various forms of domestic service, *chibaro* mine labour (Southern Rhodesia/Zimbabwe), 'political labour' (British colonies), concentration-camp labour, and 'corrective labour'. To provide a detailed account of all these different forms of labour control would be superfluous, but I would like to comment on a number of these variants, both to show some sense of how different labour regimes evolved and to indicate the senses in which postwar international migrants, and especially women migrants, can be seen as exhibiting some characteristics associated with earlier generations of unfree labourers.

Apprentice workers

The post-emancipation economies of the New World and other colonial areas provide rich sources of mixed labour organization. With the abolition of slavery (1834 in most British colonies, 1863 in the Dutch colonies, 1865 in the USA), most plantation societies operated a system of 'apprentice' labour. Normally, only children under six years were completely free. The rest of the former slaves were compelled to work without payment (except for those forms of 'hidden wage' indicated earlier) for four to six years. Their new status was distinguished from their former status by the fact that, while apprentices could not themselves be bought or sold, they could buy their own freedom and were compelled to work for a maximum of only 45 hours a week. In Antigua, the plantation owners instituted highly restrictive contracts rather than an apprenticeship system. Absence for half a day or less was met with one day's wages docked. If the labourer was absent for two days in a row, or two days in any fourteen days, one week's imprisonment, with hard labour followed. For negligence of various kinds, imprisonment for up to three months was the legal consequence.

Such was the rough class justice of the times that a breach of contract by the employer only rendered him liable to a maximum fine of £5. Other forms of compulsion directed against apprentices and former slaves included a requirement that previously free shacks now had to be rented and the rent paid by work. The movable shacks (chattels), still visible in Barbados today, date from the period when former slaves tried to escape this obligation. Even more compelling were the comprehensive extensions of the vagrancy laws. In Jamaica (in 1840) a vagrant became any man who migrated and left his wife and children without provision. In Mauritius (in 1855) the Franco-Mauritian plantocracy exacted an even harsher definition. Any able-bodied woman or man under 60 unable to prove that they followed a trade or possessed sufficient means of subsistence was required to find employment within a period fixed by the police. If the person defaulted, employment on public works was required. After a further three months, a defaulter could be sentenced to work on a plantation or in a factory for up to three years (Kloosterboer 1960: 3–16). Such were the desperate measures deployed to keep former slaves dependent on the plantation owners. The received conventional historical account is that many of these measures were unsuccessful and that in all plantation economies slaves fled to the towns in large numbers to evade the brutality of plantation work. Some West Indian historians have, however, questioned the extent to which a 'flight from the land' did indeed take place (Adamson 1972; Fraser 1981: 328–34; Green 1976; Mintz 1974).

That this experience is more general than in the West Indies, is a proposition that Cooper (1980: 1) advances in the introduction to his authoritative study of plantation labour in Zanzibar and coastal Kenya. He writes:

> In case after case, a particular class under the hallowed ideals of private property – kept land from the eager hands of ex-slaves and vigorously applied the instruments of the state and the law to block ex-slaves' access to resources and markets, to restrict their ability to move about, bargain, or refuse wage labour and to undermine their attempts to become independent producers.

Whatever the difficulties former slaves had in freeing themselves from their prior status in the post-emancipation period, the planters cried 'labour scarcity' long and loud. All over the European tropical possessions, an appeal went out for more and more hands, another cohort of helots. The demand was strongest where 'sugar was king', but it was also strongly heard where, as in the South African diamond discoveries of 1870, new sources of mineral wealth were opened out for commercial exploitation. John X. Merriman, the commissioner for Crown lands in the Cape Colony, wrote in 1876, with some asperity, of the pressure mounted by farmers and mine owners to persuade the government to import foreign labour: 'In the Cape, the government is called upon to survey mankind from China to Peru in the hope of creating and maintaining a class of cheap labourers who will thankfully accept the position of helots and not be troubled with the inconvenient ambition of bettering this condition' (cited in Magubane 1979: 77–8).

Indentured labourers

In the event it was to Asia that the colonials, hungry for labour, turned. South Africa's experiment in using Chinese mine labourers ended in political recrimination in Britain and South Africa and in a local strike (Richardson 1976), but sugar plantations in Natal, British Guiana, Fiji, Trinidad, Ceylon, Malaya, Burma, Mauritius and elsewhere successfully found agricultural labourers in India. Hugh Tinker's carefully documented account of the indentures required of Indian labourers is a stunning indictment of what, quoting Lord John Russell, he considers was a 'new system of slavery'. In the British case, the period of indentured labour lasted from 1839 to 1920. (The Dutch continued the system for much longer.)

The indentured workers characteristically signed on for five years and were given in return a free passage, medical attention, housing and a modest wage. In many cases a free or subsidized passage back to India was guaranteed after ten years. While a protector was often appointed to safeguard Indian interests, what made this system close to slavery were the mortality rates on the ships (which, for example, averaged over 17 per cent on ships to the West Indies in 1856), the poor housing and health conditions, the miserable wages and, above all, the extensive use of penal sanctions (Tinker 1974: 116–235). In one year (1892), over 40 per cent of the adult indentured population was convicted under the penal labour laws of Fiji. The ineffectiveness of the protector was indicated by the fact that in the same year only one conviction of an employer was obtained on a charge brought by his employees (Tinker 1974: 194). Tinker (1974: 383) concludes his definitive account with this statement: 'The Blacks on the West Indian plantations were known as chattel slaves; the dictionary defines a chattel as a "moveable possession", and such an ascription is also appropriate to the condition of the Indian coolies, the successors to the chattel slaves. With the legal termination of slavery, there came no end to bondage upon the tropical plantations.'

Colonial labour regimes

Where colonial powers found indigenous sources of labour unimpaired by 'pacification' or European diseases, rather than importing labourers they tapped the local reservoir to feed the insatiable appetites of the farmers, the mine owners and industrialists. As I have dealt mainly with British colonies, I provide four illustrations from other colonial areas – the French in Madagascar, the Belgians in the Congo, the Portuguese African colonies and the Spanish in Latin America. When the French took over Madagascar in 1896, they freed 500,000 slaves, but in December of that year proclaimed a legal obligation to work. A special folder or card was issued to indicate in which of the various forms of compulsory labour a male aged 16 to 60 was to be engaged. Failure to produce such a card resulted in imprisonment for three to six months, after which a further period of work on public works was prescribed, equal to three times the length of the prison service. An outcry in France about the death rate on compulsory labour and military projects led to the repeal of the compulsory labour policy (in 1900) and the setting aside of penal sanctions on contract labourers.

Yet, despite these attempts at liberal reform, Kloosterboer (1960: 107–12) convincingly demonstrates that the continuities between slavery, other forms of unfree labour and the development of a modern labour market are still remarkably persistent. For example, it was only in 1946 that in their other colonies the French finally abolished conscript military labour and *prestation*, a labour 'tax' that permitted the administration to compel all adult males to work on public projects for a number of days each year (Echenberg 1975: 171–92). But enduring though these systems of compelled labour were, French overseas laws acted as some constraint on exploitation by public authorities, a constraint that did not apply where private concessionaires were given free licence to recruit and deploy labour.

The most notorious example of private exploitation was in the Belgian Congo where King Leopold ran the area as a personal fiefdom. Millions of Congolese were compelled to collect rubber for the king who argued that the system could only be changed 'when the Negro has generally shaken off his idleness and becomes ready to work for the love of wages alone' (Davies 1966: 33–5). Brutal violence normally met any resistance proffered to the labour recruiters. The Congolese who died trying to resist habituation to the capitalist work ethic numbered in their millions. One contemporary French journalist said of the Congo at the time: 'We are tree fellers in a forest of human beings' (cited Nzula et al. 1979: 84). The *modus operandi* of the Congo Free State is best described in the words of E. D. Morel, one of the leading members of a contemporary liberal pressure group in Britain, the Congo Reform Movement:

> The aboriginal citizens of this strange creation [the Congo State] were by law called upon to provide recruits for the army, workmen for the construction of important public works, transport of stores, building up of houses and prisons, cutting and maintenance of roads and bridges, upkeep of plantations and creation and repairs of rest houses. … They were compelled to labour, *with no legal limitation either in regard to time or to quality*, in the

collection, coagulation and transport of India rubber for the profit
of their governors.

(cited in Louis and Stengers 1968: 44)

Many of the areas marked out for agricultural production in the Portuguese colonies in Angola, Mozambique and in the Portuguese
possessions off the west coast of Africa were also under the immediate
control of leaseholders whose needs for labour were serviced by the
Portuguese administrators. Failure to comply with the legal demand to
fulfil a work contract in Angola, and from 1902 Mozambique, was met
by expulsion to the islands of São Tomé and Príncipe. At the turn of the
twentieth century these two small islands produced about one-fifth of
the world's cocoa crop, a level of production that was only made possible
by the import of about 4000 labourers each year from other parts of the
Portuguese empire. The gruesome conditions on the two islands were
exposed by the writings of Nevinson (1906) and Cadbury (1910) who
likened the labour regime on the cocoa plantations to a system of
'modern slavery'. Under the impact of these and later exposés, the
Salazar regime promulgated the 1928 Codigo do Trabalho dos Indigenas
nas Colónias Portugueses de Africa, which stated that:

> The Government of the Republic does not impose, nor does it
> permit that any form of obligatory or forced labour is demanded of
> the natives of its colonies for private ends, but it does insist that
> they fulfil the moral duty which necessarily falls on them of
> seeking through work the means of subsistence, thus contributing
> to the general interest of humanity.
>
> (cited in Head 1980: 70)

In her study of the labour regime of the Sena Sugar Estates in Zambezia
province, Mozambique, Head vividly documents how the provisions of
the 1928 code were violated or twisted for the ends of the estates.
Whenever Portugal was attacked in the international forums, the first
rhetorical phrases were cited to deny that forced labour existed. But, on
the ground, it was the second half of the code's preamble and the more
detailed subsequent provisions that ruled the lives of workers and
peasants in the Portuguese territories. As Head (1980: 71) puts it:

It was through enforcing the clauses of the law, which established how Africans were to fulfil their duty to work that the Government made sure that forced labour, where voluntary labour was not available, continued to furnish the needs of private employers. Denials of forced labour practices notwithstanding, the whole thrust of the labour law and other laws which supplemented it, was to oblige men to take up regular wage work whether they wanted it or not.

Such was the bankrupt and underdeveloped nature of Portuguese colonial capitalism that it is only a small exaggeration to suggest that the administration barely had any other purpose but to act as state-registered labour recruiters supplying the needs of the sugar, copra, sisal and cocoa plantations, companies in the Portuguese possessions, and mine owners in Southern Rhodesia and South Africa. The desperate need for revenue propelled the Portuguese to negotiate a labour-supply contract for the South African mines, paid for in gold deposited in Lisbon. The number of labourers supplied was not to diminish significantly until 1976 when there was a fall in recruitment from 115,000 to 45,000 workers. The fluctuations in supply between 1890 and 1976 can be explained not by sudden moral afflictions, but by competing demands from companies operating in Mozambique, nationalist pressures from white workers in South Africa, a changing of capital/labour ratio on the mines and, finally, the initial success of Frelimo (the national liberation movement in Mozambique) in seeking to reduce the export of labourers to the mines, even though their remittances constituted at the time of independence 35 per cent of all export earnings (First 1983).

The final colonial example I consider is the *repartimiento* system in Spanish America. Broadly speaking, this system followed the establishment of the *ecomienda* system prevalent during the first 50 years of Spanish rule. The *encomendero* was allotted from 30 to 300 'Indios'[1] who had to fulfil work tasks allocated to them and/or deliver a share of their produce in exchange for the *encomendero* attending to what were defined as their material (housing, clothing, food) and spiritual (Catholicism) needs. As this system was to a large extent an attempt to recreate Castilian feudalism, strictly speaking it predates my concern with capitalist unfree labour systems. The *repartimiento* system was, however, firmly integrated into the capitalist mode of production in that the state took direct control of the recruitment and supervision of labourers; wages were paid and, in addition to public works, *repartimiento* labour was assigned to the mines (and to a lesser extent the textile industry). Though the periods of work were theoretically limited to two weeks in Mexico and four months each year in Peru, work periods were frequently and arbitrarily lengthened. One report concerned a cohort of 7000 men, women and children, destined for the mines of Potosi. Such were the conditions of work and travel that only 2000 villagers returned to their homes (cited Kloosterboer 1960: 92).

The *repartimiento* system collapsed with the movements of independence of the South American countries from the Spanish crown, but local capital, which now commanded the labour market, turned out to be no less exacting than the Spanish administration. As Kloosterboer (1960: 99) explains:

> *Repartimiento* and *mita* (Peru) were abolished but the Indians profited little. Debt bondage became the order of the day and persisted in spite of the fine sentiments expressed in the constitutions. Indeed there was a marked worsening in the position of the debt slaves. This can be mainly attributed to the fact that the place of the patriarchal Crown – which had at least tried to attain a certain degree of protection for the natives – was now taken by the *laissez faire* ideas of the new era.

That this description is not exaggerated is attested by one commentator who estimated that by the beginning of the twentieth century one-third of the Mexican people, or 80 per cent of all agricultural labourers, were debt slaves (Turner 1911: 108, 110). *Laissez-faire* was a concept that applied to employers, not workers. The bosses took care to combine low wages with high prices of essential commodities and tools, which then forced workers to pay off a lifelong (and even inherited) debt by their further work. In addition, the *obrajes* (textile mills and factories) were often locked shut with the workers inside, even on Sunday, when the priest would be admitted to administer the sacrament. In an extensive collection of many articles, Mexican and North American labour historians have shown how Mexican capitalism combined under the same roof various forms of labour – black Caribbean slaves, indigenous slaves, *naborias* (indentured servants), contract labourers, convicts, debt peons and free workers. The textile mills in Coyoacán, for example, employed side by side a mixture of free workers, slaves and prisoners who slept in the workshops and cleaned and carded the wool dressed only in singlets to avoid the sweat, dirt and fleas that additional garments would attract. A contemporary observer could see nothing to distinguish free from unfree workers: 'Every workshop resembles a dark prison; all appear half naked, covered in rags, thin and deformed' (Frost et al. 1979: 211).

The cases of French Madagascar, the Belgian Congo, Portuguese Africa and Spanish America all share certain features. The colonial state (in the form of Leopold's company in the Congo) actively organized the local labour markets and set up extensive systems of involuntary labour, legitimized by religious, moral or legal arguments. The workers so compelled sometimes coexisted with free workers at the points of production (as in Mexico). In other areas, involuntary labour in colonial capitalist states paralleled a simultaneous deployment of predominantly free labour systems in the metropolitan state. Although the anti-colonial movements after the Second World War were to challenge this definition, it was not a totally empty claim made by Portugal and France that what is now deemed their 'colonies' were overseas provinces and departments of a single polity, a unified colonial division of labour.

The overseas areas were, to paraphrase Mill's comment on the West Indies (see earlier), the places where it was found convenient to specialize in the production of tropical commodities. In the case of Portuguese Africa, one of the commodities produced (or, strictly, reproduced) was labour itself, which was sold as wage labour in regional labour markets in exchange for gold used in Lisbon to support the continuance of merchant and the beginnings of industrial capitalism. Unfree labour systems survived in the tropics for most of the twentieth century. Even when they were formally abandoned other, subtler, compelling factors ensured that many workers never fully escaped the proprietorial relationship capital commanded over labour. Nor, again, were most workers able to sell their labour freely, both in the sense that their bargaining power remained highly circumscribed and in the sense that their mobility was restricted, often by political means.

Unfree labour in core zones

It has already been suggested that Wallerstein's argument that unfree labour is confined to peripheral zones, with free labour obtaining in core zones, needs some qualification. Where extractive, infrastructural (ports, railways, roads) and manufacturing capital was able to establish itself in colonial areas, a free wage labour force (again using Marx's definition) did emerge and even the beginnings of class formation, organization and consciousness can be found (see Cohen et al. 1979). On the other hand, unfree labour is far more common in the history of metropolitan-based capital than Wallerstein would lead us to suppose.

One case concerns the so-called 'second serfdom' in eastern Europe during the sixteenth century, which showed that the transition from feudalism to capitalism was far more prolonged and far more problematic than Marx supposed. Insofar as shortages of workers compelled large farmers to concede smallholdings to their labour force, Kautsky and others saw the transformation of the peasantry as being considerably delayed – even though they believed Marx's analysis would ultimately be proved correct (Goodman and Redclift 1981: 9–10). While it is true that Wallerstein's 'trade-centred' approach often obscures questions of the relations of production, on this occasion his analysis is quite clearly 'productionist', not 'circulationist'. I concur with Wallerstein in not seeing the second serfdom as a delayed feudalism, largely because the system of 'coerced cash-crop labour' (as he calls it) involved a different set of relationships to that of feudalism. The state enforced a legal process by which part of the period spent on a large domain was devoted to production for the world market. Moreover, quoting Stahl, Wallerstein (1974: 90–100) shows that the revival of feudal exactions on the peasantry served a wholly different purpose, namely providing the basis for the primitive accumulation of capital. While Wallerstein's description of the relations of production in sixteenth-century eastern Europe is accurate, it is at least doubtful that the area can be described as a 'periphery'.

Certainly, we cannot apply the same designation to the USA, let alone England, three centuries later. Yet, as Moore (1966: 116) has shown, the whole edifice of plantation slavery in the southern USA and of the cotton crop, in particular, was both essential and totally compatible with the growth of manufacturing capitalism in the USA and England:

Though the importance of cotton for the South is familiar, its significance for capitalist development as a whole is less well known. Between 1815 and 1866 the cotton trade exercised a decisive influence upon the rate of growth in the American economy. Up until about 1830 it was the most important cause of the growth of manufacturing in this century. ... From 1840 to the time of the Civil War, Great Britain drew from the Southern states, four-fifths of all her cotton imports. Hence it is clear that the plantation operated by slavery was no anachronistic excrescence on industrial capitalism. It was an integral part of this system and one of its prime motors in the world at large.

As in the other areas surveyed above, the end of slavery did not produce a free labour force but rather one that was tightly constrained by the need for workers to eat or to comply with political and legal restrictions. The passionate denunciations by black activists and scholars arguing that the quantitative measurement of comparable conditions in slave and post-slave regimes are a 'whitewash' of slavery, do not refute Engerman's central point that 'The choice between working and starving faced by a legally-free individual seems no more attractive than a similar choice faced by a slave: and the ruling class may be able to impose legislation which can provide themselves with the same economic benefits under either system of labour' (Engerman 1973: 45–6).

Corrigan (1977: 447), who utilizes this quote from Engerman in his wide-ranging article on the sociology of unfree labour, immediately spots the further implications of the argument. Engerman uses a conventional economic vocabulary to show that the economic pressures and legislative coercion in the post-emancipation period forced workers 'off what would be their desired supply curve if choice were voluntary'. This high participation rate, combined with the reduced costs of reproduction to the employer (the free labourer now bore the costs of housing and food), meant that the level of exploitation in the USA could be increased in the post-slavery period. The post-emancipation period in the USA was also marked by the enormous growth in debt peonage, convict and contract labour.

Corrigan (1977: 442–3) also cites Starobin's (1970) work on industrial slavery, which showed that slaves were used efficiently and effectively in mines and manufacturing establishments to secure a higher rate of return than was possible using free labour. In short, the division of labour in a 'core' country like the USA, contrary to Marx's and Wallerstein's arguments, combined a system of free and unfree labour throughout its history as an expanding and leading capitalist power. The contemporary US division of labour continues to combine labour of widely different statuses.

A further refutation of the argument that the capitalist form presupposes the free wage labourer (Marx) or is spatially distributed exclusively in its core zones (Wallerstein) can, additionally, be advanced by considering the case of England, indisputably at the centre of nineteenth and early twentieth century capitalism. While he insists on the ultimate triumph of wage labour, it is worth remarking that Marx was conscious of the links between the forms of labour control prevalent in different parts of the global political economy. He observes, for example, that 'the cotton industry introduced child-slavery in England' (Marx 1976: 925). Again, he and Engels document the way in which English employers used Irish workers as an oppressed section of the reserve army, 'the cause of abasement to which the English worker is exposed, a cause permanently active in forcing the whole class downwards' (cited in Castles and Kosack 1973: 17). As is well established, the enclosure movement, the depredations of absentee landlords, the ruin of domestic industry by British capitalist interests in the period following 1800, and the famines of 1822 and 1846/7 provided triggers for mass Irish migration. The last famine occasioned the death of one million people and the emigration of an even greater number.

By 1851, there were 727,326 Irish immigrants in Britain, making up 2.9 per cent of the population in England and Wales and 7.2 per cent of the Scottish population (Castles and Kosack 1973: 16–17; Jackson 1963: 11). Child labour and Irish migrant labour were but two forms of involuntary labour in England in the nineteenth century. As Corrigan points out, the *de facto* and *de jure* status of most adult English workers continued to be defined as 'servants' until the 1875 Employer and Workan Act. Six years later, service relationships still accounted for about one-third of the paid employed population, about the same as manufacturing. Young workers, agricultural workers and domestic servants were not legally recognized as free workers until the 1920s and 1930s.

Corrigan also cites the work of the feminist historian, Leonore Davidoff, who highlighted the numerical significance of the category 'domestic servants'. The number of servants grew from 751,541 to a peak of 1,386,167 in 1891, never falling below one million until the 1930s. Other prevalent forms of compulsion included bonded miners, collier-serfs (Scotland), labourers and servants contracted at 'hiring fairs', the system of tied cottages and the provision of allotments by employers anxious to lower reproduction costs and habituate their workers (Corrigan 1977: 438–41).

In short, in the evolution of their economies, eastern Europe, Britain or the USA do not exhibit a pure form of free labour regime.

Labour-repressive systems and emergency regimes

Moore introduced the term 'labour-repressive system' in his famous account of the social origins of dictatorship and democracy. In its original form, Moore (1966: 435) used the term to argue that labour-repressive agricultural systems, such as those found in the southern USA, Japan, Prussia (and tsarist Russia, though this is not developed), provide an infertile soil for the growth of parliamentary democracy and, instead, form part of the 'institutional complex' leading to fascism. Subsequently, southern African writers deployed the notion of a labour-repressive or labour-coercive economic system in an attempt to expand the original concept to cover the situations they described (Trapido 1971; van Onselen 1976). It is easy to see the attractions of such an exercise, but we must recognize that these authors have elided Moore's stress on agriculture in order to cover the case of mining labour in southern Africa, and have also significantly deflected the specific political trajectory of Moore's arguments. My earlier discussion about the coexistence of unfree labour systems with free systems in many parts of the globe also questions the extent to which such labour-repressive economies are *sui generis*.

Nonetheless, what does unite the original and expanded versions of the concept and what also has decisive bearing on my wider argument is the insistence of the aforementioned writers on the 'political means' used to organize and perpetuate the supply of labour. Often this takes the form of intense political repression and severe restrictions on the mobility of labourers, normally the construction of worker barracks (as in South

Africa), or labour camps (as in the Soviet Union). Mention of the Soviet Union also raises the issue of whether that regime should also be considered a labour-repressive system. On the one hand, this problem can be resolved by arguing (with Trotsky) that the Soviet Union was a state capitalist society and therefore can be expected to exhibit features common to those of other early capitalist regimes. On the other hand, it is possible to concur with Swianiewicz's (1965) argument that the USSR represented but one notable example of a general tendency to deploy forced labour at the early stages of industrialization in all societies.

While I have some sympathy with both these positions, the first degenerated into a sterile set of insults traded between different left-wing sects, while the second dilutes the specific ideological and political content of the Soviet treatment of its labour force. It may be that the attempt to use the notion of a labour-repressive economy to cover the cases of imperial Germany, the antebellum southern USA, Meiji Japan, South Africa, tsarist Russia after the serf emancipation, and the Soviet Union, obscures more than it illuminates. While it correctly places at the centre of the definition the political organization of the labour supply, the category must remain a tenuous one, for the equally primary role of the state in the colonial and plantation regimes discussed earlier should not be overlooked. It would seem therefore that the mechanisms of labour control and the particular division of labour constructed by the Soviet state are best described separately, without pressing them too firmly into one or other shallow Procrustean bed.

The indictments of the Soviet labour system are now widely known in the wake of the collapse of official communism. Solzhenitsyn's bitter torrent of criticism in *The Gulag archipelago* was the most powerful voice from inside the Soviet Union denouncing the labour camps. (There were a number of accounts from cold war warriors in the West.) He graphically conveyed how *déclassé* intellectuals, 'malingering' workers and numerous national and religious minorities were shunted along the pipes of the Soviet 'sewage disposal system' towards the prisons and labour camps:

> The prison sewers were never empty. The blood, the sweat, and the urine into which we were pulped pulsed through them continuously. The history of this sewage system is the history of

an endless swallow and flow; flood alternating with ebb and ebb again with flood; waves pouring in, some big, some small brooks and rivulets flowing in from all sides; trickles oozing in through gutters; and then just plain individually scooped-up droplets.

(Solzhenitsyn 1979: 25)

In the end, however, Solzhenitsyn's account remains, as he calls it, 'an experiment in literary investigation', abstracted from the regime's own conception of its objectives. A more scholarly account is provided in a major study by Applebaum (2004). The very codicils of government provided strong interventionist principles in labour organization. The Labour Law Code, for example, obliged all people between 16 and 50 to work unless sickness or disability prevented them from so doing. There was simply no recognition of the right not to work. It is this logic that led to the regime's view that a corrective labour camp was a proper means for requiring workers to fulfil their obligations to the community, the Party and the state. The same logic led to the idea of an 'economic crime' punishable by corrective labour – until the 1970s the Soviets regarded crime as essentially a social problem exclusive to capitalist society.

The *dirigist* character of the regime was also evident in its embrace of the rationality of comprehensive planning, which in turn required an absolute monopoly over the labour market. Where compulsion was needed to develop northern Russia and Siberia, dig the canal system, mine the gold, or cut the lumber, Gulag (the central body administering the labour camps) could find plenty of unwilling recruits. These recruits were drawn from the six million kulaks whose liquidation as a class was deemed necessary, and from saboteurs, religious dissenters and nomads. According to Dallin and Nicolaevsky, two writers openly hostile to the Soviet Union, only 15 per cent of the population of the camps could be deemed 'criminals' in the conventional understanding of that label. The same two authors estimated that forced labour produced 75 per cent of gold production, while they rather loosely put the overall number of forced labourers in the 1940s at around eight, ten or twelve million. The number was so large, at any rate, that the authors believed that 'forced labour must be considered one of the main classes in Soviet Russia's social structure – a class more numerous and economically no less

important than that of office workers in industry' (Dallin and
Nicolaevsky 1948: 87). In an even more obvious product of the cold war,
Roger Baldwin (1953) and his associates extend Dallin and Nicolaevsky's
study, which they describe as 'the standard work on slave labour', to the
cases of Czechoslovakia, Hungary, Bulgaria, Romania, Albania, East
Germany, Poland, Yugoslavia and China.

In so far as it has been possible to proffer a moral excuse or rational
explanation for the Soviet labour camps, their existence has been related
to Stalin's personal political excesses, the need to fracture or eliminate
classes hostile to the revolution or to a particular emergency necessitated
by the failures of the National Economic Planning period, and the consequent need to compel infrastructural developments, heavy industry
and the rapid collectivization of agriculture. The concept of 'an emergency labour regime' implies a sudden deviation from a normally more
liberal set of arrangements. Certainly, there were peaks in the utilization
of forced labour, in 1929/30, 1937/8 and 1944–46, which far exceeded
the normal flow (Solzhenitsyn 1979: 245). But for a system that
continued for nearly half a century, until Khrushchev destroyed its worst
features in the period after 1956, the notion that the Soviets were
confronting an 'emergency' does seem a little disingenuous.

The concept of an 'emergency labour regime' is more apposite when
considering the Nazis' very different use of concentration camp and
foreign labour during the Second World War. The stunning horror of the
Holocaust of the Jews, Romanies and other *Untermenshen* has obscured
the fact that the Nazi division of labour deployed millions of foreign
labourers, in varying conditions of deprivation, in order to service the
war machine. By 1943, the numbers of *Zwangsarbeitar* (compulsory
workers) had reached 5.2 million. Some would argue that the Nazis' wild
expansionist lunges across Europe reflected the need to find further
sources of subjugated labour as much as the desire for raw materials,
strategic advantage or the assuagement of Hitler's megalomania (Homse
1967). Detailed studies of the German companies involved in the use of
forced labour demonstrate how vital such labour was, both for war
reproduction and for the super profits realized by companies like I. G.
Farben (Borkin 1978). In a review of Ferencz's (1979) book on Jewish
forced labour, T. D. Noakes summarizes the principal features of the
system. Men and women, selected for their physical fitness, were set to

work in 1634 forced labour camps under the direction of the SS. Auschwitz and its 42 branch camps alone contained 144,000 forced workers. Himmler, whose control of the party machine through the SS was absolute, was fully aware of the precious commodity he had under his control. An elaborate accounting system ensured that the companies that requested forced labour (they were not obliged to use such workers) paid the SS for every hour of skilled or unskilled labour they utilized. As Noakes (1980) explains:

> Over 200 companies availed themselves of the opportunity, employing over 250,000 inmates. They included many of the most prestigious firms in Germany: I. G. Farben, Krupp and Siemens, for example, all established works within the Auschwitz complex. The conditions in which these slave labourers worked were for the most part appalling and for the Jews they were worst of all. Over 30,000 Jews perished in three years working for the I. G. Farben Buna rubber factory in Auschwitz.

More recently, an account from the horse's mouth (the expression, I fear, insults a noble creature), in the person of Albert Speer, the minister of armaments from February 1942, makes clear that there were divisions of opinion on the question of forced labour within the Nazi hierarchy. According to his account, a debate took place as to whether Jews should be killed immediately as Aryan doctrine decreed, used first as slave labour, or worked to death. Speer's (1981) principal complaint is that Himmler used his access and control of forced labour to further his political ambitions rather than (as Speer advocated) to exploit the labour first, in a rational style based on 'American management'. In so far as several million internees were worked to death or worked before they were put to death, this aspect of the Nazi labour regime demonstrates an extreme example of a case where the employer or the state become so obsessed with immediate production goals that the reproduction of labour, which alone can ensure the long-term viability of a regime, is relegated to a second place. There is obviously a theoretical limit beyond which the cost of acquiring fresh labour supplies will outstrip the benefits derived from the economics of death – a macabre calculation that will not be made here.

The global care chain

Though camp labour on the scale of the Soviet Union and Nazi Germany
has abated everywhere but China (see below) many contemporary international migrants in wealthy societies continue to demonstrate the
historic capacity for capitalism to combine different forms of labour, free
and unfree. This applies with particular force to migrant women. Like
women in general, the migration of women has been 'hidden from
history', to use a phrase that feminist historians coined in the 1960s. No
doubt the much criticized 'male gaze' sometimes blindly failed to focus
on anything but male migrants. However, there is a more specific reason
for this omission too: early immigration statistics often identified women
as dependants of male migrants and their entry was simply not recorded.
Phizacklea (2000) has notably documented the invisibility of independent female migration and the massive growth of this phenomenon
towards the end of the twentieth century. Her early work on Caribbean
migration to the UK from the 1950s had revealed that, despite the legally
convenient description of 'spouse' or 'daughter', there were many concealed independent female migrants. Although claims that international
women migrants began to outnumber men from the mid-1970s remain
contested, Phizacklea (2000: 122) argues that the various programmes to
regularize immigration status do indeed show that there are 'substantial'
numbers of women among international migrants.

. Many women migrants crossing boundaries are employed as nannies,
domestics and sex workers, often occupying subordinated and exploited
sections of metropolitan workforces (see Ehrenreich and Hochschild
2003 for various case studies). It is an oversimplification to meld the
characteristics of these diverse women workers into one concept, yet
there is no doubt that the expression 'global care chain', which
Hochschild (2000) coined, captures some central dynamics of the
process, including the ramifications of migration for the families left
behind. The care chain involves interconnected nodes between rural and
urban areas and between poor and rich countries. The links are stronger
or weaker but they tend to reinforce, rather than obviate, existing global
inequalities. Finally, an unpaid family member tends ultimately to
displace the emotional labour expended. As Hochschild (2000: 131) puts
it, a typical global chain might comprise: 'an older daughter from a poor
family who cares for her siblings while her mother works as a nanny

caring for the children of a migrating nanny who, in turn, cares for the child of a family in a rich country'.

Yeates (2004) both accepts the value and innovative quality of Hochschild's core concept and suggests various ways of extending, refining and applying it. I want here to isolate one of her (five) qualifications to the concept and one of her new applications. As Yeates (2004: 82–3) indicates, it is wrong to imagine that subcontracting homecare is a uniquely contemporary or international phenomenon. The social history of many societies shows that aristocratic and wealthy women deployed working-class or impoverished middle-class women as governesses, nurses, nannies and servants. In other words, such relationships are not historically necessarily international, though Hochschild is clearly right to suggest that this labour had now become globalized. In terms of her additional application, Yeates (2004) makes a good case for including nurses in the global care chain, referring particularly to the example of Irish nurses coming to Britain. However, many health workers, including carers for the elderly rich, are drawn from Africa, Asia and Latin America as the market for health care has itself become globalized.

Unfree labour in the twenty-first century

The historical focus of this chapter may lead to an unwarranted assumption that in an era of globalization unfree labour has disappeared. Sadly, this is far from the case. One of the oldest non-governmental organizations in the world is the anti-slavery society, now known as Anti-Slavery International (www.anti-slavery.org). It is a depressing thought that such are the numbers of slaves involved that its mission is still essential. It rather depends, of course, on what is meant by 'slavery', where journalistic, legal, sociological, comparative and historical meanings differ widely. On the expansive definition Bales (1999) deployed, there are 27 million slaves worldwide. As indicated earlier, I am more inclined to a cautious view – seeing slavery as involving necessarily ownership, the capacity to bequeath a slave as property, no or low pay, the inheritance of the status by the next generation and a political regime that recognizes slavery as legal. Of course, there are disgraceful levels of repression, control, threat and exploitation in many labour relationships, which nonetheless I prefer to see as (other) examples of unfree labour. Within this wider category, I will say something briefly about domestic workers, sex workers, Chinese labour camps and child labour (though this is far from an exhaustive list).

One reason why we need a more complex understanding of the forms of unfree labour other than using the label 'slavery' can be found in the more intimate setting of domestic households. Even in apartheid South Africa, where the politics of race and massive economic discrepancies divided 'maids' and 'madams', the employers often saw themselves as 'helping' the domestic workers and treating them as members of the family, deploying them in intimate tasks as baby minders, wet nurses and companions to elderly relatives (Cock 1989). Anderson (2000) also found this self-righteousness on the part of employers in Europe, where employers complained plaintively that their kindness and pity were met by ingratitude. But, as Anderson (2000: 144) explains, 'maternalism' is far from a totally benign social relationship:

> Maternalism is based on the superordinate–subordinate relation-ship with the female employer caring for the worker as she would for a child or a pet, thereby expressing in a feminized way, her lack of respect for the domestic worker as an adult worker. It is encapsulated in the use of the term 'girl' to describe the adult women. It is an overpersonalization of employment relations and a refusal to properly acknowledge the employment relation, but presenting this overpersonalization as a benefit, as friendship.

Subtle exploitation is not generally found in the case of the exploitation of sex workers, many of whom are trafficked by ruthless people smug-glers. Phizacklea (2000: 132–3) provides the following data. In Thailand, two million women and children work in the sex industry, while 50,000 Thai women work in Japan. The tissue-thin labels used to describe them – 'entertainers' or 'guests' – disguises the illegality of importing sex workers to Japan. Watts and Zimmerman (2002: 1235) suggest that violence, deception and 'the misuse of power and control over women for profit' mark the trade in sex workers. Though the statistics provide a large range, they estimate the number of trafficked sex workers crossing boundaries at between 700,000 and two million. Even in a case where exploitation seems so common, notable dissent has been recorded by Kempadoo and Doezema (1998) and by Skeldon (2000) who argue that the sex industry does provide some real opportunities for job mobility, that the level of coercion is exaggerated and that in any case there is a conceptual overlap between labour migration and trafficking.

The third contemporary form of unfree labour that needs highlighting is camp labour in China. As in the Russian Gulags, Marxist doctrine dictated that the camps were established for re-education, not for punishment. The camps are known as 'laogai', Mandarin for 'reform through labour'. There is little objective information on the camps, so we have to rely largely on dissenters and exiles. One, Wu (2001), was imprisoned for 19 years and has set up the Laogai Research Foundation in Washington. He claims that there are over one thousand forced labour camps, containing a stock of population of between six to eight million. Followers of the Falun Gong movement have been particularly singled out for labour in the camps. One member of the movement, Jennifer Zeng, protested at the sale in Australia of long-eared toy rabbits carrying the Nestlé label, which she had helped to produce in a camp, despite beatings and electric shock therapy (*Sydney Morning Herald*, 28 December 2001). Wu's foundation estimates that one quarter of China's tea, 60 per cent of its rubber-vulcanizing chemicals and significant volumes of hand tools, cotton and steel pipes are produced in the camps for export.

Finally, I must allude, without space for much discussion, to child labour. The ILO estimated in 1996 that there were 250 million working children aged between 5 and 14 years, including part-time workers. Anker (2000: 2) cautioned against taking this astonishing figure too literally. In many poor countries, where schooling is not universal, part-time work by children can be a form of apprenticeship leading to productive employment or self-employment. More worrying, however, is that a significant proportion of the total are working in 'hazardous conditions' – some being brutally worked in manual labour occupations, some being trafficked and others exposed to 'forced recruitment for armed conflict, prostitution, pornography and other illicit activities' (www.anti-slavery.org).

Conclusion

I have started my account of unfree labour under modern capitalism with a description of plantation (sometimes called 'chattel') slavery, which launched the global production of tropical commodities –

principally sugar, coffee and cotton. I showed that the development of successor labour regimes, including apprenticeship, indentureship, colonial labour regimes, mine labour in South Africa and camp labour in Nazi Germany and the Soviet Union, marked the legal end of the slave trade and slavery. Contrary to Marx, I have argued that capitalism has *not* been characterized by the exclusive use of free labour but by a combination of free and unfree labour regimes. This has applied throughout the history as much as the 'prehistory' of capital and has taken a variety of forms in different areas. The very diversity of forms of unfree labour allows me to put my counter-proposition in a simple way: capitalism successfully combines labour of differing statuses. Contrary to Wallerstein, I have argued that the spatial distribution of free and unfree labour is shared between the outlying and central zones of a political economy, though clearly there is a relative concentration of free workers in the metropole and unfree workers in the colonial areas.

I showed also how the Nazi state engineered a mix of labour regimes to mitigate a war production crisis by turning millions of conquered peoples into expendable helots. Unless one adopts the position that the Soviet Union was always a state capitalist society (in which case the argument holds on other grounds), the mix of free and unfree labour is a feature that also appeared in state socialist divisions of labour, certainly in the early phases of labour-intensive industrialization. This pattern is now found too in China, 'Communist' by self-description, but showing a powerful capitalist face as it integrates its exports, including those produced in labour camps, into the global market. The period of globalization has shown no let up in the deployment of unfree labour – from outright slaves to sex workers, subordinated health workers, domestics and child labourers, the pattern has reasserted itself for those who are prepared to look beyond the glitzy adverts for production, consumption, good health and leisure to the hidden underclass that is making all this possible.

Note

1. 'Indios' (= Indians) was and is the term used to describe many indigenous South Americans. However, it arose from Columbus's misconception that in his attempt to circumnavigate the globe he had reached India. In fact, with landfall in the Americas he completed only half his intended journey.

Chapter 2

The proletariat at the gates: migrant and non-citizen labour, 1850–2000

T he period reviewed here is 1850 to 2000. The first date marks the slow death knell of slavery, the second the end of the last millennium. Europe is at the centre of the global migration history of the period surveyed. The European powers replaced the slave trade with the use of indentured labour in their plantation economies; later Europeans migrated to the 'colonies of settlement' and North America. In the period from 1850 to 1945 recruits to the European industrial zones were found from the East; after the Second World War they came from the South and colonies. Now Europe is a common destination area both for refugees from the South and for migrants from the former state socialist countries. Each of these migrations is assessed in turn in both a numerical sense and in terms of the status and condition of the migrating communities.

Indentured labour

Social institutions as powerful as slavery do not collapse instantaneously. Slavery was abolished in British colonies in 1834, but only children under the age of six were immediately freed; the remaining ex-slaves were 'apprenticed' to their masters for four to six years. It survived until 1863 in the Dutch colonies and until 1865 in the United States. Again, vagrancy laws, apprenticeship, contracts and economic compulsion still tied many of the former slaves to their old tasks. However, as a profitable and preferred means of organizing labour, the system was clearly on its way out. Moreover, the commentators and planters of the time knew it. As Adam Smith argued in *The wealth of nations*, 'The work done by slaves though it appears to cost only their maintenance is in the end the dearest of any' (cited Tinker 1984: 77). The planters had to maintain a year-round workforce in a seasonal industry, while the slaves had to be supervised, policed, housed, clothed and fed. Similarly, the British humanitarians at home maintained that 'free labour' would be more efficient than slave labour. The planters agreed. One, in Mauritius, rubbed his hands in glee at the arrival of the first group of Indian indentured labourers in 1835. 'Their cost', he gloated, 'is not half that of a slave'. The system of indentureship thus rapidly replaced slavery as the key mode of exploitation in the European plantation economies.

The indentured workers were 'free' only in so far as they could not be owned, bought or sold. The workers were highly constrained until the expiry of the contract, the breach of which was met by prosecution and often severe punishment. Potts (1990: 63–103), in her account of the evolution of the world labour market, prefers the expression 'coolieism' to describe the range of indentured and contractual systems used to recruit Asian labour, but indenture was the most common form. She (Potts 1990: 67) lists 40 countries to which the indentured workers were sent – to 23 British colonies, to the colonial possessions of France, Spain, Germany, the Netherlands, Portugal and Belgium and to the United States and its non-governing territories.

The scale and scope of the recruitment was extensive and is estimated over the 1834–1941 period (when indentureship was finally ended with the revocation of the Coolie Ordinance in the Dutch colonies) at anywhere between 12 and 37 million workers (Potts 1990: 72–3). In British India, one of the principal sources of supply, the system had effectively come to an end in 1920 partly under the weight of Indian nationalist objections, but also because the labour supply to the plantation economies now sufficed. To what degree were these indentured migrant workers able to accommodate to the countries to which they emigrated? It is important, first, to emphasize that in the case of the colonial tropical plantations, most of the inhabitants, whether indentured or not, were subjects of their colonial masters, not citizens. Forms of representation often did not extend beyond a small group of administrators, the settler groups and a few enfranchised locals. After the end of their indentures therefore, the Asian workers often shared a similar status to their fellow colonial subjects. This situation applied particularly to regions like the Caribbean where the local populations (the Caribs and the Arawaks) had largely been wiped out by European diseases or military force. The Indo- and Afro-Guyanese, for example, thus stood in a common relationship to the colonial state (Rodney 1981).

The status of indentured labourers became more problematic in countries where a substantial indigenous population survived, often with self-definitions of nationality and peoplehood that bound the indigenees to the collective ownership of the land. Such a circumstance obtained, for instance, in Fiji. At the end of colonial rule in 1970, 98 per cent of all locally born Indians had opted for Fijian citizenship. However, this did not prevent the leader of the Fijian Nationalist Party (cited in Lal 1990: 19), five years later, denouncing his fellow citizens in these terms: 'The time has arrived when Indians or people of Indian origin in this country be repatriated back to India and that their travelling expenses back home and compensation for their properties in the country be met by the British Government.'

The dilemmas of the overseas Indians as independence approached were anticipated by a discussion in the Lok Sabha on 8 March 1948, when Prime Minister Nehru (cited in Lal 1990: 20) posed these questions: 'Now these Indians abroad. ... Are they Indian citizens or not? If not, then our interest in them becomes purely humanitarian, not political. This House wants to treat them as Indians and with the same breath it wants a complete franchise for them in the countries where they are living. Of course the two things do not go together.' Nehru posed the issue in terms that we might now find too stark; after all, dual citizenship and nationality are not uncommon phenomena in the contemporary world. However, the anti-colonial movements in India, and later elsewhere, demanded total affirmations of loyalty to the local state, a fealty that the overseas Indian population was not always in a position to affirm. Thus, the East African Asians, under threat from African nationalism in Kenya and a more brutal form of kleptocracy in Idi Amin's Uganda, enjoined Britain to honour its promise of citizenship and fled to the UK in the 1960s and 1970s. By contrast, the Indian community in South Africa, suffering a common deprivation of civic rights under apartheid, had little alternative but to throw its lot in with the African majority, the Indian Congress being an important partner in the anti-apartheid 'Congress Alliance' linking Africans, Indians, 'Coloureds' and radical whites.

Settler societies: the USA and the white dominions

The plantation economies established under the aegis of mercantile capitalism predominantly deployed slave, indentured and contract labourers from Africa and Asia. However, it is perhaps important to remember Williams's (1964: 7) non-racial corrective that, 'Unfree labour in the New World was brown, white, black and yellow; Catholic, Protestant and pagan.' He shows how 'redemptioners', convicts and white servants from Ireland, Britain, Portugal, Madeira and elsewhere, were sent to the West Indies before the planters turned to Africa. (Small communities descended from these groups, like the 'Red Legs' of Barbados, still survive.)

However, the bulk of European migrants did not go to plantation colonies but to the United States (USA) and to what are sometimes described as 'the colonies of settlement'. These were New Zealand, Canada, Australia, Rhodesia and South Africa in the British case; Brazil, Mozambique and Angola in the Portuguese case; Indonesia for the Dutch; and Algeria and Tunisia in the case of the French. What links these societies together is that in each territory the European migrants were numerous enough or powerful enough to assert, or try to assert, independence from the motherland and hegemony over the indigenous populations. In short, the settlers captured the political structure from the colonial power (sometimes only for a short while) and sought to deny the local inhabitants access to that structure. For convenience I shall refer to the above-named countries as 'dominions' (which legally-speaking only refers to some of the Anglo-Saxon examples, but cogently captures the superordination that the settlers sought to assert).

From 1820 to 1927 some 37 million migrants arrived in the United States, 32 million directly from Europe (Power 1979: 10). They came predominantly from Great Britain, France, Germany, Russia, Austro-Hungary and Italy. The migrants and their descendants rapidly built up the population of the country. In 1800 the US population was only 5.3 million; by 1905 it had reached 105.7 million people (Potts 1990: 131). The newcomers immediately adopted their country of settlement as their own with scant regard to the rights of the Native Americans, and often, a disdain for settlers of non-European origin.

Although many scholars (notably Glazer and Moynihan 1983) have rightly questioned the extent to which the newcomers were able to discard their prior ethnic identities, the ideology of Americanization was nonetheless powerful enough for the immigrants to distance themselves from Europe and assert a collective citizenship. The USA is probably the most successful example of a dominion society in that it relatively easily shook off vacillating British rule during the American Revolution and widened its frontiers to include large parts of Spanish Mexico. By the Treaty of Guadalupe Hidalgo in 1848 Mexico was forced to concede more than half its territory, including modern California, Arizona, New Mexico, Nevada, Colorado, Utah and a portion of Wyoming, all inherited from Spain at its independence in 1821.

Other settler dominions also established rights to self-government, though in each case with deleterious effects on the indigenous populations. The Australians decimated the Aborigines and destroyed their way of life; the New Zealanders crippled Maori culture; the Canadians forced the Inuit peoples into reservations. In each of these three cases the British government accorded formal dominion status, namely self-government and a franchise to the settlers, while showing only token regard for the native peoples. Settlers fared less well in the remaining dominions to which British migrants went. In Kenya, the Mau Mau put paid to a wild attempt by the tiny settler group to declare 'white independence'; instead decolonization put power in the hands of the black elite. In Rhodesia, Ian Smith managed to sustain a Unilateral Declaration of Independence for about a decade, but he too was finally laid low by the force of an armed African struggle.

In South Africa, that most difficult of countries to classify and typologize, the contrary pulls of Boer and British ambitions (demonstrated by the Anglo-Boer War of 1899–1902) and the counter force of African arms inhibited the construction of a powerful dominion society. Whereas the Boers organized successful shooting parties against the helpless San and Khoi-khoi, the Zulu impis proved more formidable opponents. The fate of settler society in South Africa now hangs in the balance. Whereas the European population's political dominance is now nearly at an end, its social and economic dominance is likely to remain important.

If this view is correct, South Africa will come to resemble a Brazilian or Spanish American model in which a Creole society emerges – European by culture and language, but with a political and economic system shared by settlers, indigenees and a creolized middle stratum. In a sense this process is inevitable, for the links between the emigrants and their homelands have effectively eroded – Dutch hegemony collapsing by the early nineteenth century and the British connection being seriously weakened in 1910 with the Union Act. The only remaining question is, thus, whether the creolization of South Africa will take place with more or less violence.[1]

In the cases of Algeria, Indonesia, Angola and Mozambique, the colonizing societies of France, the Netherlands and Portugal managed to hang onto their colonies against settler demands, though sometimes by a very thin thread. The movement for a French Algeria (and against Algerian nationalism) was so powerful that it brought down the French government and was only suppressed by de Gaulle through an audacious threat of military might. The bulk of the settlers had little alternative but to return to France. The Dutch, likewise, managed to extricate themselves from Indonesia only by admitting 150,000 Netherlands citizens of Eurasian origin who were clearly unable to withstand the demands of the nationalist movement. Finally, the Portuguese settlers evacuated Angola and Mozambique on a massive scale as the anti-colonial movements in those countries began to close in on the capital cities and agricultural heartlands.

Given the highly variable and often costly outcomes of the movement of European settlers to dominion or aspirant-dominion societies, it is perhaps worth reflecting for a moment why metropolitan societies by and large encouraged this movement of their citizens abroad.

A useful example might be found in Britain. In essence, the emigration to the settler countries was seen as a solution to social problems at home and a means of expanding British interests abroad. This notion was first advanced in a state paper that Bacon delivered to James I in 1606. He suggested that by emigration England would gain 'a double commodity, in the avoidance of people here, and in making use of them there' (cited in Williams 1964: 10). The poor rates would be relieved and idlers, vagrants and criminals would be put to good use elsewhere.

Once established, the principle was extended laterally. Scottish crofters, troublesome Irish peasants, dissident soldiers (like the Levellers) were all shipped out with careless abandon. Even the reverses of British power in the United States at the hands of the colonial bourgeoisie were attributed not to a design fault but to the incompetence and capriciousness of the German monarch on the British throne at the time of the American Revolution. The movement to encourage the export of Britons abroad reached its apogee in the work of Sir John Seeley who, in his book *The expansion of England* (1883), identified emigration as the key means of effecting British imperial designs.

Migrants to Europe

First period: 1850–1945

It is paradoxical that the emigration imperialists failed to anticipate the extent to which industrialization in the core countries of nineteenth-century Europe (France, England and Prussia/Germany) would require the importation of labourers from the surrounding areas, and from abroad, in order to fuel their own growing manufacturing bases.

Marx saw this clearly in 1867: 'Ireland is at present merely an agricultural district of England which happens to be divided by a wide stretch of water from the country for which it provides corn, wool, cattle, and industrial and military recruits' (Marx 1976: 860). By 1851 there were already 700,000 disenfranchized Irish migrants in England (Power 1979: 13). To the Irish were added a significant number of Jewish migrants and refugees fleeing from the tsarist pogroms in the Pale of Settlement. Some 200,000 Jews arrived in Britain over the period between 1880 and 1914, a number that greatly outstripped the existing Jewish community of 70,000. The newcomers found an economic niche in informal self-employment, but also as industrial workers and in the 'sweated trades', particularly in the clothing industry (Kosmin 1981: 187–9).

Across the Channel, the growth in the foreign working population was similar. In 1851 there were 379,000 foreigners registered in France (1 per cent of the population), by 1886 1,127,000 foreigners were recorded. The early foreign recruits to France came from Belgium, Spain and Italy and eastern Europe, but the First World War saw the start of a pattern of labour recruitment from the colonies that was to survive until the 1970s. Looking at the Algerians alone, the pattern of recruitment of workers was as follows: 1912 (4000–5000); 1926 (69,789); 1936 (72,891); 1964 (211,675); 1968 (473,812) (Potts 1990: 134).

Germany's industrial expansion after 1870 also required large numbers of imported migrant labourers. Many of the workers in the coalmines of the Ruhr were of Polish extraction; others came from Austria, Italy, the Netherlands or Belgium. The Germans, alarmed at the prospect of 'Polandization' (*Polnisierung*), adopted a measure called *Karenzzwang*, requiring compulsory leave without pay. Combined with the *Inlands-legitimierung* (internal authorization), which tied foreign workers to a particular place of work, the German Labour Office evolved an effective set of controls over the labour market. This system gave flexibility in the boom and slump cycles and anticipated the post-1945 guest-worker system. Thus, whereas there were 1.2 million foreign workers in Germany by 1910, only 142,000 were employed in 1932 as the depression loomed (Potts 1990: 135–7).

Second period: 1945–75

The deployment of a large number of migrant workers in western Europe for the 30 years after the Second World War is well documented in the secondary literature, including in my own book *The new helots* (1987: 111–44). So, with space at a premium, I must forbear repeating anything but the barest essentials.

By the mid-1970s, when immigration restrictions were introduced in all western European countries, 13.5 million 'foreigners' were officially counted as residing in Belgium, Denmark, France, Germany (Federal Republic), Ireland, Netherlands, the UK, Sweden and Switzerland (Cohen 1987: 111–12). Notable absolute concentrations of foreign-born populations were recorded in France, Germany and the UK, while the ratio of foreigners relative to the total labour force was markedly high in Luxemburg and Switzerland.

Moore (1977) divided foreign-born workers in western Europe into four main statuses – 'community workers', 'foreign workers', 'ex-colonial workers' and 'illegal migrants'. 'Community workers' moving from one EC country to another have extensive rights embodied in EC legislation. Under provisions agreed in 1961 and 1964, they have equality of treatment with national workers in respect of remuneration, dismissal, vocational training and rehabilitation, tax and social security benefits, trade union membership and rights, access to housing, and rights to be joined by spouses and dependants.

By contrast, the other three categories of workers characteristically endure less favourable civic, legal and political statuses. Their family life is sometimes limited or prohibited, their housing is inferior, their rights as employees are often considerably worse than those of either indigenous or community workers. They are also sometimes disenfranchized and not organized in trade unions, making them relatively defenceless in political and economic spheres. This observation is less true of ex-colonial workers in Britain, France or the Netherlands who have been granted *de jure* rights superior to foreign or illegal workers. However, their legal privileges have to be set against their *de facto* status as visible minorities, subject to often severe racial discrimination.

Many of western Europe's post-1945 migrants were drawn from the Mediterranean countries – Greece, Spain, Turkey, Portugal, Yugoslavia (and southern Italy). But in each case, the mix going to individual countries was different. Greeks, Turks and Yugoslavs went to Germany; Algerians, Portuguese, Spaniards, Italians and West Africans arrived in France; while the initial influx to Britain and the Netherlands tended to come from their former colonies – India, Pakistan, Bangladesh and the Anglophone Caribbean in Britain's case; in the case of the Netherlands from Indonesia, the rest of the former Dutch East Indies and Surinam. Belgium's 'foreigners' were largely drawn from Spain, Greece (both were later to become members of the EC), Morocco and Turkey. In the case of Sweden, the predominant migration came from Finland, but Yugoslavs, Greeks and Turks joined this flow in the 1970s and 1980s in descending order of magnitude (Cohen 1987: 114).

Commentators from a number of different ideological positions – be they neoclassical economists, Marxists or the compilers of official government reports – have tended to arrive at a similar understanding of the functions of migrant labour in post-1945 European countries. The common view is that migrant workers provided an indispensable element in the labour force that helped iron out the stops and goes in European economies and filled a vital gap in the 'secondary labour market', which the national workforce was not prepared to fill at the price being offered.

Despite their use value, migrants, particularly from non-white countries, soon became the victims of xenophobia and resentment and the easy entry requirements and approved schemes for recruitment were all

phased out by the mid-1970s. The downturn in the European economies, which accompanied (but was not caused by) the oil price rises of
1973/4, the export of capital to newly industrializing countries and the
availability of unemployed local labour all militated against further
labour imports.

Undocumented workers, refugees and asylum-seekers

The distinction between refugees and asylum-seekers on the one hand
and migrants on the other has always been a difficult one to sustain both
legally and sociologically. Certainly, there is a strong element of compulsion involved in the refugee-generating areas – due to war, civic
unrest, state formation (see Zolberg et al. 1986), famine or natural
disaster. But few examples of large-scale migration are free from some
elements of compulsion – be they derived from the force of economic
circumstance or from religious or ethnic persecution.

Though it may be possible to draw a tenuous line between the res-
pective strengths of the compulsions, the crucial difference between a
refugee and an economic migrant often rests largely on the definitions
the host state accords to the movement and, to a lesser extent, on a
precise adherence to the weight of international law. The point can be
made quite easily by reference to a simple example. In the more intense
periods of the cold war those leaving the Soviet Union and other state
socialist countries were characteristically welcomed as 'political refugees'
from a totalitarian state. In the post-*glasnost* period, by contrast, western
European states are desperately policing the frontiers to brace themselves against a horde of 'economic migrants'.

One of the most important challenges to the rich industrialized countries in the field of migration over the last two decades has been the
management of the flow, and the settlement or expulsion, of such
refugees. Though the effects of this migration on western European
countries has received a great deal of attention in the literature (for
example, Joly and Cohen 1989), it is always important to bear in mind
that the overwhelming bulk of the world's 18.5 million refugees is settled
in the neighbouring poor countries. A further historical corrective to
bear in mind is that Europe, which now is the 'reluctant host' to refugees, was not too long ago the major site for the generation of refugees
and displaced persons (Zolberg 1989).

As for illegals, EU countries have historically experienced a moderate inflow compared with the USA – though, as I discuss below, the anticipated movement from the East is expected soon to create a movement of undocumented and legal migrants of North American dimensions. Partly in anticipation of this flow, but also in response to xenophobic internal pressures, extensive efforts have been made to restrict the admission of refugees, asylum-seekers and illegal entrants (Joly and Cohen 1989). The extensive harmonization of EU countries' immigration policies has rightly been characterized as the creation of 'Fortress Europe' – permitting free movement within the EU zone, but policing the frontiers more effectively against external entrants.

Migration to the oil-rich countries

Other important destinations for international migrants in recent decades have been the oil-rich countries of the Middle East and OPEC countries in which oil revenues, accelerated in the period after 1973 for about a decade, allowed the initiation of ambitious development plans. In Venezuela, for example, following the oil-price boom that contributed 70 per cent of national revenue, governmental policy switched to a pro-immigration stance. This legitimized and enhanced a stream of perhaps half a million undocumented foreign migrants into Caracas in addition to the vast numbers of internal migrants. The Venezuelan Council for Human Resources authorized the importation of a further half-million workers during the period 1976 to 1980. The migrants arrived from the Latin American countries of Colombia, Argentina, Chile and Ecuador and from the European countries of Spain, Italy and Portugal.

Middle East oil-producing countries also showed dramatic increases in imported labour power. Unskilled workers from India, Bangladesh, Pakistan and Afghanistan poured into the oil-rich countries of the Middle East, the authorities regarding their Muslim religion as an important additional reason to permit their import. In the mid-1970s, an estimated 748,000 workers from these countries arrived in Saudi Arabia, with other large numbers going to the United Arab Emirates, Qatar and Kuwait. Some of this migration is between Arab countries (for example, Egyptians in Libya; or North Yemenis, Jordanians and Palestinians in Saudi Arabia). In other cases, the bulk of the labour force comes from outside the immediate area. For example, Sudan alone provides as many as 800,000 workers to the Arab OPEC countries. In some Middle Eastern countries, the proportion of foreign workers to home workers has reached almost absurd levels: for example 50 per cent of the total population in the United Arab Emirates are non-citizens.

By contrast, much of the skilled (doctors, civil engineers, architects) and middle-level (nurses, foremen) labour has arrived from Europe, often accompanying civil construction projects. The effects of the Gulf War on this large non-citizen labour force have been little short of calamitous. Whereas most skilled European expatriates were evacuated without too much trauma, Yemenis have been forcibly expelled from Saudi Arabia, mass evacuations of Egyptians and Indians took place from the war zones, while Palestinians have been tortured and in other ways discouraged from returning to 'liberated' Kuwait. The Palestinian population of Kuwait, which numbered about 400,000, was also under severe pressure. Most Palestinians fled Lebanon or Jordan – thereby probably triggering further destabilizing events. While the Hashmenite royal house has stabilized itself under King Hussein, in the long run the regime may be displaced by the sheer force of Palestinian numbers – over two-thirds of the current population consider themselves to be Palestinian. (We can also hardly fail to be cognizant of the large numbers of Kurdish refugees generated by a combination of fear of the Iraqi regime and political aspirations for a national homeland.)

While the factors that drive the continuation of a South–North movement (famine, civil war, war, natural disasters and economic necessity) persist, we may expect the pressures from the South to continue. Within Europe, however, the headline-grabbing issue in the 1990s was the estimation of the possible extent and dangers of East–West, migration – a theme to which I turn next.

East–West migration

If we take the old 'iron curtain' as the basic line of division between East and West, roughly about 400 million people lived on each side of the divide. Churchill's expression 'the iron curtain' was, of course always something of an exaggeration in that considerable migration did take place from East to West even before the dramatic events of 1989 and 1990, especially from East to West Germany. Nonetheless, the Berlin Wall was a symbolic and actual reminder that most of the states of the

East were operating an effective 'closed border' policy, which Dowty (1987: Chapter 3) characterized as 'a new serfdom'.

Dowty suggests that a tradition of sealing the frontiers to isolate Russians from foreign influences developed even before the 1917 revolution. For example, in Pushkin's *Boris Godunov* Tsar Boris commands:

> Take steps this very instant
> To fence off our Russia from Lithuania
> With barriers, so that not a single soul
> May pass the line; that not even a single hare
> Can scurry here from Poland; that no raven
> Can come winging its way from Krakow

Soviet fears in the early years after the revolution and the ultimately doomed attempt to construct 'socialism in one country' augmented this tradition. Despite the attempts at isolation, there were four major holes in the pre-*glasnost* curtain.

- As the Second World War ended, there was a large-scale movement from the former eastern provinces of Germany to Federal Germany of the order of eight million people (Castles and Kosack 1973: 25). Over the period from 1948 to 1989 inclusive, a further 3.9 million moved from the German Democratic Republic to West Germany (Chesnais 1990: 4). This number included 840,000 illegal migrants crossing the German frontiers during the period when the wall was in existence (13 August 1961–9 November 1989).
- The Soviet Union and the former Pale of Settlement also contained a significant number of Jews who had survived the Nazi and pro-Nazi killings during the war. A steady stream of Jewish dissenters and migrants whose demands were strongly supported by the Jewish lobby abroad, particularly in the United States, were granted exit visas in response to this pressure.
- Small numbers of human rights activists, radical scientists, literary figures and other political dissenters were granted visas in response to the demands of pressure groups in the West.
- The pre-1990 'iron curtain' was also rent by another gaping hole – namely Yugoslavia. Since the early 1960s, Yugoslavs have been free to

travel abroad. In one decade (1964–73) the number of Yugoslav migrants in European and other countries grew from a few thousand to almost 1.5 million. In 1973, one in ten migrant workers in western Europe was from Yugoslavia. The two main destination countries were Germany and Austria while, seen from the sending country, migration to the West involved 1 in 15 of the Yugoslavian population (Schierup 1990: 4).

Schierup's account of the causes and consequences of migration from Yugoslavia is set within a powerful – I would even say prophetic – account of its wider political economy and place in the international division of labour. Yugoslavian history during the 1970s could well provide a prototype of the situation affecting the Soviet Union and the rest of eastern Europe in the 1990s in that Yugoslavia has been a precursor of 'permanent reform', economic restructuring and democrat- ization – in short an early example of *glasnost* and *perestroika*. As a result of an internal recognition that socialism had failed at an economic level, Yugoslavia pioneered the entry of centrally planned economies into a much closer relationship with the capitalist economies. An increasing internal disintegration paralleled that closer international integration. In Yugoslavia, as in other 'iron curtain' countries, the Communist Party apparently played not only the negative role of restricting democratic participation, but also – arguably – the more positive role of keeping the lid on potentially highly destructive national, ethnic and religious divi- sions. As a result of the release of these centrifugal tendencies, Schierup (1990) observed the emergence of regional populist bosses – increasingly dependent on transnational capital and each seeking to negotiate separ- ate deals with the Western economies. The emergence of such contem- porary figures as Boris Yeltsin closely paralleled this development.

The rational model of East–West migration

So long as there was strong demand for cheap labour in countries like Germany and Austria, the Yugoslavian system could continue without major crisis. West–East movements of capital, technology and tourists could, in effect, be bartered for an East–West movement of, hopefully, temporary migrants.

The danger for the German and Austrian economies was that the economically benign phenomenon of temporary guest workers from the East could ineluctably change to socially irksome and costly permanent settlement – a process that was visibly occurring in the case of the Turks and that was all too likely to reoccur in the case of the Yugoslavs.

The shape of a solution emerged after the recession in 1973. From 1974 to 1978, 300,000 Yugoslav workers returned from Germany in response to various incentives and negative pressures (Schierup 1990: 101). Admittedly, this large number is somewhat deceptive – 150,000 Yugoslav workers arrived during the same period, and Schierup argues that a complex pattern of oscillating migration was developing.

Nonetheless, the net loss of 150,000 was sufficiently encouraging to officialdom to evolve a sophisticated return migration programme. Many migration researchers had found that the consumption effect among returnees far outweighed their capacity for productive investment in their country of origin. Characteristically, nutritional needs, household utensils, consumer durables (radios, televisions and videos), washing machines and furniture are followed by investment in, and improvement of, property. As many of these items are of a non-productive kind, or have a high import content, remittances may simply have served to deepen a foreign exchange crisis.

However, with the aid of the OECD and the cooperation of the Yugoslavian government (Schierup 1990: 131), a more sophisticated policy emerged that linked the interest to the labour-exporting and labour-importing governments. This policy had a number of elements.

- Controlling the numbers and skills of departing workers;
- ensuring appropriate skills were acquired in the country of emigration;
- maintaining close cultural links with the emigrating workers to ensure a low level of assimilation;
- creating a stock and bond market in Yugoslavia for the potentially productive use of worker remittances;
- providing incentives to invest in agriculture, and small industry; and
- utilizing the newly acquired skills of the returnees.

This model of East–West migration is therefore set within a framework of development aid and mutual benefit. While it was accepted that there still might be considerable spontaneous settlement in the destination country, the assumption was that it could be contained to manageable limits, with both countries benefiting. The labour-importing country would benefit from the use of much-needed labour, which could act also to make the internal labour market more competitive. The labour-exporting country would lose labour surplus to its own requirements, but would gain in terms of the potentially productive use of returnees' newly acquired skills and capital. During the 1990s, it is likely that proposals of this kind can be expected from the OECD, the EC and the Soviet and German authorities.

The doomsday model of East–West migration

The rational model evolved for Yugoslavia was, however, rational and containable only in theory. Schierup ultimately concludes that the new integration of Yugoslavia into European capitalism provided no easy answers to Yugoslavian society. (Indeed, it had become evident that the political disintegration of the country was imminent.)

Nonetheless, whatever difficulties occurred there, they were as nothing compared with some of the more nightmarish projections of what might have resulted from the waves of East–West migration following the events of 1989/90. The emerging patterns of migration fell into three main categories – co-ethnic returnees to their homelands, co-ethnic returnees to communities abroad, interregional migrants and those (not in the earlier categories) seeking to escape economic and political hardships in the East.

Co-ethnic returnees to their 'homelands'

The four important subgroups involved here are the Jews, the ethnic Germans, the Greeks in Kazakhstan and Albania, and the Turks. As mentioned earlier, Jewish migration had already been significant prior to 1989, but now visas are largely unrestricted. The number of people of Jewish origin in the Soviet Union was estimated at 1.5 million. The number of arrivals in Israel during the course of 1990 sometimes exceeded 4000 a day and by early 1991 constituted about 500,000 people – one in five of the Israeli population. The nature of this migration was reported to be largely non-religious and non-Zionist in character – most entrants simply saw the opportunity to come to Israel under the Law of Return (the constitutional provision that allows all Jews immediate citizenship in Israel) as a way of escaping the Soviet Union. There was even a strong suspicion that many of the arrivees were non-Jews in the rabbinical sense (namely not descended from a Jewish mother), in terms of professed belief or in any other sense. (This must be the first occasion historically when passing for a Jew was advantageous.) The large number of entrants parallels the foundation of the Zionist state in the immediate wake of the Second World War and triggered highly alarmist reports in the Arab press. Although both Arabs and some of right wing in Israel saw the arrival of the Soviet Jews as a means of populating the West Bank and denying it to the Palestinians, in fact the Russian Jews have largely avoided the West Bank settlements.

Jews have also left in considerable numbers for Austria and, interestingly, 3000 have arrived in Germany. This small group confronted Germany with a moral dilemma in so far as it was politically embarrassing to give the impression that Soviet Jews were unwelcome. By the early 1990s, the number of Jews in Germany was 25,000, a small fraction of the half million who lived there before the war. The Jewish–German Council welcomed the new migrants as a means of rebuilding the once flourishing Jewish community and the German government has been anxious to avoid any stigma of imposing numerical limits (*Independent*, 10 January 1991).

The second major group of East–West migrants returning to their 'homeland' were the ethnic Germans. Even after the assimilation of Germany there still remain considerable numbers of German-speaking people behind the old iron curtain. By one account there are 2.5 million Volga-Germans – descendants of the people Stalin forcibly relocated to Kazakhstan (*Independent*, 1 December 1990). Another account suggests that there are now only 1.7 million Germans still living in the Soviet Union (Chesnais 1990). To this number should be added 1.6 million ethnic Germans spread across Poland, Romania, Czechoslovakia, Yugoslavia and Hungary in that order of magnitude.

What is undisputed is that the 1980s saw a huge rise in migrants from the Soviet bloc, excluding the GDR, arriving in West Germany. In all, about two million arrived over the period between 1950 and 1989, about half during the 1980s. Average monthly arrivals have been 3500 (1986),

6500 (1987), 16,900 (1988), 31,000 (1989), and 40,300 (1990). The figures Chesnais produced suggest, moreover, that the origin countries only include 82,000 from the Soviet Union. In other words, the bulk of the ethnic Germans who might wish to return to the motherland are still within the former Soviet Union.

As in the case of Israel, the German constitution allows for the admission of all ethnic Germans with minimal restrictions and checks. Given that German is a world language and that large numbers of non-ethnic Germans may be able to pass for German we may hazard a guess that perhaps another half million Soviet citizens may seek admission to Germany. There remain of course substantial numbers of ethnic Germans in Poland, Romania, Czechoslovakia, Yugoslavia and Hungary.

A third co-ethnic group wanting to return to its motherland was the Greeks. Hilton (*Independent*, 1 December 1990) suggested there were as many as 500,000 to a million Pontians – descendants of Greek immigrants of the eighth century whom Stalin forcibly sent, like the Germans, to Kazakhstan. There are also many Greeks in Albania who are desperate to link with their former homeland. Albania, notorious for the severe restrictions it placed on any contact with the rest of the world, now shows some signs of precipitating quite a large population exodus. Although there were small numbers who attempted to leave during the events of July 1990 (a few thousand), the desperation of the émigrés – clinging to the sides of boats – suggests that once the political climate is more open a high level of emigration might be expected. The Greek government is alarmed by the potential for return migration and is trying to set up a number of cultural links and economic aid programmes that will serve to stabilize the Albanian Greeks in Albania. This is unlikely to succeed. Although the Greek government does not, as far as I am aware, have a constitutional provision for the readmission of Greeks abroad, it has been the case that traditionally overseas Greeks have always felt free to return to Greece, vote in elections and purchase property. This relaxed attitude towards kith and kin abroad is likely to stop in the near future – as it has done in the case of the Italian government, which shares a rather similar historical tradition.

The fourth group joining its motherland comprised of Turks, mainly from Bulgaria. It seems that 310,000 Turkish Bulgarians left for Turkey in 1989 alone (Chesnais 1990: 4).

Co-ethnic migrants to communities abroad

A similar form of migration, but one in which the ethnic groups do not have a homeland to return to applied in the case of the Armenians. The Armenian population of the Soviet Union was numbered at 3.5 million. Most were settled in Soviet Armenia itself, but about one quarter of the group – 500,000 in Azerbaijan and 400,000 in Georgia – are much more unstable. Chesnais (1990: 17) surmises that everything points to a large proportion of these populations becoming emigrants going either to the United States or to France (which have populations of Armenian origin of half a million and 300,000 respectively).

The second major group without a homeland is the Romanies (known as 'gypsies'). The Romany population of the East is estimated at between 2.5 and 4 million people excluding Romania. They are likely to be particular victims of xenophobia, ethnic conflict and the rise of nationalism. While in some respects they would represent a similar pattern to that presented by the Armenians, in that there are reasonably large Romany populations in Italy, Spain and France to which they can go, more likely they will become serious victims of waves of prejudice and anger in their own territories and will have only a restricted capacity to move. A good example is the case of Romanies in Romania, who were victimized during the ethnic conflicts from 1989 onwards.

The number of Romanies in Romania – probably underdeclared in the census there as elsewhere because of prejudice – is between two and six million. Visitors to many parts of eastern Europe may casually observe that Romanies are on the move. As is well known, they already attract hostility in Western countries and are unlikely to be welcomed either as political refugees or as potentially productive economic migrants. Their situation, therefore, is likely to be equally fraught, whether they end up in the East or the West.

Cross-border movements within the East

Not all migration will be East–West in the sense of crossing the old iron curtain. Many coreligionists or co-ethnic groups may very well wish to re-establish their rights of settlement in other eastern European countries.

This situation applies particularly to Poland, where about half a million Soviet citizens of Polish origin anticipated returning. According to a report in the *Independent* (29 November 1990) 'Poland's plenipotentiary for refugees, Colonel Zbigniew Skoczylas, expects two or even three million Russians, Ukrainians, Belorussians and others to flood westwards into Poland if and when Soviet travel restrictions are lifted. ... He is also preparing for possible mass defections by Soviet soldiers and their families based here [in Warsaw].' It is also important to emphasize that there are very large discrepancies of wealth, power and misfortune within the eastern European bloc. So, whereas the situation in Poland may look fairly desperate by comparison with German standards, there are nevertheless very large numbers of Romanians seeking to emigrate both to Poland and Hungary. The Poles estimated that Romanians were entering Poland at the rate of 35,000 to 50,000 a day in November 1990, while the number of Romanians going to Hungary moved from 13,000 in 1988 to 30,000 in the next year. With the collapse of the Ceausescu government, and more particularly the massacre of students in June 1990, the numbers increased dramatically. One estimate is that 800,000 people left Romania in the first eight months of 1990.

Other migrants from the East

Three major factors will heavily influence interregional and international movements from the East. These are first ethnic conflicts, especially in the Transcaucasus between the Armenians and the Azerbaijanis, and forced expulsions and frequent attacks on ethnic minorities in Uzbekistan, Kazakhstan and Kirgiziya. Second, *perestroika*, namely economic restructuring, will allow market forces to let rip, thus permitting much freer travel within countries. Large slum development and homelessness are expected to arise while unemployment levels reached 30 million in 2000. This led to increased pressure for emigration, both interregional and East–West. Third, the citizens of the Soviet Union suffered more than their due share of ecological disasters, some natural like the Armenian earthquake, which made half a million people homeless, and some man-made, like the Chernobyl nuclear disaster (when 135,000 were evacuated) and the killing of the Aral Sea, which threatens subsistence over a massive region. Again this led to increased pressures for emigration.

Conclusion

In trying to define the status of many of the migrant, non-citizen workers over the period considered, I suggested in an earlier work (Cohen 1987) the category of 'helot' – a term used to capture the subordinate situation of such workers. Technically, the workers concerned are not slaves in that the employers claim no absolute proprietorial rights over them and they cannot be bought or sold. At the same time, helots characteristically do not enjoy full social and civic rights compared with citizen workers.

The continued large-scale deployment of such workers in the most advanced industrial countries challenges the proposition Marx advanced that the capitalist mode of production invariably requires 'free' labourers. Of course, Marx saw the workers' 'freedom' in a very special sense – free from their own means of production (land, tools and livestock) and free only to sell their remaining asset, labour power. In this sense, migrant non-citizen labourers share a common relationship to capital with native workers. However, it is clear that a worker's freedom cannot be conceived in so circumscribed a manner. Whether a worker is free to join a trade union, free to vote, or free to establish and maintain a family relationship are all aspects of a modern notion of freedom. The citizenship of a modern state also confers a host of rights and benefits ranging from access to health care, social security, unemployment insurance, a pension, disability, sickness and injury allowances to protection in respect of minimum wages, unfair dismissal and arbitrary state power.

Even in so abbreviated a historical review as the one provided above, we notice a wide variety of possibilities with respect to such rights and benefits being accorded to migrant workers. In the plantation societies European mercantilism established, indentured labourers were highly disadvantaged by the terms of their contracts and even after they had served out their indentures they were able only to attain the status of colonial subjects. Their descendants had to await the process of decolonization to reach citizenship and, even then, many experienced discrimination and expulsions as a result of the restricted definitions of nationality that emerged. By contrast, those European migrants who successfully established dominion societies appropriated the boundaries of nationality and citizenship for themselves, normally at the expense of the native peoples and sometimes at the expense of non-European migrants.

Characteristically, migrant workers flowing the other way, that is to Europe, failed to enjoy such benefits and rights of full citizenship, or had to fight to attain equality with the indigenous population. Such a situation obtained, for example, with respect to ex-colonial workers, non-national workers and illegals in Europe and the United States. Refugees and asylum-seekers also have had great difficulties in asserting their claims to equality under the Geneva Convention of 1951 or the Bellagio Protocol of 1967.

Increasingly restrictive EU legislation and harmonization of immigration policy, which commenced on 1 January 1993, enhanced rights of mobility in the EU at the expense of non-EU nationals – both those from the East as well as those from the South. Populations from the East that share a common ethnic heritage with states in the West (Germans, Jews, Turks and Greeks) will initially be advantaged, but this 'honeymoon' period is likely to be short lived and will not apply at all to ethnic groups that do not have state power in the West (Armenians, Romanies, Kurds) or to other migrants.

While migration from South and East is likely to be highly restricted, there will nonetheless clearly be some demand for helot labour. In considering the continued functionality of such a group, it is perhaps a useful way to understand capitalist societies by suggesting that they do not require free labour or, for that matter, unfree labour, but work best through a judicious mix of labour of different statuses. If we see this from the prism of 'the logic of capital', the systematic requirements are for a constant new flow of subordinate labour – slave, followed or paralleled by indentured, forced, non-citizen, illegal, colonial, 'Third World' and former state socialist. As one cohort of helots is exhausted, another is found to take its place. Not only does this provide a useful supply of cheap labour that can be inserted into the production process (and extruded from it) as the stops and goes of the economy dictate, it also acts as a classical 'reserve army'. Existing workers are thus disciplined by the possibility of replacement by helot labour or the export of their jobs to a low-wage area.

A 'capital logic' position should also be contrasted with a view from below. A crucial part of the argument – and one I have had little opportunity to develop here – is how the migrants themselves respond to their situation and organize in defence of their collective interests. This counter-movement by helot labour – in the direction of acquiring the status of citizen labour – both limits the extent and possibility of complete exploitation, but also, by the same token, propels the perpetual search for a cohort of replacement helots.

What are the future trends? The sheer quantities of people on the move in both East and South are expected to accelerate to such dimensions that they are unlikely to be peacefully absorbed into Western European states. In the East, economic restructuring is leading to homelessness, slum development and unemployment. However, some nightmare scenarios would take the argument much further, suggesting that hyperinflation and the current shortages of food in the former Soviet Union might lead to mass poverty. In this circumstance, the political pressures on the current administration in the Russian Federation may very well be intolerable and military intervention perhaps accompanied by further balkanization will result. Mass migratory movements may very well follow such a development.

The Soviet Union attempted to give vent to some of the demands for East–West migration by passing a permissive emigration law (in 1991). This removed for the first time legal restrictions on exit and brought the Soviets into line with the situation that was pertained in Yugoslavia since 1972. Even assuming that there will be no mass migration arising from starvation and political disorder, if the Russian propensity to migrate matches the Yugoslavian case, we are talking about two million migrants. However, this is almost certainly likely to be an underestimate of those who may wish to leave.

Unlike Tsar Boris Godunov, Gorbachev reversed totally the inclination to close Russia off from the rest of the world and was apparently only too happy to let go those who wished to leave. However, demand from the West will be limited to some co-ethnic groups, those with technical, language and other qualifications and, finally, a small tranche of helot labour. A much larger pool of intending migrants may wish to move west, along with refugees from the South. Despite their centrality in the history of global migration, European politicians and populations are in no mood to welcome them.

Note

1. The first democratic elections took place in 1994. Writing a decade later
   allows me to venture that South Africa's prospects for political stability and
   modest economic growth look positive. However, crime levels are high, as
   too is unemployment. Using the Gini index of inequality and comparing the
   top with the bottom deciles of the population generates the highest level of
   inequality in the world. This should be set against the upward mobility of a
   significant black middle class and the general success of a 'coloured' (that is
   mixed identity) artisan class in the Cape. In other words, the question posed
   cannot yet be definitively answered.

Chapter 3

Shaping the nation, excluding the Other: the deportation of migrants from Britain

I n recent years, historians, social theorists and literary scholars have developed an impressive theoretical armoury with which to illuminate the question of how a national identity is formed and how it becomes distinguished from other national entities. Traditional discussions of racism, xenophobia and nationalism have now been complemented by notions of 'Otherness and difference', 'boundary formation' and 'identity construction'. Though there are important differences in nuance between contemporary thinkers, since the publication of Anderson's influential book, *Imagined communities* (1983), in a sense we are all 'constructionists' now in that it is difficult to imagine any contemporary scholar insisting on the biological determinacy of race, the immutability of national character or the primordiality of ethnicity (see Jackson and Penrose 1993). After providing a brief exegesis of some of the more recent theory, I use the case of expulsions and deportations from Britain to show how immigration policy was deployed, both in a metaphorical and more literal sense, to give shape and meaning to an emerging British national identity.

Theory

Literary theorists and cultural anthropologists have used notions of 'Otherness' and 'difference' with dramatic effect to show how Eurocentric views of the world came to be dominant. For example, Pratt (1986), a scholar of comparative literature, showed how travellers' descriptions of the San of southern Africa (called 'Bushmen') codified difference and fixed 'the Other' in a timeless present. All actions and reactions of the 'native' were thought to be habitual and predictable. The ethnographic present gave a history to the observer (characteristically the European, the insider, the self), but denied coevality to the observed (the outsider, the alien, 'the Other'). By suggesting that members of the Other were incapable of change, they cease to be amenable to reason and become unable to change, adapt or assimilate.

While useful in showing how non-Europeans were denied an historical consciousness, notions of the Other have also been used to portray how Europe distanced itself from the rest of the world's regions. This process was probed notably by Edward Said (1991) who argued that the Orient had a special place in Europe's experience as its main cultural contestant and a source of rival civilizations, languages and cultures. The Orient was the source of Europe's 'deepest and most recurring images of the Other. ... European culture gained in strength and identity by setting itself off against the Orient as a sort of surrogate and even underground self' (Said 1991: 1–2). If the Orient represented a redoubtable yet ultimately subordinated enemy, Africa, the Pacific islands and the indigenees of the Americas were so easily enslaved, conquered or infected with European diseases that their inhabitants (and descendants) became lodged in the European consciousness as inferior beings placed on the lowest rungs of a static hierarchy of racial excellence.

Despite their allusive, metaphorical and literary qualities, discussions about Otherness have undoubtedly helped us understand the general processes of identity formation at national and international levels. A closely related strand of theory looks at how boundaries are formed between peoples. Again I will start with Said's observation (1991: 4) that a group of people living on only a few acres of land will set up boundaries between their land, its immediate surroundings and the territory beyond, often designated as 'the land of the barbarians'. It is not required that the barbarians accept the 'us–them' label for the distinction to work. The difference may be arbitrary or fictive: it is enough that 'we' have set up the boundaries of 'us', for 'them' to become 'they'. 'They' have a culture or an identity incompatible with ours. As Said reasons, 'To a certain extent, modern and primitive societies seem thus to derive a sense of their identities negatively.'

Said's contention can be greatly extended by reference to an established and more complex anthropological debate started by Frederick

Barth's discussion of ethnic boundaries. For Barth (1969) boundaries could be real or symbolic, visible or invisible. The markers that divide could include territory, history, language, economic considerations, or symbolic identifications of one kind or another. In addressing the question of which markers the social actors would use, Barth used the metaphor of a boundary 'vessel'. The contents of the vessel would determine the firmness or weakness of the boundary and the significance of the diacritic that differentiated the 'us' from the 'them'.

The literary scholars and the tradition Barth pioneered essentially considered group identity formation without reference to nationality and state formation. The attempt to make the boundaries of nationality, identity and territory coincide is, of course, all nationalists' central political project. Despite the nationalists' claims, Anderson emphasized that the nation remained an imaginary identity construct, as real in people's minds as it is in the world. The nation is an 'imagined community' with four principal qualities: it is *imagined* because the members of even the smallest nation will never know most of their fellow members, yet in the minds of each is the image of their commonality. The nation is imagined as *limited* 'because even the largest of them has finite, if elastic boundaries beyond which lie other nations'. (In other words, no nation claims to be coterminous with humankind.) It is imagined as *sovereign* in that it displaces (or at least severely undermines) the legitimacy of organized religion or the monarchy. Finally, it is imagined as a *community* because, regardless of actual inequality, the nation is conceived of as a deep horizontal comradeship (Anderson 1983: 15–16).

While I share the view that identity boundaries are more indeterminate, malleable and variable than is commonly surmised, national identities differ from other group identities by involving the achievement of, or aspiration to, statehood. However, once the state is brought back in, the extent to which national identities can be reshaped, reformed and recombined simply through a form of 'cultural politics' becomes far more problematic. I argue, therefore, for a greater historical specificity, a more exacting focus on the different diacritics used to define the self and the Other and an appreciation of the key role of major political and social actors who selectively construct the walls that separate, or selectively permit access through the turnstiles and gateways linking the inner and outer worlds. In the case of the boundary between the British and the

Other, I suggest that immigration policies and practices (and, in particular, deportations) can be used to tell which forms of distinction (religion, language difference, economic competition, fear of dangerous political ideas, assumed racial difference, imperial arrogance or whatever) were associated with the growth of an English (and, more diffusely, a British) national identity.

A second limitation of recent theory (particularly of the literary variety) is that much of it grew up as a critique of colonialism and imperialism and consequently centres on the relations between European and non-European societies. By correcting the monochromatic view of the latter, Said and others fell into the error of falsely assuming an historical, moral and practical unity among Europeans. As I show below, the level of official British suspicion and hostility to European continental immigrants makes this assumption far from accurate. Despite these two limitations on recent theory, the core insight remains. This I would summarize as follows: 'We know who we are by who we reject'. Or – to be more pertinent to my current argument – 'we know who we are by who we eject.'

Beginnings of state control

When did the English state's right to control entry and exit become established? T. W. E. Roche, the historian of the immigration service, argued that immigration control commenced with William the Conqueror who, in the wake of his successful invasion, set up castles along the south coast to prevent somebody else emulating what he had just done. The five key control points, the 'Cinque Ports', were at Hastings, Romney, Dover, Hythe and Sandwich: the process of passing through these ports gave birth to the word 'passport'. The policing of the frontier became an important aspect of royal power to be executed by the monarch's most trustworthy vassals. William the Conqueror and Henry I were particularly preoccupied with excluding papal delegates and with threats to their own power from rivals who had taken refuge abroad. The assassination of Henry at Canterbury by Becket's four knights only arose because they were not successfully intercepted at Hythe. In the second year of Henry II's reign, all 'aliens' were abruptly banished on the grounds that 'they were considered to be becoming too numerous' (Roche 1969: 13–15).

The early thirteenth century showed the first signs of an exclusive English identity being shaped. When the French king, Philip Augustus, seized Normandy in 1204, some English magnates were in the uncomfortable position of having to choose between two liege lords on either side of the Channel. The ex-Norman baronage was now sufficiently indigenized to see Normans as 'foreigners'. The attempted invasion of Dover by Louis the Dauphin provides one illustration. When this was threatened in 1216, the port's custodian, with the decidedly Gallic name of Hubert de Burgh, provided a ringing declaration of early nationalism: 'As long as I draw breath I will not surrender to French aliens this castle, which is the key in the lock of England' (Roche 1969: 17–18).

Middlemen minorities

The notion of a 'French alien' was especially innovative in that (though they had lost Normandy) Poitou still remained under the control of the English crown and many officials and nobles of continental origin sought and found preferment in England under Henry III's rule (1216–72). For much of his reign, Henry was tolerant of continental merchants, moneylenders and foreign wool workers. He afforded them protection so long as they made suitable contributions to the crown. However, as W. Cunningham (1969: 70) cynically remarked, 'they were protected only to be plundered.' Even this conditional haven did not last. The final years of Henry's reign saw increasing hostility to three groups – the Flemish, some of whom were granted a 'denizen' (resident alien) status but most of whom were deported; the Caorsine 'usurers' who were expelled at the insistence of the Church; and the Jews.

With respect to the last, in the first half of the twelfth century anti-Jewish riots had occurred in Westminster (on the day of Richard the Lionheart's coronation), in Dunstable, Stamford, York and Norwich. However, the full force of royal disapproval was to await Edward I's rule. Within two years of his accession, Jews found guilty of usury had to wear a placard around their necks. Then, in 1290, the entire resident Jewish population, some 15,660 people, were deported. They were not allowed to return until 367 years later during the Cromwellian period.

The Jewish role as the classical 'middleman minority' (as the sexist sociological term has it), was supplanted by the Lombards, the Hansards and the Flemish who fared little better at the hands of the rapacious crown or mobs manipulated by City magnates who owed money to their creditors. In a particularly excruciating test of political correctness, members of the Flemish colony at Southwark were enjoined to pronounce the words 'Bread and Cheese' in the proper London pronunciation. Those who failed were summarily executed.

But deportations and expulsions were rare in the fourteenth and fifteenth centuries. The Lombards were protected by the Pope, the Black Death meant that Edward III needed to rebuild the population of England and, at the end of the period (when the unsettling Wars of the Roses had finally ended) a new era of international trade between England and Flanders had been opened up.

Religion

The liberalism of human mobility that followed trade liberalization was, however, short lived. The religious oppression and intolerance that started in the mid-sixteenth century over much of Europe soon ramified at the English court and in the Privy Council. At the accession of Mary (1553), all 'strangers'[1] were commanded to leave the realm. These included Walloon weavers who professed a Calvinist faith and were returned to the continent. Another example can be found in the Privy Council papers of 1562, which refer to the expulsion of an unfortunate 'Dutch heretic', one Hadrian Hamslede, who is described as 'being found obstinat in dyvers erronious opinions' (Dasent 1890: 127).

Although Elizabeth (1558–1603) allowed the weavers that Mary had expelled to return, she used the royal prerogative to expel other religious dissenters fearing, in particular, a pro-Catholic revival. For the same reason, she also restricted movement out of England by her own subjects to prevent them being schooled at the Catholic seminaries in the Netherlands, Reims and Rome that were dedicated to training missionaries for the English field. In 1585 alone, 14 Catholic priests were deported; Philip II suspected some of preparing the ground for an invasion. Three years later, when the long-feared Spanish Armada finally materialized, Elizabeth again used her power to expel Jesuits and 'Spanish agents' (Bindhoff 1961: 235–6; Roche 1969: 39).

In the seventeenth century, the power to deport seems to have been progressively conceded to the Privy Council, though the notion of a royal prerogative still survived.[2] The principal targets remained religious dissenters, especially Jesuits. For example, in 1618, 'by letters patent of comission', James I (James VI of Scotland) gave the power to six or more privy councillors 'to exile and bannish out of and from his Majesty's realmes of Englaund and Irelaund ... so manie jesuits, seminarie priests and other eccelesiasticall persons whatsoever made and ordayned accordinge to the order and rites of the Romish Church' (LCHMT 1930: 338). The Lord Chancellor, Lord Treasurer, Lord Privy Seal and others set about their task with determination, the Acts of the Privy Council recording no less than 49 Jesuit priests so expelled in the 1620–21 session alone. The Privy Council also formalized the procedure. A deportation order signed in December 1620 was issued in the recognizably modern form of a warrant to constables and other officers.

Revolutionaries and the 'alien menace'

In his history of the Home Office, Sir Edward Troup (1925: 125) suggested that 'in the eighteenth century the right to exclude had fallen into abeyance'. However, an important legal landmark was initiated by the British government's apprehensive reaction to the French Revolution. In 1793, Grenville's Aliens Act was passed, which gave parliamentary sanction for the expulsion of aliens for the first time. The Act provided, *inter alia*, for the transportation of an alien who returned after being expelled. If the alien were so impudent as to return yet again, the Act allowed capital punishment.

The most prominent victim of Grenville's Act was the French politician and diplomat, Talleyrand, who had been elected president of the French assembly in 1790. When the revolution debouched into the period known as 'The Terror', he had swiftly fled to England. Talleyrand was deported to the USA in 1793, but argued in his memoirs that he was expelled so as to show that the Aliens Act was no dead letter. Under Clause XVII of the Act, all principal secretaries of state were empowered to issue a deportation under specified conditions. This provision was strengthened in 1803 when expulsion was allowed on 'mere suspicion'; this sweeping power prevailed until 1836.

Lord Loughborough's speech in defence of the 1793 Act was instructive in alluding to the crisis that had faced Elizabeth in 1588 when the country was threatened by 'religious fanaticism'. Now, he opined, England was threatened by 'the fanaticism of infidelity'. This referred to the progress of French revolutionary ideas including 'atheism' and 'anarchism'. In the Act there is a clear legal distinction made between an alien and a denizen (privileged foreigner), its provisions not being applicable to 'foreign ambassadors' or to an 'Alien who shall have Letters Patent of Denization'.

The 1793 Act was only rarely deployed and intermittently re-enacted (in 1816, 1826 and 1836). Indeed, the evaporation of the tensions that followed the defeat of Napoleon, led Troup (1925: 125) to consider that the measures against aliens, 'fell into desuetude'. Powers of deportation were, however, renewed in 1848 in readiness for another 'alien menace' from continental revolutionaries. The Removal of Aliens Act of 1848 gave the home secretary and the lord lieutenant of Ireland the right to expel foreigners if it were deemed that they threatened the 'preservation of the peace and tranquillity of the realm'. Nine years later, Palmerston insisted on the repeal of the 1848 Act on the liberal grounds that deporting aliens on this vague basis would lead to an abuse of power.

The relaxed attitude of the period 1815–90 came to an abrupt end with another 'alien menace' – the influx of Russian and eastern European Jews. The discriminatory May Laws in Russia (1882) had precipitated the first big wave of migrants to the UK. Press and popular opinion was not slow to respond, albeit with contradictory arguments. According to the *Manchester City News* of 2 April 1887, 'Jews [are] advanced socialists who sympathise with the Paris Commune and Chicago martyrs.' On the other hand, English trade unionists and socialists frequently represented all Jews as wicked capitalists. A royal commission on alien immigration, which reported in 1903, accepted the force of various popular accusations against the Jewish immigrants. For example, the commission regarded it as 'an evil' that 'immigrants of the Jewish faith do not assimilate and intermarry with the native race' (Roche 1969: 66). Fierce controls were proposed. In fact when the Aliens Act of 1905 was passed in parliament the restrictionists did not have it all their own way. The act limited the powers of expulsion granted to immigration officers to the exclusion of 'undesirables'. These were defined as previous deportees, fugitive offenders, the mad and the destitute. Moreover, those refused admission had the right to appeal to an immigration board whose members were often surprisingly sympathetic.

The authorities thought potential 'undesirables' were to be exclusively found among the steerage passengers. The restrictionists in the Home Office were unhappy, not at the stunning demonstration of class justice that allowed those who could afford cabin fares to escape examination but at their limited powers to stop what they saw as mass immigration. That noses were out of joint in the Home Office can be discerned in Sir Edward Troup's history of the department. As the permanent under-secretary of state at the Home Office over the period from 1908 to 1922, Troup was probably the most important of what might be termed the 'hidden frontier guards' in the first quarter of this century. He claimed that the 1905 Aliens Act was disliked on the purely pragmatic grounds that it was difficult to administer, but it is clear that he and his immediate colleagues identified fully with the restrictionists. Competition from the 'aliens from eastern Europe', he asserted, 'lowered the wages in some of the unorganized trades to starvation point and their habits had a demoralizing effect in the crowded areas in which they settled' (Troup 1925: 143).

While other minorities, including Indians, Africans and Romanies, were all victims of restrictionist attitudes, there is little doubt that the main targets of animosity just before the First World War were the Jews. The term 'alien' was effectively the turn of the century newspeak for 'Jew'. Chamberlain campaigned on an anti-alien platform, the anti-Semitic British Brother League was established, while the journal, the *Alien Immigrant*, thought it 'scarcely necessary to labour the point that the first generation of children of Russian Jews in the East End are only English by legal fiction' (Landa 1911: 137). The Jews also had no friend in court, for W. Haldane Porter, the chief inspector under the Aliens Act and 'the founding father of the Immigration Service' was covertly associated with Major Evans Gordon, one of the most vocal of the anti-alien agitators (Kaye and Charlton 1990: 6). One commentator on the 'alien invasion' dropped all restraint and penned this verse offering the alternatives of voluntary departure or death:

> Be he Russian, or Pole, Lithuanian or Jew
> I care not, but take it for granted
> That the island of Britain can readily do
> With the notice: 'No aliens wanted'.
> I would give them one chance – just one week to clear out

And if found in the land one hour later
Then – death without trial or fooling about
Whether Anarchist, banker or waiter.

A curious gentility surrounded these odious sentiments. *The People* published them in February 1909 under the *nom de plume* of 'a lady' and the columnist 'Mr Will Workman' described them as 'a rousing patriotic stanza'.

Wartime expulsions and the aftermath

Administrative discretion and popular agitation, however, had their limitations. The frontier guard, Sir Edward Troup, was clearly a great deal happier with the logic of the military mind. In 1914, the Committee of Imperial Defence discussed the issue of aliens in Britain. The Aliens Act of that year – which placed rigid controls over the registration, movement and deportation of all aliens – was rushed through in a single day, 5 August. It was introduced in the House of Commons at 3.30 p.m. and gained royal assent by 7 p.m. Troup (1925: 143, 152) had no doubts as to its efficacy and justification: 'the base was laid for the effective control of aliens which was maintained throughout the war. ... [Before the war] all attempts on the part of the Home Office to exclude persons who had not identified themselves with English life and remained in sentiment *really* foreigners proved abortive' (emphasis added). Troup saw no difficulty bureaucratically in separating 'the real foreigners' from 'the English' (he ignored the rest of Britain). Subsequent historians have shown that it was not quite so easy in practice to segregate the sheep from the goats, due to the almost hysterical levels of Germanophobia that the outbreak of the First World War had generated (Holmes 1988; 1991). George V felt constrained to drop all German family titles and adopt the name 'Windsor'. German Knights of the Garter were struck off the roll; grocers with German names were accused of poisoning the public while *The Times* ran a series of 'loyalty letters', in which German or German-Jewish public figures were enjoined to declare themselves. (Those who refused found themselves cold-shouldered.) Another telling example, in the light of Britain's international reputation for the care of domestic animals (the RSPCA was founded as early as 1824), was that dachshunds were stoned in the streets of London. Spy stories also abounded.

After the sinking of the *Lusitania* off the coast of Ireland in May 1915, with the loss of 1201 lives, all restraints on the frontier guards of British identity were off. The previous autumn the government had initiated the repatriation of women, children, elderly men, invalid men of military age, ministers of religion and medical doctors of German origin. Henceforth, women and men over military age with a German background were obliged to show why they should not be expelled – a stunning administrative diktat significantly reversing the traditional burden of proof. According to Holmes (1988: 66), over the 1914–19 period 28,744 aliens were repatriated, of whom 23,571 were Germans. Cesarani (1987: 5) offers even higher figures: 30,700 Germans, Austrians, Hungarians and Turks over the 1914–18 period, together with 7000 Russians, probably all Jews.

The xenophobia of the war years no doubt helped in recruitment and in manufacturing a patriotic consensus in support of the increasingly costly, blood-drenched and futile war. But no amount of jingoism could keep pace with the losses at the front. In January 1916, the British government introduced conscription. Conscription placed particular pressures on three minority groups: the Belgians, the Russian Poles and the Lithuanians. The Belgians on the whole took up an offer for repatriation worked out jointly between the Belgian and British governments. The Russian Poles, who were mainly Jewish, split three ways. Established Anglo-Jewry persuaded some of their coreligionists to show their gratitude to their country of settlement by enlisting. But many Russian aliens, a substantial number of whom had not taken out British nationality, saw no good reason to support Britain's anti-Semitic ally, the tsar, whom they considered responsible for their enforced flight. A third group, with socialist views, simply saw the war as a capitalist conspiracy, which any self-respecting internationalist should denounce (Holmes 1988: 101–6). The frontier guards in the Home Office and War Office pressed the issue: the Russians and Lithuanians should serve either in the British army or in the armies of their original citizenship. The Lithuanians became wedged in a particularly tight vice. The conscripts split into two bodies: in 1917, 700 joined the British army, while 1100 returned to serve in Lithuania, then part of the tsar's empire. With the Russian revolution came another turn of the screw. Only 300 of the Lithuanian returnees were permitted to come back to Britain, on the grounds that the remaining 700 could not prove they had fought on the side of the allies or had not fought for the Bolsheviks. The Treasury withdrew the small allowances made to their families in Britain and 600 of the Lithuanian returnees' dependants (all women and children) were deported.

The aftermath of the extensive wartime expulsions and repatriations saw the frontier guards riding high. The ejection of 'enemy aliens' became an election pledge for Lloyd George in 1918 and, by April the following year, 19,000 Germans had been repatriated. Given the fanning of popular sentiment, it was no surprise that the emergency wartime powers over aliens were largely retained in the Aliens Restrictions (Amendment) Act of 1919. An order in council in 1920 reserved the home secretary's right to deport someone if he considered it 'conducive to the public good', a phrase that still echoes through the corridors of the Home Office. The home secretary Edward Shortt also insisted on additional clauses to exclude or deport aliens who encouraged sedition in the armed forces or promoted industrial unrest.

These clauses reflected the ruling elite's general apprehension imme-diately after the war. The Bolsheviks were triumphant in Russia and the rot looked like spreading to Germany. Anti-British riots had occurred in a number of colonies. Socialist political organizations were making great headway in the USA. And, in Britain, suffragettes chained themselves to the railings of Buckingham Palace, a soviet was briefly established in Glasgow and the first major race riots had broken out in Liverpool and Cardiff against a background of a police strike. Truly, hands must have wobbled in the gentlemen's clubs as they reached out to grab the port.

The frontier guards lashed out. Eighty 'Bolshevik sympathizers' were deported in May 1919. The Labour MP for Whitechapel complained that the Home Office was sending out Russian Jews almost weekly. Excluding dependants, 31 were expelled in November 1920, 49 in December 1920 and 58 in March 1921. Some of the 1917 conscripts who had elected to serve in the Russian army returned to Britain illegally: 40 were found and deported; 29 others were sent to Brixton Prison (Cesarani 1987: 7, 13).

As home secretary, Shortt's administrative powers included, but also transcended, the enforcement of a court's recommendation for depor-tation following conviction. This form of dual power (impossible in any

country where a written constitution separates administrative and judicial powers) allowed the home secretary to order a deportation even
when the court had not made such a recommendation or, indeed, had
acquitted an alien defendant. The home secretary saw no problem. He
maintained that deportation should not be treated as a judicial issue, 'but
rather as a matter of administration'. Deportation was not punishment
for a particular offence, but 'administrative action taken on behalf of the
public'.

During the 1920s and 1930s, the 1919 Act was extended on an annual
basis, despite an attempt in 1927, thrown out in parliament, to have the
powers accorded to the home secretary made permanent. Reformers and
pressure groups – most notably the Board of Deputies (the British
representative body of Jewry) – managed to establish an independent
Aliens Deportation Advisory Committee in 1930. The Home Office held
to its old line of 'administrative discretion' in cases of illegal entry and
overstaying (beyond the time allowed at the port of entry), but the home
secretary agreed to refer all other cases to the committee on the basis of a
'private understanding' and after 'radicals' like Harold Laski (a politics
lecturer at the London School of Economics) had been dropped from its
membership. When the committee had the temerity to question the
home secretary's judgements in 33 cases, the committee was quietly side-
tracked then discontinued.

That the committee was batting on a sticky wicket can be deduced
from the attitudes of the top civil servants at the Home Office: for
example, in a departmental memo to the home secretary in 1924,
Troup's successor as permanent under-secretary of state at the Home
Office, Sir John Pedder, explained why he systematically delayed looking
at some classes of applications for 'far longer' than the statutory minimum time of five years' residence. This was because his experience
suggested:

> that different races display very different qualities and capabilities
> for identifying themselves with this country. Speaking roughly, the
> Latin, Teuton and Scandinavian races, starting some of them, with
> a certain kinship with British races, [are] prompt and eager to
> identify themselves with the life and habits of this country and are
> easily assimilated. On the other hand, Slavs, Jews and other races

from Central and Eastern parts of Europe stand in quite a different position. They do not want to be assimilated in the same way and do not readily identify themselves with this country. Even the British-born Jews, for instance, always speak of themselves as a 'community', separate to a considerable degree and different from the British people.

(Cesarani 1987: 17)

While Sir John wrestled with his comparative studies of the differential rate of assimilability of various 'races', another committee of the Home Office planned for future encounters with other alien beings. In the light of the negative Isle of Man experiences with internment during the 1914–18 conflict, the Committee of Imperial Defence concluded in 1923 that there was no point in depriving the enemy of its able-bodied men if it took a large number of your own to look after them. It was thus agreed (with the exception of a limited provision for exactly 5490 internees) that, in any future conflict, expulsion would be far better than detention (Gillman and Gillman 1980: 23).

As the Second World War loomed this policy looked dangerously simplistic: 30,000 German-Jewish refugees had been admitted, while other Germans had put down roots, hoping to be naturalized. In 1938, the Home Office still clung to the 1923 ruling suggesting that all enemy aliens who came to Britain after 1 January 1919 should be 'required to return to their own countries'. Clearly, forcible repatriation of the Jews would be politically indefensible, so the Home Office, rather than abandon its expulsion plans, proposed a system of appeals against deportation. But what if these appeals were successful and the individuals concerned were still considered a security risk? Surely internment, the rejected policy, was bound to be reinstated?

In fact, some of the repatriations were affected, for 110 women and eight children were sent back to Germany between December 1939 and January 1940. Later, the policy and practice of detention and internment during the Second World War paralleled, and then soon exceeded, the hopeless mire of detentions during the First World War.

The racialization of immigration: deportations, 1945–78

After the Second World War the British Nationality Act of 1948, the

signing of the European Convention on Establishment and the Immigration Acts of 1962, 1968 and 1971 supplemented the state's powers of
deportation (in the Aliens Acts of 1905, 1914 and 1919). With the single
exception of the European Convention, which gave rights to proposed
deportees in certain categories to make representations to the courts, the
effects of all this legislation were to extend the reasons for deportations
and to widen the categories of people who could be expelled. In
particular, Commonwealth citizens, especially black Commonwealth
ones, were gradually legally 'reduced' to the status of aliens.

The succession of immigration measures was harsh by any standards,
but the virtually naked appeal to 'race' as a differentiating category
between those who were immune from deportation and those who were
subject to this state power made the policies more odious. In particular,
the 1971 legislation gave a right of abode to 'patrials' (nearly all of whom
were white) and denied that right to 'non-patrials' (nearly all of whom
were black, brown or yellow).[3]

The moment in the post-1945 period that has come to symbolize the
racialization of the 'immigration issue' was Enoch Powell's infamous
speech in Birmingham in April 1968. Powell developed the theme of 'an
alien wedge', which threatened the notion of legality that had hitherto
informed the British national culture. While the numbers in the alien
wedge were important, more pertinent were the character and effects of
black settlement. Powell continued, 'in fifteen or twenty years' time the
black man will hold the whip hand over the white man.' As Paul Gilroy
(1987: 85–8) comments, this image inverts the customary roles of
master and slave, thereby accepting historical guilt, but immediately
counteracts guilt with fear. Later in the speech, the masculine black
remains (either in the form of 'charming wide-grinning piccaninnies' or
as 'negro workers') but the white is transformed into a vulnerable little
old lady. She is taunted by the cry of 'racialist'[4] by the blacks, who also
push excreta through her letter box. Powell is distraught; he is 'filled
with foreboding'. Like the ancient Roman he sees 'the River Tiber
foaming with much blood'. Moreover, all of this is a 'preventable evil'
visited upon the UK 'by our own volition and our own neglect'.

What effects did this curious speech and the enormous row it provoked have on the question of deportations and removals? First, and
most important, it lent force to the gathering view that black Com-

monwealth citizens were as 'alien' as the foreigners and aliens of old. Instead of evoking the empire and Commonwealth, or common military service against the Nazis, the differences between white Britons and non-white Commonwealth citizens were now stressed. This extended also to the East African Asians who, as UK and Colonies passport holders, had the untrammelled right of entry. Many believed that successive colonial secretaries had promised them protection should their situation in independent African countries become intolerable. Powell, however, angrily denounced these historic rights and denied any suggestion that Britain had any responsibilities. Suddenly, the East African Asians were India's responsibility, despite their UK citizenship. Notice below how Powell (cited by Goulbourne 1991: 117) used the notion of 'belonging' to elide the force of international law and separate the 'them' from the 'us':

> When the East African countries became independent there was no suggestion, let alone undertaking, in parliament or outside, that those inhabitants who remained citizens of the UK and Colonies would have the right of entry into this country ... the practice of international law which requires a country to readmit or admit its own nationals applies in our case only to those who belong to the UK and not to other Commonwealth countries, whether classified as citizens of the UK and Colonies or not.

In short, the first effect of Powell's intervention was to draw the frontiers of identity more tightly around the British Isles and to try to renounce any responsibilities inherited from empire. Next, despite his phantasm of a foaming river of blood, like all good politicians, Powell did not project a message of complete fatalism. The 'evil' was 'preventable'. For his supporters, the problem was how. The 1971 legislation probably went as far as it could in explicitly diminishing the former privileges of Commonwealth citizens. To play with 'Powellism' more openly was both unrespectable and possibly dangerous, with unpredictable outcomes in the politics of the streets and perhaps open racial violence.

But Powell had touched a nerve of popular sentiment (across party lines), which sanctioned tougher action by the frontier guards. This is most dramatically evidenced in the use of the powers the home secretary was given (in practice exercised by immigration officers) to 'remove' alleged 'illegal entrants' by administrative fiat. Whereas the power to 'remove' was conditional and very rarely used in the case of Commonwealth citizens prior to the 1971 Act, once the Act had come into force (on 1 January 1973) the numbers of alleged illegal entrants removed from the Commonwealth were soon comparable to the number of aliens removed (Table 3.1).

Table 3.1: Alleged illegal entrants removed, 1973–86

Year	Foreign	Commonwealth	Total
1973	35	44	79
1974	33	80	113
1975	76	78	154
1976	127	137	264
1977	184	312	496
1978	275	263	538
1979	330	255	585
1980	589	319	908
1981	357	283	640
1982	223	208	431
1983	179	195	374
1984	188	237	425
1985	n.a.	n.a.	528
1986	246	44	704

Source: Correspondence with the Home Office Research and Statistics Department (1992).

Cultural swamping: Conservative governments, 1979–92

While the Labour Party was fearful of appearing 'soft on immigration', there was little doubt that there was a qualitative distinction in immigration matters between the two major parties during the Thatcher years. This turned on the Conservative Party's more intimate association with the ideas that Powell's 1968 'rivers of blood' speech had brought to the surface. For example, in her much quoted television speech in February

1978, Mrs Thatcher linked herself firmly to that tradition. Referring to trends in New (the official code name for 'non-white') Commonwealth and Pakistani immigration, she said:

> That is an awful lot, and I think it means that people are really rather afraid that this country might be swamped by people of a different culture. The British character has done so much for democracy, for law, and done so much throughout the world that if there is any fear that it might be swamped, then people are going to be rather hostile to those coming in.

This was precisely the message that a large part of the British electorate wanted to hear. Paradoxically, however, for a politician whose popularity lay in the claim that she always did what she promised, Mrs Thatcher was already making an anachronistic appeal. The immigration legislation of 1961 and 1971 had already throttled off all primary ('breadwinner') immigration from the so-called New Commonwealth, and the British Caribbean population, including their descendants, was actually declining. All that was left with respect to controlling the inflow was making it as difficult as it could possibly be for Indian, Bangladeshi and Pakistani spouses and dependants to join their breadwinners in the UK. The Home Office, the British visa officials in Asia and the immigration officers at Heathrow obliged with a series of petty, vindictive and obstructionist measures.

Some of the unrequited hostility of Mrs Thatcher's supporters was slaked by these actions, while xenophobia directed against asylum seekers provided a second outlet. Finally, however, a series of highly publicized deportation cases provided much symbolic satisfaction to the anti-foreigner and anti-black brigade. The increased use of deportations can in some measure also be seen as a sop to the Tory right that had demanded 'voluntary repatriation' at a noisy intervention at the Tory conference in October 1983.[5]

How were expulsions carried out in the post-1979 period? It may be useful first to provide some quantitative data on deportations during the three Thatcher terms of office (from 1979 to 1990) and for the first two years under the leadership of Mr Major, which commenced in November 1990 after her enforced resignation (Table 3.2).

Table 3.2: Removals and deportations under Conservative governments, 1979–92

1979	1382	1986	1880
1980	1872	1987	2700
1981	946	1988	2961
1982	863	1989	4500
1983	1365	1990	4330
1984	1545	1991	5600
1985	1665	1992	6100

Sources: Home Office Statistical Bulletins (various years); reports of the Immigration and Nationality Department, Home Office (various years); correspondence with the Home Office.

A cursory examination of the statistics shows that there was a strong and increasing propensity to use the powers of removal and deportation during the successive Conservative administrations commencing in 1979, the total more than doubling over the period. The number of deportation orders served (and the much smaller number ultimately enforced) also went up dramatically. According to figures provided by the Joint Council for the Welfare of Immigrants in the 1979–83 period, orders made went up by 145 per cent and those enforced by 64 per cent compared with the previous Labour Party government's period.

The quantitative data, however, tell only a part of the story. As pertinent as the figures themselves were four more qualitative changes in the policy of expulsions: first, an increased propensity to deport and detain asylum seekers requesting refuge in the UK; second, a greater determination in the Home Office to see through highly-publicized and often controversial cases 'to the end'; third, an attempt to restrict the role of MPs to intervene in deportation cases; finally, the passing of additional legislation tightening the powers of deportation even further.

Home Office attitudes

The immigration authorities' proliferating use of deportation orders triggered determined opposition from the Church, from newly formed pressure groups, from left-wing fringe parties and from the friends and neighbours of those who were threatened. This took the form of a sanctuary and anti-deportation movement. I will provide just one example of this phenomenon, chosen on the one hand not to provoke automatic sympathy with the victims, but on the other to demonstrate the hardening of attitudes at the Home Office.

First let me give some background. Roughly one-third of deportation orders follow a drugs conviction. The courts have the power to recommend deportation and in anything from one-third to one-half of drugs related cases they do so. Almost invariably the Home Office complies, but even where the court does not recommend deportation, the Home Office can still proceed with a deportation order. This is what happened in the case of Andy Anderson and Farida Ali, whose campaign against deportation was taken up by the Greater Manchester Immigration Aid Unit. According to the campaigners, Mr Anderson arrived in the UK from Jamaica in 1976 and was given permanent residence in 1978. He married a British citizen and had two children born in the UK. All his family were in the country. In 1987 the couple were convicted for possessing and supplying cannabis. Ms Farida Ali (his spouse) was given a 12-month sentence; her husband – who had one previous conviction for supplying – was imprisoned for four years. In September 1988, while in prison, he was served with a Home Office notice that his presence in the UK 'was not conducive to the public good'. His appeal was rejected at an immigration tribunal (with one out of three members, who happened to be black, strongly dissenting) and by the High Court.

In this case the trial judge had not ordered deportation, but the home secretary decided to deport, despite very favourable reports from the prison governor, the prison education officer, the probation officer, the prison chaplain and even an immigration officer sent to interview Ms Ali. The campaigners argued that the mass of positive evidence was ignored because Mr Anderson was black and a Rastafarian. The relevant minister at the Home Office, Mr Peter Lloyd, refused to withdraw the deportation order, but offered to pay the fares for Ms Ali and the children to join him in Jamaica! As the campaigners' contended, it was extraordinary that the government of the day was prepared to pay a British citizen to go into exile.

Although it is more than likely that a convicted drug dealer does not constitute most people's idea of a good citizen, this case illustrates several general features. First, any residual notion that Commonwealth origin provided a privileged status was firmly disabused. Second, the hidden frontier guards at the Home Office considered their own assessment of the case for deportation superior to the advice of prison officers, care workers close to the individual and even to the court itself. Third, in their determination to proceed with deportation, the fates of three British-born citizens (the wife and two children) counted for little.

The restriction of MPs' rights

Conventionally, members of parliament have a right (indeed a responsibility) to represent their constituents in immigration matters where they or a constituent's relative or friend has fallen foul of the immigration authorities. The principal forms of intervention available to MPs are two: first, the 'stop' procedure, initiated in the 1960s, whereby a removal direction is delayed pending representation by an MP and the further consideration given to the case by the relevant minister of state at the Home Office. Second, MPs can ask the minister to allow a person entry 'outside the immigration rules', a power of administrative discretion allowed in the 1971 immigration acts. Taking these forms of representation together, Table 3.3 indicates the number of representations made.

Table 3.3: Representations by MPs on immigration cases

1979	10,395	1984	13,164
1980	10,029	1985	16,024
1981	8,945	1986	17,511
1982	9,931	1987	11,842
1983	11,456		

Source: Parliamentary reply to Mr Jeremy Corbyn MP, 12 April 1988.

There is no doubt that many of these representations were conscientious responses to genuine cases of distress. In fact, some MPs became notoriously sympathetic to the anti-deportation cause and often pursued cases even where there was no obvious constituency connection. Again, the power to ask for a 'stop', particularly if a number of members made this request, delayed matters for long enough for an ordinary visitor – perhaps without the necessary visa – to see their families.

By July 1983, the minister of state at the Home Office, David Waddington, had had enough. He wrote to all MPs stating that he would only consider the first representation and this would have to come from an MP with a constituency interest. Then, in May 1985, he initiated a brief experiment that only lasted two weeks, requesting that MPs should intervene in port-of-entry cases within 24 hours. With the assistance of the Tamil Refugee Action Group and the United Kingdom Immigration Advisory Service, the MPs swung into action to beat the deadline, only to find that the Home Office was unable to respond equally as quickly. The experiment was abandoned (Morgado 1989: 14).

Rattled by this fiasco and the continuing flow of correspondence, in October 1985 Waddington accused MPs of 'abusing their right to make representations' and during the course of 1986 he issued four successive sets of 'guidelines' with which he asked MPs to comply. He failed in his attempt to get the chief immigration officers at the ports of entry, rather than his own office, to be responsible for giving reasons for refusal. But he succeeded in halting the grant of an automatic 'stop' in cases where visas had been required and where there was 'a clear attempt to seek entry through clearly bogus application for asylum'. The minister's mail-bag was lighter by nearly 6000 letters (see Table 3.3) in the year following this new ruling. He also was able to press the ruling that removal would be deferred only by 12 days if an MP intervened. Subsequently, this period was reduced to eight days.

Further immigration legislation

The Nationality Act of 1981 was not so much an immigration act as a way of reconciling (and multiplying) definitions of nationality to conform to the evolving practice of immigration law, particularly the determination of who had the right of abode in the UK. With respect to my current concern with deportations, it is worth drawing attention to the difficult (though thankfully rare) situation that, after the act, could result for those who are deported without having gained a *jus soli* status, a citizenship derived from their birthplace.

One such case concerned a London-born baby, Sidrah Syed, who happened to be born just four months after the implementation of the 1981 Act on 1 January 1983. His father, Shahid Syed, had come to the UK as a student in 1975 and worked for British Gas as an accountant after graduation. When his work permit was not renewed in 1983, he, his wife and baby Sidrah were faced with deportation to Pakistan, a country that Sidrah had no formal right to enter. In essence, the 1981 act has created the possibility of statelessness for minors and may continue to generate great complexity at the level of international relations in sorting out the consequences of deporting a stateless minor.

Seven years later, the Conservative government passed the Immigration Act of 1988. Lord McNair in the House of Lords lambasted this legislation as: 'another mean-minded, screw-tightening, loophole-closing concoction imbued with the implicit assumption that almost everybody who seeks to enter this demi-paradise of ours has some ulterior, sinister, and very probably criminal motive and the sooner we get rid of him the better'. In truth, the justification for another round of national legislation did seem rather thin. The government could not detect widespread abuse of the system or the influx of large additional numbers demanding entry. (According to the Home Office's own figures, 1986 was 'the lowest calendar year since Commonwealth citizens first became subject to control in 1962'.) So, it appears that, once again, the legislation was directed towards the ideological right, which, like the hydra-headed Cerberus of classical times, needed continual supplies of honey cake with which to be quietened. One small example, which reinforces this interpretation, is the abrupt insistence in the act that polygamous wives should no longer have the right of abode in the UK. This is both a demonstration of cultural arrogance and an illustration of the mean-mindedness to which Lord McNair referred because there were only about 25 such claims each year.

With respect to deportation, the 1988 act did contain some real teeth. Clause 4 severely limited the availability and scope of appeals for all those without UK citizenship and also constrained the right to appeal against deportation for those who were seeking refugee status. In the case of an overstayer who had been in the UK for fewer than seven years, no appeal would be allowed. In effect, the government appeared to be viewing the courts as getting in the way of running a smooth immigration control system and interfering in the minister's discretionary powers. A speech by Mr Renton in the House of Commons strongly reinforced this impression when he referred to the courts as a 'thicket within which the immigrant [*sic*] is well protected. He goes from one appeal to the next while the years drag on, at the end, after eight or nine years it is almost inevitable that he will be given leave to remain in Britain.'

The home secretary also interpreted the act as having allowed changes at the administrative level. He averred that immigration officers at the inspector level (instead of staff at the Immigration and Nationality Department) could issue deportation orders. Under the 'supervised departure' power accorded to them, immigration officers were allowed to offer the alleged offender a speedy exit, rather than waiting 14 days in prison for all the formalities to be completed. Some 70 per cent of deportees in 1989 took this option.

Three immediate effects of the increased power granted to the immigration officers were visible. First, the number of deportations went up dramatically – nearly 1000 people were deported in the first months of 1989 alone; in one court case the judge alluded to a threefold increase since the act came into force. Second, the police got involved to a much greater extent on the grounds that, as a Home Office spokesperson claimed: 'It is useful for immigration officers to have police along for their expertise. They attend in an advisory capacity' (*Evening Standard*, 29 November 1989). Joint raids by the police and immigration service also increased. One, on British Petroleum's headquarters in London, turned up 39 allegedly illegal cleaners, who were served with deportation orders. Finally, a number of cases appeared where immigration officers exercised their newly assigned powers with such indecent haste that they deported British citizens. One instance concerned the unfortunate Mr Koyobe Alese, a 25 year-old British citizen, born and educated in Britain and whose parents live in northwest London. Stopped for a driving offence, he gave a false name that the police could not find on their computers. They tipped off immigration officers who refused to believe him even after he had given his correct name. Somewhat distressed and bemused, he found himself at Lagos airport the next day (*Independent*, 29 April 1989).

These high-handed actions by immigration officers showed a scandalous disregard by the Home Office for the decision of Lord Justice Woolf in the High Court on 21 February 1990 that the home secretary had no right to delegate the power to issue deportation orders to immigration officers and that consequently 500 deportation orders were legally invalid. Individual immigration officers and the Home Office itself appeared to ignore this decision even though their own lawyers (in a confidential memo leaked to a newspaper in April 1989) had anticipated the judgment.

Conclusion

Who, historically, have the British authorities vomited out, ejected from the body politic? As I have skipped through the centuries, the cast list has grown quite bloated. Former French allies, Jews, Lombards, Hansards, Flemings, Calvinists, Catholics, Spanish agents, continental revolutionaries, Jews (again), Germans, Romanies, Bolsheviks, black Commonwealth citizens, illegal entrants, overstayers, drugs dealers and, finally, a black Briton who had committed a driving offence – all these have been deported by executive authority, judicial recommendation or administrative decision.

The very diversity of the deportees' backgrounds questions any mono-focused characterization of the character of the state and the motivations of its agents. At various times appeals to national security, economic competition, religious uniformity, ideological rigidity, cultural distinctiveness and racial purity have structured their fears. In short, the Other is a shifting category. We need greater historical specificity to distinguish between Hubert de Burgh's refusal to surrender Dover to the 'French aliens' in 1216 and (say) Enoch Powell's classification of black Commonwealth citizens as 'an alien wedge' more than 500 years later. Who becomes the alien, who the Other, who has to be feared, despised and deported varies greatly. But all are victims of a malevolent version of the old game of 'pass the parcel'. The parcel gets dumped into the lap of the group that the selves, or more exactly the defining agents and agencies of British identity, most need at that time to distance themselves from and to repulse.

Before the last war all manner of people fell victim to this unpleasant game. From the 1950s to the 1980s the victims have primarily been black and brown people from the Commonwealth. Unfortunately, many from these communities are still subject to the racial discrimination in Britain, which I in no way wish to discount or minimize. However, it became apparent in the late 1980s that the frontier guards were constructing a new alien menace. These were the 'undeserving asylum-seekers' from the Middle East, Turkey, Asia, eastern Europe or the New Commonwealth. Colour was now less relevant. These new barbarians at the gate were not 'genuine refugees' but disguised 'economic migrants', we were told. The media and political depiction of contemporary asylum seekers and refugees indicated that they were being framed for their role as the Other in the new millennium.

Notes

1. The category 'strangers' did not, presumably include the 'denizens' – privileged aliens who had been granted the right to live and conduct their business in England by royal agreement.
2. The barrister and legal expert in immigration law Andrew Nicol (1981: 9–10) pointed out that, as recently as 1971, section 33(5) of the Immigration Act stated: 'This Act shall not be taken to supersede or impair any power exercised by Her Majesty in relation to aliens by virtue of Her prerogative.' In practice, the royal prerogative seems not to have been exercised since Elizabeth I, though Nicol is wrong in saying that the last occasion was in 1575. As indicated earlier, Elizabeth signed deportation orders at least as late as 1588.
3. The legislation fell just short of an explicitly racial classification scheme (along, say, the lines of the apartheid regime), by allowing the notion of 'patriality' to include marginal numbers on a non-racial basis. Thus, patrials were those citizens of the UK and Colonies who had been ordinarily resident for five years or more, or acquired their citizenships through naturalization or registration (a small number of non-white citizens were so qualified), as well as those whose birth, adoption, parenthood or grandparenthood made them citizens through descent (overwhelmingly a white category).
4. 'They cannot speak English, but one word ["racialist"] they know.' Powell's well-known pedantry is a dead giveaway here. Even in 1968, it stretches all credulity to imagine that the verbally inadequate 'piccaninnies' would 'chant' the linguistically proper but passé term 'racialist', rather than the more common form 'racist'.
5. David Waddington, the Home Office minister responsible for immigration, strongly resisted the demand for a national programme of repatriation: 'The government is not in the business of telling people who have made their lives here, who perhaps have even become British citizens: You are unwelcome. Here is some money. Clear off!' (*Financial Times*, 14 October 1983). But behind this public reaction, there in fact existed modest government support for at least two repatriation schemes.

Chapter 4

Constructing the alien: seven theories of social exclusion

T he level of public hostility in recent years in the European Union towards 'foreigners', 'outsiders', 'immigrants', 'third country nationals', 'Muslims', 'gypsies', 'those from the Third World' (the labels and targets fluctuate) is now all too evident. Although there are depressing similarities, there are certainly also important variations in the strength, character and timing of this hostility when we look at different European countries. In Germany and Britain, for example, xenophobia has long roots. In France, with its stronger tradition of citizenship and assimilation, it has come as a relatively recent realization that some groups – particularly from the Maghreb and West Africa – are unlikely to be accepted and peacefully absorbed. In the southern countries of Europe (Spain, Portugal, Italy and Greece) with their complex Mediterranean history of trade and migration and a familiarity with emigration rather than immigration, the general recognition of alarming levels of xenophobia is a post-1990s phenomenon.

There are complex and overlapping ways of understanding the phenomenon of xenophobia among social psychologists, historians, social theorists and literary scholars who have developed a large theoretical armoury with which to bombard the problem. I cannot hope to do full justice to the rich array of possible alternatives, but want nonetheless to provide an exposition and develop a modest critique of seven broad strands of relevant and stimulating theory. I do not wish to reject any particular position, but I shall lay special emphasis on those more recent ideas that I find more innovative. The seven strands, which I deal with in turn below, comprise discussions of: (a) prejudice, (b) racism, (c) Otherness and difference, (d) boundary formation, (e) the construction of social identities, (f) the reconstruction of nationalism and (g) diasporic formations among minorities.

The nature of prejudice

In the Anglo-American tradition the study of prejudice has essentially been a preserve of social psychology. The mechanism involved is quite simple. In the case of negative prejudice (remembering that technically there can also be positive prejudice) there is an attribution of commonality to a total group. 'They are all like that', 'they are dirty', 'they are thieves' or 'they are taking our houses/jobs/women away'. The collective ascription will sustain, even when a rational observer can point to evidence in the opposite direction. In that case the prejudiced person will claim that this is 'an exception': the general rule holds good. These elements of irrationality and refusal to listen to contrary evidence have suggested to social psychologists that particular kinds of personalities are prone to prejudice.

The most notable and still influential study along these lines is that of Theodor Adorno et al. (1950). There they surmised that certain people were prejudiced because this met certain needs in their personalities. Those who were exceptionally prejudiced were held to have 'an authoritarian personality'. They were submissive and obedient, but rejected outgroups in an angry and hostile way. Such sentiments applied not just to one out-group but to many. The in-group was celebrated as the normal, while all out-groups were seen as deviant. Characteristically, a number of out-groups were aggregated. In a number of European countries, for example, all Muslims, North Africans, West Africans, Indians and Bengalis were normally classed together as coming from 'the Third World'.

Although studies of prejudice are important vehicles for understanding current expressions of xenophobia, one should remember their limitations. Adorno and a number of other refugee scholars were preoccupied with trying to find an underlying explanation behind the Nazi and fascist regimes. They found this in an attack on 'reason' and the Enlightenment itself, which they saw as leading logically to totalitarianism – a theme Bauman (1991) picked up later – and in an abnormally repressive and insecure personality shaped by childhood experiences. Clearly, this stress on individual pathology is inadequate. Subsequent scholars have pointed to the social context as being a more significant cause of the development of an authoritarian personality. Peer group pressures and expectations, a threat to employment prospects and a general decline or perceived decline in living standards may all trigger the expression of prejudices at both personal and collective levels (Cashmore 1988: 227–30).

What do we mean by racism?

Because the term has been used as an epithet rather than a concept – in street demonstrations rather than lecture theatres – we have to be very cautious in deploying it in a scientific sense. I fully accept that when people experience discrimination because of racial appearance or assumed biological differences (technically, labelling through pheno-typification or genotypification), using the term 'racist' to describe the perpetrators of such discriminatory acts is perfectly proper and appropriate.

Difficulties in deploying the term arise, however, when differences and prejudices are acknowledged to be socially, culturally or ideologically constructed – either by the social actors themselves or by observers and commentators – *without* explicit reference to appearance or biology. The proliferation of meanings of 'racism' in such contexts has led two well-known scholars to provide a divided entry in a *Dictionary of race and ethnic relations* (Banton and Miles 1988: 247–51). Both accept that 'the word has been used in so many ways that there is a danger of it losing any value as a concept' but, whereas Michael Banton is content to abandon the term in modern settings, Robert Miles wants to continue to employ the term, with the following explanation: for him racism 'is the attribution of social significance (meaning) to particular patterns of phenotypical and/or genetic difference which, along with the characteristic of additional deterministic ascription of real or supposed other characteristics to a group constituted by descent, is the defining feature of racism as an ideology' (Banton and Miles 1988: 250). Additionally, these characteristics must be evaluated negatively and justify unequal treatment of the defined group.

The problem remains that in addition to overtly racist acts, we are often concerned with forms of exclusion that do not obviously or instinctively seem to fit the 'racism' label, even if we treat 'racism' as a generalized ideology of difference. In short, it seems doubtful that the word 'racism' (used in English only from the 1940s) can be deployed to describe all forms of discrimination. Some of the strongest discriminatory sentiments – for example anti-Muslim feelings – deploy cultural and religious categories to target their victims with little or no allusion to colour or descent. Of course, anti-Semitism, anti-Muslim sentiments or the exclusion of white migrants like Albanians, Bosnians or Russians from behind the old iron curtain can all, with a degree of theoretical inventiveness, be reconstituted as forms of 'racism'. Indeed, a number of authors have sought to do so in some or all of the cases mentioned. They usually rely on the power of simile to make their case. The argument would go something like this. Of course groups like the Albanians are not a separate 'race'. But we all know that 'races' are artificial social constructs anyway and, as they are treated like a different race and alluded to in race-like ways, they are 'racialized' and can thus be considered the victims of 'racism'. In short, we can have 'racism' without 'race'.

Other authors have sought to reduce all cognate phenomena to 'race' or 'racism' by a process of rather indiscriminate aggregation. One example is provided by Sarup (1991: 89), who writes of Britain: 'It is evident that many racists have the capacity to link the discourses of Englishness, Britishness, nationalism, patriotism, militarism, xenophobia and gender difference into a complex system which gives "race" its contemporary meaning.' This tendency reached its apogee in the title and subtitle to a book, namely *Racialized boundaries: race, nation, gender, colour and class and the anti-racist struggle* (Anthias and Yuval-Davis 1993). The aggregation procedure is not so much wrong as it is tenuous – stretching the elastic band of 'racism' around a fatter and fatter bundle of related (yet importantly distinct) phenomena so thinly that the band is in grave danger of snapping and flying off out of sight. Despite my doubts that racism can be used currently with any conceptual precision, there are at least two innovative and insightful accounts of racism that bear further analysis.

In the first account considered, Bauman (1991: 62–82) seeks to refute Taguieff's notion that racism and heterophobia (fear of difference) are closely related phenomena. Instead, he proposes a suggestive trichotomy:

- *heterophobia*, a phenomenon of unease, anxiety, discomfort and a sense of loss of control commonly (and normally in the sense of sanely) experienced when confronted by the unknown;

- *contestant enmity*, a form of antagonism and hatred generated by the social practices of identity-seeking and boundary-drawing. Here, the contestants dramatically separate, or keep a required distance from one another. Separation is necessary precisely because the alien threatens to penetrate the opposing group and to blur the distinction between the familiar and the strange; and
- *racism*, which differs from contestant enmity by not admitting any possibility for a certain group of human beings to become part of the rational order. Endemic blemishes and deficiencies make the group unreachable by scientific, technical or cultural manipulation. Racism demands discrimination, territorial exclusion or (as in the case of the Holocaust Jews or Roma) extermination.

Without developing a full critique of Bauman, I would simply add that curiosity[1] and contestant enmity might mediate heterophobia through mutual interest. Only racism proper (in his sense) is beyond rational challenge.

The second innovative account of racism to which I want to allude is Goldberg's *Racist culture* (1993), a treatment by a philosopher who is closely aware of the comparative experiences of racism in South Africa, Europe and the USA. A lengthy book is not going to be easily summarized for my purposes, but I take Goldberg's principal starting point to be that race and racial thinking have become increasingly normal and diffused among many social actors in most societies. Therefore, whatever the scientific, technical or logical difficulties we (namely commentators or academics) encounter in using the terms 'race' and 'racism', it is our job to trace the way in which the notion is inscribed in people's consciousness and lends meaning and direction to their everyday conduct.

Like a tenacious tracker dog, Goldberg makes a creditable job of following all the labyrinthine trails and tracks where his rabbit of racism leads. Sometimes he doubles back on himself; sometimes he seems to lose the scent. On many occasions he closes in, but perhaps inevitably never manages to catch the creature by its throat and shake it to death. In the manner of a Bugs Bunny in a conceptual forest, Goldberg's rabbit of racism somersaults free, then multiplies, appearing again and again in different guises – one time as the anthropological 'primitive' or 'tribal', on the next occasion as 'the Third World', on the third occasion as an urban 'underclass'. Though Goldberg would probably be unhappy at the medical comparison, I could not help but think of a free floating virus, where the particular disease contracted is contextually specific and takes different forms, but the virus itself remains potent and continually mutates.

If I have understood Goldberg correctly (and I am not sure I have), he posits the idea of a free-floating set of exclusionary possibilities that attach themselves to different objects ('hosts' in my analogy), and are therefore expressed in different discourses and forms. When sufficiently distinct they become different 'racisms' (with emphasis on the plural). This notion would work quite well with my subject matter in Chapter 3 of this book as a theoretical explanation of the way in which different groups have been targets of deportation at different periods. Whereas most historians would insist on providing a causal explanation specific to each period and group, Goldberg's analysis of different, but logically connected racisms would allow an underlying pattern to emerge. He is aware of the danger of attributing a timeless functionalism to racisms and argues that, although success is not guaranteed, resistance to racisms is possible, even if only along the lines of a gruelling guerrilla campaign (Goldberg 1993: 224, 226):

> Resistance to racisms consists in vigorously contesting and disput-
> ing exclusionary values, norms, institutions and practices, as well
> as assertively articulating open-ended specifications and means for
> an incorporative politics. Where racisms are openly and volubly
> expressed, it is likely a matter of time before a more or less
> organized resistance by its objects, often in alliance with other
> antiracists, will be promoted in response. ... Antiracist means may
> include confrontation, persuasion, punishment for racist expres-
> sions, or sometimes imaginatively rewarding anti- or even non-
> racist expression.

Otherness and difference

A different strand of theory arises from notions of 'Otherness' and 'difference'. Though often vague, literary theorists have used them with dramatic effect while cultural anthropologists have deployed similar concepts to show how Eurocentric views of the world came to be dominant. For example, Pratt (1986), a scholar of comparative literature, shows how travellers' descriptions of the San of southern Africa (once pejoratively called 'Bushmen') codified difference and fixed 'the Other' in a timeless present. All actions and reactions are thought to be habitual and predictable. The ethnographic present gives a history to the observer (characteristically the European, the insider 'the self'), but denies coevalness to the observed (the outsider, the alien, 'the Other').

Such an atemporal attribution can be bent to a positive depiction of national character – as in Carlyle's description of the English[2] – but is also highly amenable to racism in the sense used by Bauman. By suggesting that members of 'the Other' are incapable of change, they become unamenable to reason, incapable of change, adaptation or assimilation. This notion of a fixed and negative Other is, as I have shown (Cohen 1994 and Chapter 3 in this book), very close to the thinking of officials at the British Home Office who, as late as the 1920s would have found it inconceivable that seven or eight of the descendants of what they called the 'unassimilable' Slavs and Jews would become ministers in Mrs Thatcher's cabinet 60 years later. Early in the twenty-first century one member of this group, Michael Howard, became the leader of the Conservative Party. There is a similar essentialism in (say) Enoch Powell's descriptions of British people of Caribbean descent who were assumed to be incapable of change in their new environment despite the fact that most are now born and raised in Britain (according to the 2001 census).

Useful then in showing how those outside the charmed circle are denied an historical consciousness, 'the Other' has also been used to show how Europe distanced itself from other world regions. Said probed this process brilliantly in *Orientalism* (Said 1991: 1–3); he argued that the Orient had a special place in Europe's experience in being its main cultural contestant and a source of rival civilizations, languages and cultures. The Orient was the source of Europe's 'deepest and most recurring images of the Other. ... European culture gained in strength and identity by setting itself off against the Orient as a sort of surrogate and even underground self.' Though Said's thesis ruled the day for two decades, specialist historians of India were always aware that there was considerable cultural intercourse between the British and the Indians until the nineteenth century, though it diminished thereafter in the wake of imperialism and Social Darwinism.

The evidence of extensive social interaction was brought to the reading public's attention by Dalrymple's (2003) brilliantly realized popular history of eighteenth-century India, centred on the love affair between a British representative of the East India Company and a Mughal princess. However, as Dalrymple makes clear, this liaison was not a one-off. About one-third of British men were living with Indian women, there was continuous intellectual discourse between enlightened Europeans and the scholars and poets of Lucknow (Dalrymple 2003: 271), while Anglo-Indian or British women joined the Avadhi harem. One woman, a Miss Walters, had a mosque built for her by the nawab (the local governor's title). Dalrymple (2003: 270) has a telling description of hybridity in Lucknow:

> If the Nawab sometimes amazed foreign visitors by appearing dressed as a British admiral, or even as a clergyman of the Church of England, then the Europeans of Lucknow often returned the compliment. Miniature after miniature from late-eighteenth-century Lucknow shows Europeans of the period dressed in Avadhi gowns, lying back on carpets, hubble-bubbles in their mouths, as they watch their nautch girls dance before them. Some Europeans even married into the Nawabi royal family.

The Orient was thus a rather more complex construction in the European imagination than Said allowed. The extent of creolization in Africa, in the Caribbean and in South America also suggests that the spectacles of imperialism have tinted European views in a rather monochromatic way. Nonetheless, it is undeniable that Africa and the indigenes of the Americas were so easily enslaved, conquered or infected with European diseases that their inhabitants (and descendants) became lodged in the European consciousness as inferior beings placed on the lowest rungs of a static hierarchy of racial excellence.

Yet, despite the degrading heritage of disparagement, Europeans sensed some affinity with Africans even if they sought to deny and repress their attraction. Missionaries were terrified of being converted by the heathen; Victorian scholars like Burton provided suspiciously prurient ethnographic descriptions and the novelist Rider Haggard's heroes were always being tempted by magnificent and sensuous women, sometimes diplomatically transmogrified into paler-complexioned examples, as in *She* ('who must be obeyed'). Sadomasochism lurked not far beneath Victorian surfaces. As Brantlinger (1986: 215) shows, Kurtz in Conrad's *Heart of darkness* displays many of the resultant contradictions. In his unrestrained lust and hunger for power he displaces his own 'savage' impulses onto Africans. As Europeans penetrated the heart of darkness, symbolized by the Congo River, they discovered 'lust and depravity, cannibalism and devil worship; they also discovered, as the central figure in the shadows, a Stanley, a Stokes, or a Kurtz – an astonished white face staring back.'

This unexpected twinning of Anthropos, this recognition of commonality behind the difference, is paralleled in psychoanalytical writings by Freud's discovery of the unconscious and Jung's theory of subconscious archetypes. These represented a collective personality manifested in dreams, myths and religions (and also in the fantasies of the psychotic). It is notable that Jung's work on archetypes was based on fieldwork among native Americans and Kenyans. In both the literary and psychoanalytical articulations of the Other with the self, the self is on a journey of discovery that turns into a quixotic, reflexive and surprising journey of self discovery. The externalized becomes internalized, because it had always been there.

'One only knows who one is by whom one is not.' Although expressed in a very simple form, this proposition fits well with the more complex discussion of the self–Other relationship I have highlighted. As the 'asylum-seeker', 'foreigner', 'stranger' or 'alien' is silhouetted and identified, the native majority are, so to speak, delineating one or other aspect of themselves. Their national identity is thereby being continually defined and redefined. The processes of exclusion and rejection uncover and reveal and become constitutive of the national identity itself.

Despite their allusive, metaphorical and literary quality, discussions of Otherness are inherently more heuristic, subtle and optimistic than many discussions of racism (or 'racisms', to accept Goldberg's corrective). The latter are often pessimistic and denying of the human spirit and characteristically assume that dominant groups are likely always to maintain their hegemony and self-regard. While it is true that some writers seek to articulate an anti-racist strategy, their nostrums remain ultimately unconvincing because of the overwhelming sense of the inevitability and ubiquity of 'racism' that they have previously depicted. By contrast, discussions of Otherness easily admit more liberating possibilities of self-examination and auto-critique. Psychological insights can expose the aspects of the self that resemble the Other or how the self displaces and projects onto the Other. Equally, an appeal to conscience, common humanity or self-interest can be used to reduce perceived difference. The ethical and progressive possibilities of this strand of theory are particularly marked in Sampson's (1993: 175) plea to engage in *Celebrating the Other*, the title of his book:

> We are obliged to work together with others in a responsible way because who and what we are and who and what they are [are] intimately and inextricably linked. We cannot be us, nor can they be they without one another: our responsibilities, then, are not simply to avoid the Other but of necessity and in recognition of this inherent bonding, to work together on our collective behalf.

Boundary formation

A closely related strand of theory looks at the processes of boundary formation. In trying to describe how some distinctive objects are made by the mind, Said (1991: 54) suggested that a group of people living on only a few acres of land will set up boundaries between their land, its immediate surroundings and the territory beyond, often designated as 'the land of the barbarians'. It is not required that the barbarians accept the 'us–them' label for the distinction to work. The difference may be arbitrary or fictive: it is enough that 'we' have set up the boundaries of 'us', for 'them' to become 'they'. 'They' have a culture or an identity incompatible with ours. As Said reasons, 'To a certain extent, modern and primitive societies seem thus to derive a sense of their identities negatively.'

Said's basic contention can be greatly extended by reference to an anthropological debate started by Barth's (1969) notion of ethnic boundaries. For Barth, boundaries can be real or symbolic, visible or invisible. The markers that divide can include territory (see my later discussion of nationalism), history, language, economic considerations, or symbolic identifications of one kind or another. But there are a number of other potential markers – perhaps, Wallman (1986: 230) claims, as many as 14. She further avers that once having listed the range of boundary markers, the problem still remains as to when, whether and which markers the social actors will choose.

In addressing this question Barth had used the metaphor of a boundary 'vessel'. The contents of the vessel would determine the firmness or weakness of the boundary and the significance of the diacritics that differentiated the 'us' from the 'them'. Wallman's important addition to this tradition is to suggest that differences between peoples only turn into ethnic boundaries when 'heated' into significance by the identity investments of either side (irrespective of the actors' consciousness or purpose). In the case of the boundary between the British and the Others, I suggested (Cohen 1994) that the diacritics include race, religion, language, ethnicity, nationalism and symbolic identifications of many sorts (like dress, appearance, accent, manner, the flag and the monarchy) on the part of the British.

The tradition Barth pioneered essentially considered ethnic group boundaries without reference to state formation. Parallel work by historians and political philosophers has made useful inroads into the supposed 'naturalness' of national boundaries. One historical account by Sahlins (1992) focuses on the Cerdanya region of Catalonia, divided between France and Spain in 1659. His micro study reveals just how problematic is the assumption that nationality is (or should be) coincident with territory. Locals found themselves insiders, outsiders, and then insiders again in bewildering mixes. They became 'political amphibians', donning two or three masks of nationality – sometimes finding that when they sought to discard one or other, their assumed identity embarrassingly 'stuck to their skins'.

The political philosopher, O'Neill (1993a), is equally convinced that far from normally being coincident, boundaries and national identities are characteristically permeable and variable. Boundaries can be made more or less permeable while national identities 'can be reshaped, reformed and recombined'. Her and Sahlins's stress on the indeterminacy, malleability and variability of identity boundaries perhaps goes rather further than I have suggested in the case of the British frontiers of identity, but I share their arguments that boundaries are legitimated not legitimate, that key political and social actors selectively construct the walls that separate, or selectively permit access through the turnstiles and gateways linking the inner and outer worlds. Such selectivity is often supported by an economic ideology, as in the stunning neo-liberal hypocrisy that defends trans-boundary free trade and capital flows but restricts population mobility (see Barry and Goodin 1992 and Chapter 9 in this book). Again, as O'Neill (1993b) emphasizes, moral philosophy could not defend an interpretation of sovereignty that constitutes an arbitrary limit to the scope of justice. Yet that is precisely what a national boundary does. It constrains crossing (whether for asylum, travel, migration, abode, work, settlement, or to take up citizenship) but permits transnational economic interaction without transnational powers of taxation or a convincing transnational programme to relieve poverty. In short, while there may be such things as *just* (fair) borders, generalized and taken-for-granted claims to impermeable boundaries made by nationalists cannot be ethically sustained.

The construction of social identities

In recent years, cross-cultural studies in history, sociology, anthropology and psychology have greatly enhanced the study of identity. The key point of departure for much discussion is the 'real world' observation that nationalist, regional, racial and ethnic mobilizations are occurring globally and pervasively. At the same time, within (and to some degree between) national, racial or regional units of identification are other kinds of social groupings – organized often on the axes of age, disability, gender or class. These too are claiming rights or advantages in the name of their particular social affiliation. Such are the persistence, universality and simultaneity of these claims that some academics argue that the construction, reproduction and reshaping of identity is the crucial pre-occupation of our era.

Understanding the concept of identity means at least briefly alluding to the ways in which humankind situated itself in nature. Virtually all the major intellectual breakthroughs of the modern world have threatened simplistic notions of self-regard and the over-inflation of our egos. This process probably started with Galileo, who decentred the earth itself when he demonstrated that the planets and the sun did not revolve around us. His compatriots sought to hang him for this bad news. Equally, Darwin showed that man was not a uniquely privileged creature, but simply one species that survived. Other dominant species preceded us; others may follow us. For his pains, the fundamentalists and creationists ban Darwin's work or anyone who adheres to his theory. In his insightful article, Hall (1991) lays emphasis on three key thinkers who fix our current notions of identity – Marx, Freud and Saussure. In each a process of decentring, of humbling and rendering humankind into relative insignificance, takes place – in Marx through the power of economic forces, in Freud through the role of the unconscious and in Saussure through the underlying system of language.

These observations have yielded four major insights, which have informed my use of the notion of identity:

- First, in the contemporary world, identity is fragmented, a process that started with the fragmentation and humbling of the human ego itself. Whereas some Eastern philosophers welcomed this insight, the fragmentation of identity proved too threatening for the children of the Enlightenment. In their attempt to recover their identities, or to overcome identity irresolution, groups lash out, often violently, at other neighbouring groups. This is what makes the fragmentation of modern identity-constructs both so important and so potentially dangerous.

- Second, in seeking to overcome fragmentation, there is an important class of identity-constructs that focuses on exclusive *territorial* claims. These I have considered as 'nationalism' and have discussed earlier.

- Third, the modern study of identity has yielded convincing evidence that the phenomenon of multiple social identities is much more common than previously had been assumed. These data have dished the old 'essentialisms' – for example, the Marxist idea that all social identity could essentially be reduced to class identity. This does not mean that class-consciousness does not exist, but rather that there are other competing claims for affiliation that cannot be reduced to epiphenomena. Thus, gender, age, disability, race, religion, ethnicity, nationality, civil status, even musical styles and dress codes, are also very potent axes of organization and identification. These different forms of identity appear to be upheld simultaneously, successively or separately and with different degrees of force, conviction and enthusiasm.

- But how do individuals attach themselves to, or withdraw from, any one label or category? This question leads to the fourth major insight I deploy – the notion of situational identity. The basic idea here is that an individual constructs and presents any one of a number of possible social identities, depending on the situation. Like a player concealing a deck of cards from the other contestants, the individual pulls out an ace, a two or a knave – namely a religion, an ethnicity, a lifestyle – as the context deems a particular choice desirable or appropriate.

There are obvious limits to the manipulative use of situational identity. It is relatively easy to change a religion or one's clothes. It is less easy to change one's accent, manner and language, though Eliza Doolittle managed it in G. B. Shaw's *Pygmalion*. It is very difficult to alter one's physical appearance, one's phenotype. Difficult, but by no means impossible – as is demonstrated by the large sales of skin and hair-altering products and by the successful strategy of 'passing', even in such racially divided societies as the USA and South Africa. There are some cultures where the possibility of mistaking one phenotype for another has led to mutilation at an early age to inhibit cross-identification (facial scarification by the Yoruba of southwestern Nigeria is one example).

The fragmentation, territoriality, multiplicity and situationally specific aspects of identity all need expression. One way of understanding racist and nationalist claims is that they seek to simplify complexity, reduce diversity to singularity and provide an artificial unity in the face of a plural reality.

The reconstruction of nationalism

The attempt to make the boundaries of nationality and identity coincide is, of course, the nationalists' project. I cannot begin to analyse the thousands of scholarly tracts on the sixth strand of theory considered here, namely nationalism. But it is relevant to notice that an influential book (Anderson 1983) treats the nation as an imaginary identity construct, though as real in people's minds as it is in the world. As I indicated in Chapter 3, for Anderson (1983: 15–16) the nation is an 'imagined community' partly because, regardless of actual inequality, its members can conceive of themselves as sharing a form of comradeship. These ties of solidarity are, to be sure, somewhat situational and intermittent – for example, when a fellow national is recognized abroad, when sporting contests arouse popular passions, or in times of war.

This last element of nationalism is a particularly potent explanation for the extraordinary loyalty that the idea of nationalism can command. Women and men apparently willingly die for their nations and go through endless sacrifices to get a nation-state (a territorialized identity) of their own. One can hardly look at a newspaper's front page without seeing an example of this phenomenon, be it in ex-Yugoslavia, the former Soviet Union, Africa, Asia or Europe. The progress of the idea (but, some might add, also its dilution) over the last 60 years can be measured by a simple head count of those nations that have acquired recognized status. When the UN was formed after the Second World War, its membership comprised 51 nation-states; by 2005 there were 191 members.

Numbers alone cannot tell the whole story. There are two additional factors fuelling nationalism in the contemporary world – the rise of nativist sentiments in response to increased immigration and a more familiar splintering into nation-states following the break up of an empire, in this case that of the Soviet Union. An innovative way of understanding nativism in Europe is advanced by Husbands (1994) who revives the notion of a 'moral panic' first proposed by Stanley Cohen (1972) to characterize public overreaction, fanned by a news hungry media, to deviant youth movements. Husbands suggests that anxieties about national identities in Britain, Germany and the Netherlands (and, by inference, France) have analogous features to a moral panic. Sensitivities about Muslim fundamentalism, political asylum and illegal migration have fostered fears of a 'cultural dilution' of the majority's cherished ways and threatened the collective psychic wellbeing. As Husbands concedes, there is not a perfect fit between the upsurge of national moral panics and changes in economic and social conditions that would help give the concept some predictive force. Nonetheless, a creative use of the concept provides a useful way of coming to grips with the exaggerated responses to the challenges posed by the presence of non-nationals in European societies.

There is an instructive contrast between nativist ideas in Britain and France. While there are some similarities between the ideas of the British National Party and those of Le Pen, the more educated English right talks of cultural threat while its French equivalent fears the invasion of harmful microbes into healthy biological specimens. Perhaps this is because the classical bias of the New Right English intelligentsia contrasts with the natural science bias in France. However, both are building elaborate bastions against insidious alien forces. I simply respond to such notions by pointing to the naïve, ahistorical and simplistic ideas of the nation to which such thinkers apparently subscribe. Society and nation (like culture and biological organisms) have always been, and continue to be, enriched and invigorated by diversity and difference.

While panics by their very nature flare up then evaporate, I think it a reasonable supposition that in countries like Britain, France and Germany undiluted nationalism will not provide a long-term palliative for anti-foreigner fears, particularly if the ideologues seek to offer the 'nation' as an *exclusive* focus of loyalty and identity. This is for two principal reasons. First, the named countries are locked into regional blocs and tied by their dependence on world trade and foreign investment – thus an excessive anti-foreigner position would compromise their national interests. Second, in mature nation-states a Pandora's Box of multiple loyalties and identities – nationalist, ethnic, religious, linguistic, cultural and gender based – has already been opened. All compete for attention and it is unlikely that nationalism will be able to subordinate all the remaining foci of affiliation and identification.

Of course one has to concede the ultimate possibility that the admixture of strangers can eventually fundamentally alter and even subvert a host culture. But in both Britain and France we normally are talking of small fractions of the population (fewer than 6 per cent are of New Commonwealth origin in the UK and a similar figure for residents of Arab origin in France). The implication that the adults of these minorities share nothing in common with European society is wholly fallacious and, of course, the children of such minority groups are already strongly socialized into the language and social norms of their host societies. To proclaim intellectually that hostility to such small groups is legitimate and 'natural' is the moral equivalent of celebrating the virtues of a bully in a playground.

I need say little enough about the second factor fuelling the wave of nationalism characteristic of the early 1990s, namely the break-up of empires and federations. A similar phenomenon accompanied the end of the Ottoman, Austro-Hungarian, British, French, Portuguese and Dutch empires. Of the 26 members that joined the UN over a three-year period, no less than 18 were formerly part of Yugoslavia or the Soviet Union (see Table 4.1). In a number of these new nation-states, the displacement of populations, contests about how to develop exclusive citizenships and even ethnic cleansing accompanied their birth and recognition.

Table 4.1: Members joining the United Nations, 1991–3

1991	Democratic People's Republic of Korea, Estonia, Federated States of Micronesia, Latvia, Lithuania, Marshall Islands, Republic of Korea
1992	Armenia, Azerbaijan, Bosnia and Herzegovina, Croatia, Georgia, Kazakhstan, Kyrgyzstan, Moldova, San Marino, Slovenia, Tajikistan, Turkmenistan, Uzbekistan
1993	Andorra, Czech Republic, Eritrea, Monaco, Slovak Republic, The former Yugoslav Republic of Macedonia

Source: United Nations.

Diasporic formations among minorities

My final strand of theory will consider changes in patterns of international migration at the turn of the century, in particular the revival, refurbishment and invention of diasporic formations. I have dealt with the general theme of diaspora at book length elsewhere (Cohen 1997). Here I want to consider just two aspects of diasporas. The first is the cultural one. Diasporic communities have always been in a favourable position to interrogate the particular with the universal. They are better able to discern what their own group shares with other groups and where its cultural norms and social practices threaten majority groups. Such awareness constitutes the major component of *sechal* (being 'street-wise' in Yiddish), without which survival itself might be threatened. This vulnerability may also be the basis of success in trade and business, which is so often noted in the Indian, Armenian, Jewish and Chinese diasporas (Kotkin 1993). It is perhaps because of this need to be sensitive to the currents around one that diasporic groups are also typically over-represented in the arts, cinema and entertainment industry. Awareness of their precarious situation may, finally, also propel members of diasporas to advance legal and civic causes and to be active in human rights and social justice issues.

In the case of some diasporas knowledge and sensibilities have sometimes enlarged to the point of cosmopolitanism (or universal humanism) while, at the same time, traditional cultural values have often been reasserted. This capacity to combine universal and particularistic discourses has proved attractive to many ethnic groups and not merely to those traditionally defined as diasporas (Dufoix 2003). The result is a proliferation of identity politics and cultural alternatives that the nation-state, some commentators fear, cannot contain. For example, Dickstein (1993: 539–40) argues, from a liberal US position, that 'many groups in America risk destroying the delicate balance between a common culture and a particular difference.' Far from resolving the issue, 'multiculturalism' has provided a platform for separatism and has propelled the frightened majority into its own forms of cultural nationalism. In the conditions of late modernity there is, Dickstein (1993: 535) suggests, a significant difference from the minorities of old:

> Once, minority groups had been desperately eager to join the mainstream, to become assimilated. They were looking for simple justice, not ultimate approval. Now, an angry, self-destructive separatism, an assertion of group pride at the expense of practical goals, often replaced the old desire for legal equality. Minorities no longer looked to be admitted to the club; instead they insisted on changing the rules. ... Cultural conflict from the trivial to the transcendent became the order of the day: from the gestural politics of media events and feel-good symbols to the moral politics of irreconcilable differences, righteous demands, and absolute beliefs.

A second feature of contemporary diasporas is their potential ability, not always realized, to connect to original homeland politics and to bring homeland politics to their places of settlement, an aspect of diasporas that has been described notably by Sheffer (2003). This too has caused adverse comment and harsh reactions by policy makers. Although the events of '9/11' are used to explain many repressive acts by state office holders, security issues arising from diasporic consciousness have long provided a cover for state intervention in Europe.

One need go back no further than August 1994 when the get-tough minister of the interior, Charles Pasqua, ordered mass pick-ups of Islamic 'fundamentalists' in France. The crackdown on the Islamic Salvation Front, the Algerian militant Islamic party, ramified into an essentialist conflict between the Enlightenment and the Middle Ages, between light and darkness, between good and bad. As Malik (*Independent*, 26 August 1994) suggested, 'Islam is one of the most powerful demons in French political iconography and Pasqua seems to have manipulated this to justify a wider campaign against immigrants.' Malik shows how French political debates have celebrated the secular, rational, republican tradition that has symbolized the content of French citizenship since the revolution, while excoriating Islam's obedience to theological strictures rather than to national laws and its theocratic principles fusing state, religion and ethics. Islam's enormous contributions to the world's art, architecture, mathematics and notions of jurisprudence (to mention the more obvious expressions of universalism) are reduced to insignificance Even the liberal paper *Libération* argued that Pasqua's actions were necessary 'to prevent French territory from being a base camp for Islamic terrorism' (*Independent*, 26 August 1994).

The terrorist attacks in New York in September 2001 much sharpened similar debates in the USA. After '9/11', patriotism, never a philosophy that has relied much on a reasoned defence, went into a mindless liftoff. Wal-Mart sold 250,000 US flags on 12 September 2001, while the US public re-elected a president who proclaimed an ill-defined 'war on terror' and invaded Iraq without legal sanction or immediate cause. The security aspects raised by diasporic mobilizations were highlighted by the conservative academic Samuel P. Huntington (2004), always a good weather vane for concerned policy makers on Capitol Hill. According to Huntington (2004: 290, 291):

> Increased and diversified immigration to America is multiplying the number of diasporic communities and their actual and potential political significance. As a result conflicts abroad between

opposing homelands increasingly become conflicts in America between opposing diasporas. ... An ineluctable dynamic is at work. The more power the United States has in world politics, the more it becomes an arena of world politics, the more foreign governments and their diasporas attempt to influence American policy, and the less able the United States is to define and to pursue its own national interests when these do not correspond with those of other countries that have exported people to America.

In short, a number of nationalist politicians (and a number of observers) see diasporas in the twenty-first century as positively threatening and potentially dangerous to both the social fabric and the security of host states.

Conclusion

I have used the expression 'social exclusion' in this chapter, even though Brussels bureaucrats adopted the phrase in the 1980s as an official and somewhat bland platitude concerned with the growth in anti-foreigner sentiment in Europe. My reason for so doing is that the expression provides a neutral organizing concept for phenomena that have been too easily rendered into a *reductio ad monochromium*. My target has particularly been those who cry 'racism' at every expression of discrimination and hostility. This is not to say that there are never occasions when such a description is perfectly apposite. However, my argument is that 'racism' needs to be used more precisely and more rarely to capture particularly odious forms of social exclusion. Doing anything else both weakens the force of the term and fails to capture other, more subtle and complex, forms of segregation that rely on *sub rosa* and often more respectable appeals to cultural homogeneity, the protection of political liberalism, the defence of sovereignty or the necessity for security.

By looking at a number of ways of understanding exclusion and xenophobia I drew on insights from a variety of disciplines, elaborated on popular discourses and described contemporary policies pursued by governments. At least two important lessons have emerged. First, in the past, too much attention has been paid to identity formation among minority ethnic groups without looking at the shifts in popular consciousness and cultural practices among majority populations. These dominant populations have often assumed to have inherited an identity fixed by history, tradition and habitus. In fact, such identities are often fragile and easily manipulated by threat and, often more importantly, the perception of threat. Second, angry denunciations of racist practices – real, imagined or exaggerated – often corner people who are not self-evidently racists by ideological conviction. Mere contiguity does not elide difference, unease, anxiety or discomfort. Anti-racist practices and the celebration of Otherness are aspired states to be reached by social engagement, political action and continuous dialogue with all who are open to the conversation. To neglect potential allies and to assume that harmony is normal feeds complacency and self-righteousness without addressing the many hateful forms of social exclusion.

Notes

1. A brief personal experience may be illustrative. When I lived in Nigeria, I had occasion to walk in the poorest streets of the city of Ibadan. The children had clearly never seen an *oyimbo* (white man) close up before and darted in and out pinching me while furiously rubbing at my skin with a wild mixture of excitement, inquisitiveness and consternation. They hoped, their parents explained, to rub off the lighter colouring to reveal the proper skin underneath. Within the bounds of their knowledge, the children's actions were driven by curiosity and rational enquiry, not by racism or heterophobia.
2. Carlyle wrote: '[The Englishman's] ... spoken sense is next to nothing, nine-tenths of it is palpable *non*-sense: but his unspoken sense, his inner silent feeling of what is true, what does agree with fact, what is doable and not doable, – this seeks its fellow in the world. A terrible worker; irresistible against marshes, mountains, impediments, disorder, incivilization; everywhere vanquishing disorder, leaving it behind him as method and order' (cited in C. Hall 1992: 283).

Chapter 5
Trade, aid and migration

For many years international migration attracted scholarly interest from a number of cognate disciplines – economics, demography, human geography and sociology. However, since the early 1990s the subject has moved from the academy to the realm of 'high politics', providing a focus of concern for politicians, international agencies and strategic thinkers (Cornelius et al. 1994; Meissner 1993). A prominent account in this vein was written by a former director-general for emigration in the Ministry of Foreign Affairs in Rome, Nino Falchi (1995), who argued that international migration has the potential to cause disequilibria on a global scale. Strategic discussions on how to 'manage' and contain global migration flows have centred on two questions. Can prosperity induced by enhanced trade with labour-exporting countries reduce the need and desire for labour migration? And can aid targeted at the same countries and regions produce a slowdown in migration?

The context for such concerns is that national politicians are under increasing pressure from their electorates to supplement failing or compromised systems of border controls (together with associated measures like detentions, deportations and welfare denials), particularly in the light of enhanced security concerns. Proactive measures like targeted development aid, the liberalization of trade regimes, direct foreign investment, the design of rotational migrant labour systems, the creation of transitional zones, 'safe havens' and offshore processing of migrants are all receiving attention from researchers and policy-makers. The measures source countries take to promote or impede emigration flows also may have a significant impact on international migration. In this chapter, I concentrate my discussion on the migration effects of trade and aid.

International trade and migration: general discussion

As Nayyar (1994: 31–8) reminds us, neoclassical theory of international trade is mostly about the movement of goods and not very much about the movement of capital or labour across national boundaries. In so far as it is concerned with international factor movements, the focus is on capital mobility, so that labour mobility is, at best, a corollary.

Orthodox trade theory starts from David Ricardo's notion of 'comparative advantage', which seeks to explain the pattern of trade between countries in terms of differences in factor endowments. In the conventional two country, two commodity, two factor model, the labour abundant country's export of labour intensive goods constitutes a 'virtual' (but not actual) export of labour, while the capital abundant country's export of capital intensive goods constitutes an implicit (but again not actual) export of capital. If, instead of goods, we think of factors of production moving from countries from where they are relatively abundant to where they are relatively scarce, the basis for trade in goods would narrow and vanish over time. The movement of capital from rich to poor countries and the movement of labour from poor to rich countries are theoretically, therefore, perfectly substitutable.

Despite this general theory, international trade in goods and movement of factors would tend to be *substitutes* for each other only if differences in factor endowments *are* the basis for trade. If, by contrast, we assume that international trade is attributable to other structural differences between economies, it is possible that trade in goods and movements of capital between countries are *complements* rather than substitutes for each other. Work in the 1960s and 1970s on technological gaps, product cycles and wage differentials indeed concluded that international trade and international investment complement each other. This provided an explanation for the very large-scale and simultaneous expansion of international trade in goods and international capital movements over the last three decades of the twentieth century.

In sharp contrast to this well-established literature on trade and investment, Deepak Nayyar (1994) argued that the theoretical literature on the relationship between international trade and international movements of labour is poorly developed. Fragmentary attempts have been made to generalize intranational rural–urban migration models to an international scale, but these are fundamentally flawed by the central fact that we do not have anything like a free movement of labour across frontiers, the actions of states in regulating exit, entry and the lengths of stay of

migrants creating the most notable distorting factors. Determinants of
the timing, character, duration and the volume of international labour
movements have remained relatively unexplored by economists.[1]

Discussion of the relationship between labour mobility and trade can
proceed instead through a rather arbitrary citation of historical
examples. For instance, it is apparent that forced and free migration to
the plantations and mines of Southeast Asia, southern Africa and the
Caribbean during the nineteenth century stimulated international trade
flows (the sugar, slaves and manufactured goods of the triangular trade).
The overseas Chinese outside the PRC, numbering some 55 million,
have brought a vast movement of goods and capital in their wake
(Seagrave 1995). British settlement in the Dominions can also be interpreted in the same way. (We thus have three 'complementary cases'.)
Although this selection of historical examples is somewhat arbitrary it
suggests that the historical relationship between international trade and
international migration was often mutually reinforcing. There is no
doubt too that many labour-exporting states continue to see their
migrants abroad as advance guards to further their export plans for
goods other than labour.

The crucial change from these historical examples is that since the
1970s there has been a rapid liberalization of trade in goods associated
with a progressive dismantling of restrictions on the movement of capital
across borders, *together with* an intensification of restrictions on the
movement of labour. If these restrictions work (it is a moot point as to
how effective they are or will be), the international trade in goods and
international labour movements are potential substitutes for each other.
Where immigration controls are effective, capital-abundant but labour-
scarce countries will tend to export capital and employ cheap labour
abroad – or simply import goods that embody the cheap labour – rather
than import labour.

Philip Martin (1992: 30) recognizes the two broad conclusions of
classical economic theory (that *migration can substitute or complement
trade*) but adds three other possible relationships between trade and
migration. These additions arise because politicians intervene in the
policy-free world that I have so far constructed:

- *Migration patterns can affect trade policies*. Martin gives the example of the *maquiladora* (assembly plant) programme, which permits US firms to export components to Mexican border plants and pay duty only on the value-added in Mexico. This was a trade policy that postdated the USA's termination of the Bracero Program (regulating the import of cheap agricultural and manual labour from Mexico) in 1964.

- *Migration policies can affect trade patterns.* Policies that encourage rotational migration usually increase trade between the source and temporary host countries because migrant workers need transport, banking and related services. Trade in goods also tends to expand under guest-worker programmes.
- *Trade policies can influence migration patterns.* Martin's interesting example is the US sugar industry. US policy limits competition by levying a low tariff on the first tranche of sugar imported from countries that have been given the right to export sugar to the USA, but protects its industry by imposing a high import-stopping tariff on any additional imports. The first measure decreases immigration potential, the second increases potential movement.

Development–migration 'paradoxes'

It should already be apparent that policies and theories play out in a number of contradictory ways. Russell and Teitelbaum, in a number of contributions conducted under the aegis of the World Bank (see Russell 1992; Russell and Teitelbaum 1992: 33–5; Russell et al. 1990a; Russell et al. 1990b; and Teitelbaum and Russell 1994), fix on two central 'paradoxes'. They point to the common assumption that rapid economic growth in sending countries can best moderate the economic pressures underlying recent increases in international migration. To this end, they continue, many have advocated economic transfers via aid, investment and trade from high-income to low-income countries as a tool of immigration policy to augment immigration control. Russell and Teitelbaum also refer to the 'Marshall Plan for Mexico' proposed by some US politicians; European plans for foreign assistance to and investment in North and sub-Saharan Africa, the Middle East and central and eastern Europe; and to the findings of the US Commission for the Study of International Migration and Cooperative Economic Development (USCSIMCED).[2]

Despite these assumptions and policies, Russell and Teitelbaum (1992) aver that many aspects of the assumed relationship between international migration and economic development are overly simplistic and include two 'disconcerting contradictions', paradoxes that 'surprise many advocates who are unfamiliar with the evidence'.

The first paradox lies in the contradiction between the short- and long-term effects of economic development on emigration. The 'long term' implies a period of generations, or many decades, while the 'short term' is of the order of a decade or two. The paradox is as follows: *over the long term, rapid economic development in poor countries can be expected to moderate the pressures that produce high propensities towards emigration,* currently and prospectively. Rapid economic development over several decades could provide job opportunities for fast-growing labour forces; expand career opportunities for highly-trained professionals and business people with appropriate skills; give governments the financial resources necessary to improve education, health, infrastructure and social services; reduce the large differentials in earnings between developing and industrialized countries; and help alleviate the population pressures that fuel emigration in many countries.[3]

In the shorter run, however, the effects of successful and rapid economic development tend to the opposite direction: they increase the propensities for emigration. Russell and Teitelbaum suggest that rapid development is profoundly destabilizing to the old social and economic orders. Rural modernization increases agricultural productivity but ruptures traditional social networks and economic relationships, thereby encouraging rural–urban movement, which is often a prelude to international migration. The rapid growth of cities that accompanies development produces saturated labour markets and inequitable income distributions, as well as a revolution of rising expectations and access to the information and resources on the fringes of these urban economies. The cost of rural–urban movement declines with the improved transport and communications that usually accompany successful economic development. Equally, rising individual and household incomes make the migration option more accessible to a greater number of people. Hence, *economic development tends to promote and accelerate emigration over the 'short term',* namely ten to twenty years.

The second paradox may be summarized as follows: although all industrialized countries have embraced explicit policies and formal mechanisms to further economic development in the poor countries, in practice their economic policies often tend, directly or indirectly, to neutralize these efforts. Most industrialized countries proffer concessionary financial assistance to developing countries and many offer preferential trade access to their domestic markets. However, concessionary assistance flows are too small to be decisive. Domestic pressure groups anxious to protect their own interests heavily influence trade policy in most industrialized countries. The outcome of domestic political pressure is often a policy framework that damages the development potential of low-wage countries. Even explicitly preferential trade provisions like the Caribbean Basin Initiative and Lomé Conventions often exclude or limit labour-intensive goods (like shoes, garments and labour-intensive agricultural products) for which the less developed countries have an obvious comparative advantage. The contrary effect of the US sugar lobby has been mentioned above. The policy required reductions by nearly 75 per cent in the USA's imports of sugar from the Caribbean. (The largest supplier, the Dominican Republic, saw its quota decline from 774,000 tons to 204,000 tons over a short period, which inevitably led to an increase in emigration pressures.) Other examples are the EU's Common Agricultural Policy (CAP) and the agricultural import policies of Japan, which have both direct and indirect negative effects on development in emigration countries. A joint OECD/World Bank study (Goldin et al. 1993) concluded that the then newly completed GATT could lose African nations US$ 2.6 billion annually, while the industrialized nations could gain US$ 135 billion annually in world income.

Trade and migration: case studies

The above argument is comparative and generalized. The overwhelming bulk of the detailed country-by-country research on the relationship between trade and migration has been conducted in two settings – USA/Mexico, particularly in reaction to the North American Free Trade Agreement (NAFTA), and in the newly industrializing countries (NICs) of East Asia.

A case study of NAFTA

NAFTA (which came into force on 1 January 1994) provides probably the most important official trade link between a high-income and low-income country. The income discrepancy between the USA and Mexico is roughly 9:1, very close to the global North–South 10:1 wage gap. If free trade can slow Mexican migration to the USA, which in the 1980s approached three million (some 20 per cent of Mexico's population growth), then free trade may also be a means to reduce migration between countries with similar wage gaps.

As has been established, economic theory posits that developing nations will tend to export products (commodities that embody comparative advantage) or people (one of the factors of production). Martin (1993) uses this homely illustration: if the USA is more effective at keeping out Mexican tomatoes than Mexican tomato pickers, then it should come as no surprise that Mexicans migrate to the USA. In the US–Mexican case, pure classical theory should see the USA exporting capital-intensive goods to Mexico, Mexico exporting labour-intensive goods to the USA, wages eventually converging, and an end to Mexico–USA migration in search of higher wages.

But how does an emigration country like Mexico increase its trade and exports sufficiently to create the jobs that deter emigration? A number of scholars (Díaz-Briquets and Weintraub 1991a and 1991b; Martin 1993) argue that many of the solutions lie within the emigration countries themselves. They are enjoined to abolish defensive 'import-substitution economies' and join the global trade race. They are urged to adopt market- and export-oriented economic policies that offer incentives to invest, and prudent monetary and fiscal policies that assure a stable economic environment. Good governance, a reduction in graft, and political stability would, it is said, give investors long-term confidence in the future of the economy. However, the recent worldwide movement to adopt such economic policies is cut-throat (think of competing against China) and disruptive, displacing workers in formerly protected industries and contributing to the worldwide increase in migration. *Economic restructuring thus increases emigration pressures by undermining internationally uncompetitive industries.*

Martin (1993) concluded that Mexico–USA migration would increase in the 1990s, with or without NAFTA, for two reasons: job displacement and the acceleration of existing migration. Job displacement refers to the unemployment in Mexico caused by freer agricultural trade with the

USA. For example, faced by the juggernaut of US agribusiness, small-scale Mexican corn and bean farmers will be unable to compete, and unless jobs were created for them in the rural areas where they lived, some of those displaced by freer trade will head for the USA.

The acceleration argument is that most job creation in Mexico would be in the border areas that are highly accessible to the USA. This is where almost all the *maquiladora* plants are already located. Based on existing evidence of the results of the Border Industrialization Program, locating more foreign-investor owned plants in this region will touch off a new mass migration of Mexicans to the northern border area. *Maquiladoras* (and for that matter plants in export processing zones elsewhere in the world), tend to hire new entrants to the labour force. These are mostly young women who experience high rates of turnover. Male unemployment is barely touched and even the best jobs in the *maquiladoras* pay only one-fifth to one-sixth of US wages. Moreover, the prospect of jobs in the northern towns has stimulated internal migration to the area from people whose job aspirations cannot be met short of exporting hundreds of thousands of US jobs to Mexico.

Mexicans dominate legal and illegal migration to the USA. Mexico accounted for about one-quarter of the 7.3 million immigrants to the USA in the 1980s and almost half of the 1990 arrivals. How much might NAFTA add to these flows? Martin (1993) predicted that between 800,000 and one million additional illegal Mexican immigrants could arrive in the USA because of NAFTA. He suggested that the increased migration due to NAFTA would be limited to at most an additional 100,000 migrants annually. If 10 per cent of them were to settle, NAFTA could produce an additional 10,000 unauthorized Mexicans settling in the USA each year. The crucial part of his argument, which is illustrated in Figure 5.1, is that this upward pressure, shown as a 'hump', is a relatively short-term phenomenon. Thereafter, returns to Mexican trade are predicted to slow emigration pressures significantly. It is notable that Martin's projections were in perfect harmony with the first of the paradoxes World Bank researchers identified, an argument again echoed in the findings of the US Migration Commission. However, we are now in a position to say that the short-term 'hump' followed by a steep long-term decline (depicted in Figure 5.1) was too dramatic a projection. Using 2004 figures, Jeff Passel (2005) estimated that there were 10.3

million unauthorized foreigners in the USA in March 2004, a rise of nearly two million on the 2004 figure, a net increase (that is, deducting departures and the number legalized) of nearly 500,000 a year.

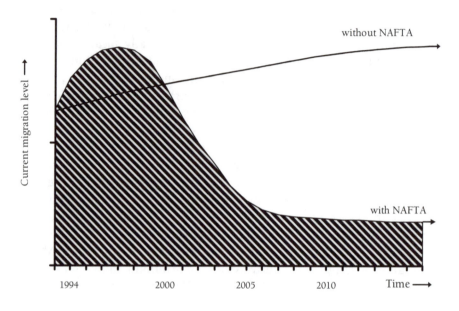

Figure 5.1: Projected Mexico–US migration with and without NAFTA

Source: Martin (1993: 360).

Confining ourselves to the illegal figure alone, 57 per cent were Mexicans, yielding a figure of 285,000 per year since 2000, vastly different from Martin's projections of 10,000 settlers or 100,000 migrants per annum. To give some context to this figure, Passel (2005) estimated that there were about 36 million foreign-born US residents in 2004, almost 30 per cent of whom were unauthorized.

It is difficult to explain this large discrepancy from the theory. Certainly, the effects of job displacement and the 'honey pot' attractions of the border zones were underestimated. However, at least some of the factors that may encourage emigration from Mexico are due to major political initiatives like land reform and privatization. The wild fluctuations and downward spiral in the value of the peso, the rebellion in the South and the collapse in legitimacy of the ruling party, the PRI, all suggest that one should be cautious about accepting an analysis based purely on economic projections.

Trade and migration: Asian examples

Two contrasting examples from Asia are provided to illustrate some of the difficulties in inferring the connection between migration and trade in an Asian setting. On the one hand, the Philippines remains firmly tied to a labour-export model, one promoted by government initiatives, commercial labour recruiters and household decisions, not to mention demand-pull factors in the destination countries. On the other hand, Korea seems to have reached a migration 'turning point'[4] where the number of imported labourers exceeds the number of emigrants. (Note that emigration does not cease when a 'turning point' is reached. All that is implied is that South Korea has attained a migration balance.)

(a) Philippines

In the case of the Philippines, trade and migration are not substitutes, a conclusion that can be drawn from Figure 5.2 below, which show trade and migration moving in harmony. The reasons for this outcome are more fully explained in Chapter 7 later in this book, so I merely provide a summary here. Since 1980, real wages in the Philippines have deteriorated across all skill levels, including high rates of unemployment among school leavers and university graduates (Abella 1993). Declines in wages were experienced both as absolute falls and felt more deeply when nearby countries in Asia (the 'golden tigers' of Singapore, Korea, Hong Kong and Taiwan) were displaying strong growth. Other nearby countries like Japan had wage rates that were ten times higher than those pertaining in the Philippines (in fact the ratio was approximately the same as that between the USA and Mexico).

Many families responded to their declining living standards and growing relative deprivation with respect to neighbouring Asian countries by fuelling a culture of emigration. Sons and daughters were selectively educated and enskilled with the intention of encouraging emigration, which, in turn, would protect the family's investment in housing and land in the Philippines. Government strategies also moved to a pro-emigration stance in response to the apparent impossibility of competing with the Asian tiger economies and in recognition of the enormous benefits that were conferred by remittance income returned by Filipinos abroad. By 2004 more than seven million overseas workers had returned US$ 8.5 billion to the country's economy. In effect, a dual strategy emerged of supporting manufacturing and agricultural exports where possible and encouraging labour emigration at the same time. This complementary strategy is mirrored exactly in Figure 5.2.

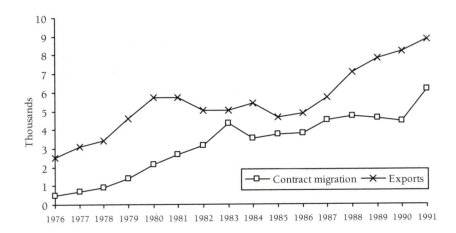

**Figure 5.2: Contract migration and exports from the Philippines,
1976–91**

Source: Abella (1993: 263).

(b) South Korea

In contrast with the Philippines, South Korea provides a 'substitute case'.[5] There, the decline in labour outflows started in 1983, the figures of contract workers showing a steep fall. Measured in thousands, the outflow was as follows: 1983 (196.9), 1984 (187.8), 1985 (152.7), 1986 (95.3), 1987 (86.3) and 1988 (83). As Florian Alburo (1994: 57) argued, by 1990 Korea had 'already graduated from being a massive exporter of contract labour'.

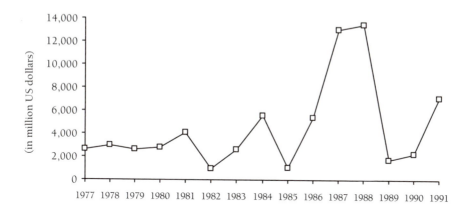

Figure 5.3: South Korea: value of exports

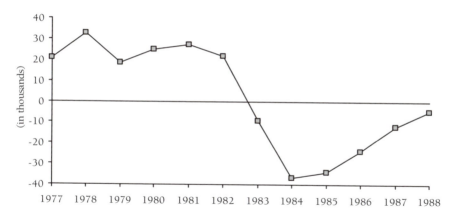

Figure 5.4: South Korea: number of migrant workers

Source: Alburo (1994: 68).

Looking at the other side of the coin, South Korea shows the most striking increase in the value of trade during the period from 1970 to 1990, which even by Asian standards is quite spectacular. Expressed in billions of US dollars the figures are as follows: 1970 (0.8), 1980 (17.5), 1985 (26.4), and 1989 (74.2).

According to Alburo (1994: 65), 'Korea's experiences illustrate the pattern where an increase [in labour outflows] takes place at some fast clip until a peak is reached, followed by a decline in outflows in migrant workers.' The data represented in Figures 5.3 and 5.4 provide support for his argument, particularly over the crucial 1984–1989 period when a migration balance was achieved.

Though there must be some doubt about the quality of the data, the broad trends are sufficient to demonstrate that in the case of South Korea some of the assumptions of classical theory appear valid. I have, however, added some surmises below, not on the basis of any particular knowledge about Korea but because Korea is unusual in showing so marked a substitute effect. The likely reasons for the substitute effect can be summarized as follows:

- In association with other factors, like those listed below, a successful response to trade liberalization eventually forces the reduction of labour exports and an increase in labour imports.
- Korea's rise in exports was not gradual, but sudden and steep and the exports contained a substantial element of value-added by Korean labour (electronics, steel, shipyards and cars all had high local labour content).
- Because of the political and social prejudices associated with the extensive import of foreign workers, the government has tried to retain the local labour force and actively discourages emigration and recruitment.
- Wages, conditions of work and lifestyles are sufficiently attractive to retain local workers.
- The local culture, religion and language are sufficiently distinctive not to encourage emigration.
- Political stability, even if under an authoritarian regime, is sufficient to give confidence to local savers, shareholders and foreign investors.

Aid and migration: general links

Following a joint meeting with the UNHCR, the ILO produced the single most targeted discussion on the relationship between migration and aid (Böhning and Schloeter-Paredes 1994). (The editors of the report use the term 'Official Development Assistance', which I will continue to refer to as 'aid'.) The starting point of the ILO discussion is that aid was the only international instrument whose impact on the propensity to emigrate had never been explored before in any detail. While this is true, the assertion that aid is 'perhaps the only remaining means of changing the circumstances in poor emigration countries to enable their citizens to choose freely whether to stay or to leave' is clearly exaggerated.

One contributor to the Böhning and Schloeter-Paredes volume (1994: 246–52) recognized that 'massive amounts of aid would be needed to achieve the economic growth necessary to keep economically-motivated migrants at home'. In the case of Central America, to eliminate economic incentives to emigrate aid would have to be almost US\$ 100 a year for each person alive today for 20 or 30 years. In the case of Europe it is very difficult to determine how much aid would be needed to reduce economically motivated East–West migration. Per capita income differences today range from 20:1 (the Swiss to Albanian ratio), but are more typically in the 10–15:1 range. If western Europe were to grow by just 2 per cent a year, and eastern Europe by 5 per cent, the per capita income gap might close to 3–4:1 by 2020. To keep eastern Europe growing 3 per cent faster than western Europe over 30 years, it is calculated that *annual* investment and aid flows of between 20 and 40 billion US dollars would be needed.

If we look purely at the effect of trade in similar vein to the 'hump effect' surmised by Martin earlier, East–West emigration pressures would rise over about two decades as the impact of free trade with the West takes effect. Unemployment in Poland, for example, increased almost twenty-fold to two million between 1989 and 1991, and the Polish unemployment rate was projected to rise to 3.5 million, or almost 20 per cent of the labour force, 12 months later. The prognosis is for more unemployment and thus more reasons to emigrate – factories continue to shed workers and, in single-industry areas, there is no alternative but to move; agricultural restructuring will displace older workers who are not entitled to unemployment benefits; and government deficits will make it hard to employ newly graduated teachers, nurses and people with similar skills. Will workers wanting to leave eastern Europe find jobs in western Europe?

Until 2005 there were relatively few opportunities to work legally, but a growing number of employers and labour intermediaries were willing to assemble crews of illegal workers. In this manner, young eastern

Europeans were absorbed into the underground economies of agriculture, construction and some manufacturing and services. Molle et al. (1992; 1994: 39–72) speculated that two million Poles might emigrate in the 1990s, including 1.4 million to western Europe. A micro indication of this was seen in the number of Polish 'asylum-seekers' arriving in Britain, which increased towards the end of the twentieth century. The participation of 'tourist' Poles in the informal house renovation industry in Britain was the subject of an instructive feature film. With the accession of Poland to the EU in 2005, the number of legal Polish migrants coming to western European countries increased dramatically.

The question of whether aid can be a substitute for migration was addressed in the Böhning and Schloeter-Paredes (1994) volume mainly by using a number of case studies – on Poland, East–West more generally, the Horn of Africa, Central America, Tunisia, the Philippines and Turkey. Let me quote the key finding from each example.

- *Poland*: while foreign aid can be used, for example, to launch needed infrastructure projects that can 'temporarily employ the unemployed … the only real solution to the issue of emigration must be brought about in Poland itself' (Böhning and Schloeter-Paredes 1994: 67).
- *East–West*: 'macroeconomic improvements will affect migration behaviour. New job opportunities, improved conditions of employment and higher incomes will reduce the number of economically motivated migration decisions in the long run' (ibid.: 96–7).
- *Horn of Africa*: 'the effectiveness of international assistance in preventing forced displacements of population is hampered by obstacles arising at four distinct levels [local, national, international and UN-related] … a limited approach may have negative consequences' (ibid.: 111).
- *Central America*: the main precondition is 'the restoration and maintenance of political order in the region. … The economic incentive to emigrate from the sending countries in Central America cannot be eliminated in the short term' (ibid.: 147).
- *Tunisia*: 'job creation and the reduction of migration pressure require the range of cooperation to be broadened' (ibid.: 175).
- *The Philippines*: '[aid] can be helpful directly, as well as indirectly, by enhancing the developing economy's capacity to export labour-

intensive products and attract private capital: these replace the pressure to emigrate on the part of unskilled and semi-skilled workers' (ibid.: 199).

- *Turkey*: 'there exist a number of pilot programmes which can be evaluated as to feasibility and effectiveness. Commitment from both sides might render emigration pressure obsolete within about two decades' (ibid.: 237).

So, can aid reduce migration? On my scorecard, of the seven experiences covered there are two 'yesses', 'two maybes' and three 'noes'. One 'yes', the Philippines, should probably be discounted on the grounds covered earlier in the chapter. To be sure, one can easily miss nuances by selective quotation, but nonetheless there are insufficient data to support the more optimistic conclusions of the editors, or of Martin (1994) who strikes a buoyant note about the possibilities of reducing migration by aid in his epilogue to the book. What *is* common ground is that in addition to aid, foreign direct investment and trade liberalization are also important parts of the picture.

Another powerful variable that a number of contributors mentioned is the not so little matter of political freedom. This is at the heart of Astri Sukhre's (1994: 13–38) argument, for she fundamentally questions the overly economic assumptions of the other contributors. In fact, Díaz-Briquets and Weintraub (1991a: 119–50) are closer to her argument than she concedes. They note that the Central American economies experienced rapid economic growth during the 1960s (GDP increased at a 5–6 per cent average annual rate), uneven but generally rapid growth in the 1970s, and slow or negative growth during the 1980s. During the 1980s, foreign aid poured into the region and refugees poured out, suggesting an *inverse* relationship between aid and emigration.

However, it is evident that political and military considerations drove the bulk of aid that flowed into Central America during the 1980s, for the superpowers supported opposing sides in Nicaragua and El Salvador. Using purely economic measures, if a US$ 20,000 investment is needed to create each new job in Central America, then two billion US dollars a year in aid would be necessary to prevent unemployment and under-employment rates from worsening. (In the early 1990s they were about 30 per cent.) Since the region received a staggering 1.3 billion US dollars in 1989 alone, such an increase in aid might seem feasible. But with the end of the cold war, neither Congress nor the Clinton administration showed the remotest interest in pressing for aid on the scale mentioned.

The case of Central America can be used to demonstrate a third 'paradox'. Now that the end of the cold war permits aid to be used to stimulate economic development and reduce migration pressure (as opposed to perpetuating civil war), the commitment to supplying aid, and the volume of aid itself, have rapidly declined.

Aid and migration: the Mediterranean and Turkey

Since migration flows into Europe are from an increasingly diverse source of countries, it is difficult to select appropriately sensitive cases to examine in more detail. However, it is probably fair to say that the Mediterranean and Turkey comprise Europe's 'leakiest' frontier. Given that there are increasing pressures in the EU to permit – and under some programmes, like student exchanges – to encourage free movement between the countries of the EU, it is understandable that concern is concentrated on one of the weakest walls surrounding 'Fortress Europe', namely the southern frontier.[6] The Mediterranean is a particularly sensitive area, for three reasons:

- Europe's southern frontier has always been uncertain, right from classical times when the Greek god Zeus ravaged a Phoenician princess called 'Europa'. The Mediterranean basin provided an interactive crucible for subsequent civilizations – the Roman, Judeo-Christian and Islamic – intimately linking what we would nowadays call the Middle East, the Maghreb and southern Europe. It is doubtful whether 'Europe' could be meaningfully distinguished from 'the Mediterranean' until perhaps the late fifteenth century.
- Southern European countries were, until recently, overwhelmingly emigration rather than immigration countries. For this reason Italy, Spain, Portugal and Greece have imperfect and relatively recent legal, bureaucratic and practical control of their borders.
- France, Portugal and Spain have continued to have a much stronger relationship with their ex-colonies in Africa than (say) the British have retained with theirs. A continuous mesh of training, educational, cultural and aid projects thus link the Mediterranean to Europe.

Bruni and Venturi (1995: 389–90) point to the basic demographic differences between the Mediterranean's European and African shores. In the former, the annual rate of increase in population was 0.8 per cent over the period from 1950 to 1980, while the projected rate was 0.4 per cent to the year 2000. The corresponding African shore figures were 2.6 and 2.3 per cent. Between the 1950s and the 1990s the number of children on the African side of the Mediterranean more than doubled, while the European school population had become lower than it had been in the 1950s.

(a) The case of Tunisia

A number of measures on trade have been adopted to bring North Africa into line with the free market. Algeria and Morocco have privatized many state enterprises; Morocco joined GATT in 1987; and Algeria abolished the state monopoly on trading. However, Tunisia alone seems to have reached a migration turning point (a migration balance), but less by design than by unintended consequence. During the 1980s, there were an additional 53,000 workers joining the labour force each year, but only 40,000 new jobs. The gap was largely met by exporting workers to Europe, Libya and the Gulf. Political disagreements with Libya in the 1980s and again in 1995, together with European deportations and restrictions, have resulted in the repatriation and return of Tunisian nationals. In short, unlike in South Korea, a migration balance was not achieved primarily through autochthonous economic development.

Nonetheless, the economic achievements of the Tunisian people are considerable. As Hadj Amor (1994) states, Tunisia now faces a development dilemma. It needs foreign capital, but it is considered too rich to receive large amounts of concessional aid. Loans, however, add to the country's debt and interest burdens. Amor argues that the international community should write off some of Tunisia's external debt so that foreign investors would be more inclined to invest in Tunisia. He advocates channelling additional foreign aid to the country through a new regional bank for northern Africa. No doubt, there is some special pleading involved in this argument, but an interesting proposition arises. Foreign aid has historically been targeted on countries where there is a military or strategic interest or where the country concerned has met humanitarian criteria, like exceptional poverty. It may instead be possible to define a group of deserving countries that, with aid, may reach or maintain migration 'turning points'.

(b) The case of Turkey

We can turn now to our second example, Turkey. Schiller (1994) reviews Turkey's economic and emigration record and concludes that aid could help to reduce emigration pressures there. Turkey followed many other developing nations down the import-substitution road during the 1960s and 1970s, and this strategy produced rapid growth but insufficient jobs. As wage gaps between the protected manufacturing sector and rural areas widened, the stage was set for rural–urban migration. When there was an opportunity to migrate abroad, many of these previously internal migrants became migrant workers in western Europe. Like the Philippines, Egypt and several other emigration nations, Turkey used its strategic location to extract high levels of aid from industrialized countries during the cold war. However, most of Turkey's aid in recent years has come in the form of World Bank loans, which Turkey must repay in the same foreign currency (dollars and Deutschmarks) in which the funds arrived. Turkey had a foreign debt of US$ 49 billion in mid-1991, which required US$ 3 billion in foreign currency earnings to service. Germany and the EU provide additional assistance to Turkey, usually in the form of grants.

Turkey may be unique in the level of technical assistance it receives, especially from Germany. Germany is helping Turkey to introduce its 'dual apprenticeship training system', which involves classroom learning as well as paid work and training in a workplace. Germany is also providing credit and training for returning Turkish migrant workers who wish to start businesses in Turkey. German aid has prompted fundamental revisions to Turkey's vocational training system commencing in 1991. Under the law, non-governmental bodies are responsible for administering the training system, which is to be financed by the requirement that 20 per cent of each firm's gross revenues are to be spent on vocational training. These vocational training reforms are being combined with an extension of compulsory schooling from five to eight years. It is hoped that by massively increasing the number of trained workers self-sustaining growth will be stimulated. What this summary suggests is that Turkish migration to Germany has not been reversed, but that some kind of equilibrium has been reached, through four means:

- greater acceptance of about two-thirds of the Turks who originally arrived in Germany as guest workers. This applies particularly to residential and employment rights, but there is still considerable resistance to conceding citizenship, dual or German;
- the voluntary return and repatriation of the remaining third during the economic downturns of the 1970s and 1980s;
- the provision of aid and training packages for Turkey; and
- changing the constitutional provisions for the recognition of asylum-seekers and tightening up other immigration procedures.

Towards a more sophisticated causal model of migration

Although the limits of using neoclassical economic theory – to evaluate either trade or labour flows – have been hinted at from time to time, it is time now to be more explicit. The neoclassical economists' models are normally based on push–pull reasoning and cost–benefit analysis. But too many of the conclusions fall under the *ceteris paribus* assumption (that everything else is thought to be equal).

Neoclassical models see people as exaggeratedly calculating and profit maximizing. They mistakenly assume that potential migrants have unlimited access to relevant information with which to make well-supported decisions on the value of a move and on the best alternative destinations. In fact, information is frequently imperfect and the migration decision is often based on expectations and myths rather than on rational calculations. Too little attention is paid to the reference system on which potential migrants base their calculations, which time frame they use (for example, current wage differences or life-time earnings), for whom the calculation is relevant and how non-monetary factors are appraised. Neoclassical models have also failed to integrate properly the different causal layers of the migration outcomes – the micro level where the decision is formed, the meso level where immigration laws or visas constrain and channel movements and the macro level where long-term economic, environmental and demographic changes are relevant.

Massey and his associates have produced a commanding synthesis of migration theory that has gained wide acceptance by migration scholars. They (Massey et al. 1993: 454) argue that:

> Because theories proposed to explain the origins and persistence of international migration posit causal mechanisms at many levels of aggregation, the various explanations are not necessarily contradictory unless one adopts the rigid position that causes must operate at one level and one level only. We find no *a priori* grounds for such an assertion. ... It is entirely possible that individuals engage in cost-benefit calculations; that households act to diversify labour allocations; and that the socio-economic context within which these decisions are made is determined by structural forces operating at the national and international levels. Thus, we are sceptical both of atomistic theories that deny the importance of structural constraints on individual decisions, and of structural theories that deny agency to individuals and families.

The neoclassical economic model implied a clear empirical prediction that, in principle, the volume of international migration is directly and significantly related, over time and across countries, to the size of the international gap in wage rates. However, later refinements of the neoclassical model make clear that the pertinent factor in migration decision-making is the *expected* earnings gap, not the absolute real-wage differential. This immediately allows some room for miscalculation, misinformation and irrationality. The refined model (developed by Todaro and his successors) predicted that individual and household characteristics that were positively related to the rate of remuneration or the probability of employment in destination areas would increase the probability of migration by raising the expected returns to international movement. Hence, such standard human capital variables as age, experience, schooling, marital status and skill can be used reliably to predict the likelihood of emigration (Massey et al. 1993: 455). When Massey et al. (1994: 709) came to test the theory by examining the results of 300 empirical studies on North America, the results were disappointing:

> If neoclassical theory is correct, we [would] expect this factor [expected income] to play the predominant role in the decision to

migrate, and to account for most of the variation in the likelihood of migration. Although expected income is indeed positive and significant, *it does not explain the bulk of the variation nor is it even the strongest effect in the model.* ... Even controlling for differences in expected incomes, such other factors as migrant experience and network connections play an important role in structuring the migration decision. Thus, neoclassical theory is clearly supported, but results suggest that, by itself, *it does not constitute a complete explanation of the migration decision* [emphasis added].

The newer theoretical alternatives (Massey et al. discuss) are often concerned with two major causal arenas – networks and migrant experiences on the one hand, and household decisions on the other:[8]

- *Network and migrant experience theory* proposes that once someone has migrated internationally, he or she is likely to do so again, leading to repeated movements over time. Again, the probability of international migration should be greater for people who are related to someone with prior international migration experience, or who lives abroad. Moreover, the likelihood of movement should increase with the intimacy of the relationship (having a brother in Britain is more likely to induce a Bangladeshi to migrate there than having a cousin, neighbour or friend). Migration should also be related to the quality of the social capital embodied in the relationship (having a brother who has lived in Britain for ten years is more valuable to a potential emigrant than having one who has just arrived and is not yet established). Having a network is likely to reduce the costs and risks of movement. If network theory is valid we should be able to trace the vectors of transmission. For example, dependent sons whose fathers are international migrants should be more likely to emigrate than those whose fathers lack foreign experience. At the community level, people should be more likely to migrate abroad if they come from a community where many people have migrated and where a large stock of foreign experience has accumulated than if they come from a place where international migration is relatively uncommon.
- *Family and household theory* focuses on these units, rather than on the individual, as the relevant decision-making unit. It posits that

migration is a response to income risk and to failures in a variety of markets (insurance, credit, labour, food prices, land), which together constrain local income opportunities and inhibit risk spreading. Risk minimization, or risk diversification, is seen as the underlying motivation because rural households often live under uncertain and irregular income conditions. As it can be essential to spread the risk among several family members, migration often functions as a component in the household's diversified income strategy. Migration of one or several of the household's members can in this perspective serve the following purposes among others; as an alternative source of income if the harvest from the family's farming should fail; as insurance against large fluctuations in the prices of agricultural products; as a way to allocate extra resources for financing investments in the household's farm; or as an extra insurance against loss of income due to illness, old age or unemployment within the family. Because women make up almost half of all international migrants, there is also an important gender dimension to household decisions. Gender relations can be decisive for the households' decision-making, for the emergence of a migrant network and for the composition of the migrant flows.

Family and household strategies: the Senegal River Valley

The study of family and household strategies has meant an important step forward for economists studying the causes of migration (Stark 1991). However, anthropologists and sociologists have long been aware of this important locus of decision-making. One obscurely published, but commendably well-researched study has focused on households and communities in the Senegal River Valley (Findley 1993). Her principal findings were that:

- the *demographic* composition of a household provided an important measure as to which households were likely to contain migrant members;
- *access* to kin and informants who had migrated before provided an incentive to migrate;
- such access was more import than literacy rates (nearly all in the Senegal River Valley are illiterate);

- migration is *learned* behaviour – the Sonike of the Senegal River Valley are the established migrants, though other communities in the area soon caught on when they perceived the benefits gained by the Sonike from having a large migrant, especially international migrant, population;
- migration was not generally a response to poverty: rather households were seeking to *diversify* their economic base;
- migration was *not* slowed by the provision of irrigation. Indeed, families served by irrigation were *more* not less likely to send their families abroad – this cast doubt on the French government's huge investment in the Manatali dam project;
- 'the likely effects of efforts to diversify the economy and to link it to the external monetary economy via increased commercialization should only further increase the flows to France relative to other destinations' (Findley 1993: 24);
- international migration can be seen as an attempt to insert the family into the global economy, 'a tendency little influenced by the local farm situation or crop cycles from year to year'.

Conclusion

Discussions about the relationship between international trade and migration have in the past centred on concerns in industrialized countries about pressures to emigrate from the South, thereby threatening social and political conditions in the North. The major issue is whether policies to liberalize trade, especially imports from developing countries could sufficiently strengthen the economies of the South so as eventually to lessen those emigration pressures. Unfortunately, the evidence that this is possible is confined to a few success stories in East and Southeast Asia. Most poor countries have in fact been experiencing a diminishing share of world trade and of direct foreign investments. From this perspective, migration and trade are seldom clear alternatives (see Abella 1993).

The positive evidence we have to suggest that trade can be substituted for migration seems to depend, moreover, on internal economic successes. The most notable contemporary example of this is in South Korea, where unprecedented growth in exports (increasing eighty-fold over a period of 20 years) led to a migration 'turning point'. It must also be remembered that achieving a migration balance does not mean that emigration stops, merely that it is counter-balanced by immigration. (The UK presents a comparable historical example.) It may still, of course, be argued that spreading the benefits of trade will allow migrants an increasing choice of destination, thereby reducing migration pressure on any one destination country.

The weight of evidence suggests that trade and migration are often complements rather than substitutes. Certainly, this has historical support (though admittedly this would require a more comprehensive selection of cases). But there are other dynamics involved. A number of source countries have decided that labour exports add an important strength to their export portfolio. They do not see a fundamental distinction between commodity and labour export and actively encourage or sanction the recruitment of labour. Ghosh (1995) also suggests that labour mobility is essential for trade in services whenever the producer must move to the consumer to deliver the service. The temporary migration of unskilled, semi-skilled or skilled workers, in manual or clerical occupations, from poor countries to rich countries, may be necessary to deliver labour-intensive services. The temporary migration of people with professional expertise, technical qualifications or managerial talents from rich countries to poor countries may be necessary to deliver capital-intensive or technology-intensive services. In either case, the temporary movement of labour across national boundaries represents a situation where the producer of a service moves to its consumer. In other words, as the economy globalizes trade in services will grow and international companies will have to recruit globally to compete. They can be expected to put a great deal of pressure on immigration authorities to accept contract workers.

With regard to aid (and the related issue of foreign direct investment) it seems clear that only a great deal of money, concentrated at the right spots and sustained over a long period (15 years or more) is likely to make much difference to emigration flows. There may be excellent reasons to advance aid – to alleviate suffering, to promote trade or for strategic purposes – but if the aim is to reduce migration, then the aid will be of little use if there is too little of it, if it is too dispersed or if it is for too short a period. Aid can also make it unnecessary for the recipient country to modify economic policies that slow down growth. Compassion fatigue and impatience with the operations of the main international aid agencies concerned with migration flows also suggest that the industrialized countries are more willing to provide short-term relief than the longer-term assistance necessary to deal with the root causes of emigration.

Another inescapable conclusion is that doctrinal economics does not work in this field. There is no use reciting the *mantra* of 'the market' if one factor of production, namely the movement of labour, is politically constrained from forming part of the global market place. Because of the weight of this institutional obstacle and because neoclassical economic theory has, in any case, severe limitations when applied to migration studies, a richer and more subtle theory of migration has to be assimilated. In this chapter I have provided just some hints of the complexity of the newer theories now advanced. One important implication that arises from network theory in particular, is that once international migration has commenced it cannot easily be stopped, let alone reversed. Another is that policies targeted at blunting or diverting the migration aspirations of a single (often male) breadwinner will not work. I believe it is right to see the household as the key focus of the migration decision; in that unit a number of potential migrants have to have their aspirations considered. Moreover, absolute poverty at the individual or household level is not the point at issue. More potent propelling forces are emulation, risk minimization and the perception of relative deprivation. In short, raising the income of a single breadwinner alone will not satisfy the household at large.

Notes

1 I need to make an honourable except of Barry Chiswick who has played a pioneering role in the economics of migration. His collection of articles (Chiswick 2005) is a convenient starting point to his work.
2. I will refer hereafter to the 'US Migration Commission' or to USCSIMCED. It is worth noting too that Teitelbaum was a member of USCSIMCED, so his work for the World Bank tends to overlap closely with the Commission's findings.
3. It is a widely reported finding that economic development has a much more potent effect on fertility rates than do birth control measures. This has little to do with contrasting religious traditions, as the similar low-fertility cases of Singapore and Italy demonstrate. Teitelbaum and Russell (1994: 241) warn

against any simple association between high fertility rates and the propensity to migrate. The association is valid only after *sustained* fertility, more than 15 to 20 years, is superimposed on a youthful demographic structure. By contrast, policy-makers should not expect a quick turnaround in migration flows should fertility rates decline. In Malaysia and Thailand emigration rates increased despite the commencement of declines in fertility.

4. Abella (1994: 3) cogently summarizes three migration 'turning points'. The first is reached when economic development leads to the rate of net outflows reaching the rate of labour force growth. The second is when outflows are in balance with inflows (the South Korea case). The third begins when sectoral shortages are noticed (but are not filled by local workers because of their resistance to what are perceived as unacceptable jobs or because they lack the skills demanded). This phase ends when governments succumb to pressure from employers to accept further immigration or sanction illegality.

5. It is worth noting that Japan presents historical analogies with Korea. Thailand and India represent similar, though less marked, examples of countries that have reached or nearly reached migration 'turning points'. Alburo (1994) offers a useful comparative analysis covering the Philippines, South Korea, Thailand, Bangladesh, India, Indonesia, Pakistan and Sri Lanka.

6. I have taken two Mediterranean countries as examples of South–North migration), but we should not overlook the Oder–Nesse line (East–West migration) as another poorly constructed, ambiguous and weakly policed frontier. It is worth making clear that despite official encouragement of internal free movement the 1993 figures showed that only 1.4 per cent of the total EU population were EU nationals living in a country other than their own. By contrast, many illegal and legal professionals and labour migrants were working in EU countries from 'third countries' with historic, colonial or economic links with particular members of the EU.

7. Since British rule in Hong Kong has now ended there may be an inclination to question its inclusion in this list. The point here is that Hong Kong has reached a migration balance (and its GNP per capita exceeded that of the UK for a period). Of course political instability can upset migration balances.

8. Massey et al. (1993) in fact also discuss world systems theory, institutional theory and a notion of cumulative causation. I have elided these (partly for reasons of space) and also amalgamated 'migration experience' and 'networks' into one alternative. (They are separated in the original.)

Chapter 6

Citizens, denizens and helots: the politics of international migration flows after 1945

I mmigration policies in the twenty-first century are marked by restrictions and increasingly tight definitions of nationality and citizenship. It is thus sometimes difficult to remember that the climate of decision-making in the post-1945 period was very different in North America and most European countries. In France, for example the leading demographer at the influential Institut national d'Études démographiques, Alfred Sauvy, pronounced that France needed at the minimum to import 5,290,000 permanent immigrants to renew its labour force, stabilize the skewed demographic structure arising from wartime losses and reinforce its claims to Great Power status (Freeman 1979: 69).

Across the Channel, the budding Labour Party politician, James Callaghan (later to become prime minister), ignored the potentially xenophobic reactions of his working-class supporters and proclaimed in the House of Commons.

> We are living in an expansionist era. Surely, this is a Socialist government committed to a policy of full employment? In a few years' time we in this country will be faced with a shortage of labour, and not with a shortage of jobs. Our birth rate is not increasing in sufficient proportion to enable us to replace ourselves. ... We are turning away from the shores of this country eligible and desirable young men who could be added to our strength and resources, as similar immigrants have done in the past.
>
> (cited in Cohen 1987: 124)

In Germany, the postwar constitutional provision for reunification allowed millions of East Germans to cross the frontier. These expellees

and refugees, together with those from the former eastern territories of
the Reich and demobilized soldiers, all unprotected by the weakened
labour movement, 'provided ideal conditions for capitalist expansion,
and were the essential cause of the economic miracle' (Castles et al.
1984: 25). With expansion, West Germany's demand for labour
increased dramatically. Though a more cautious attitude prevailed on the
question of according citizenship to 'foreign' newcomers, a massive
guest-worker programme from Turkey and elsewhere was initiated.

In the USA, in addition to the strong continued demand for migrant
labour (flowing especially from the neighbouring areas of Central
America and the Caribbean), temporary labour programmes, initiated to
offset wartime shortages, were allowed to continue into the postwar
period. For instance, the Bracero Program, designed to supply agricultural labourers to southwest agribusiness, commenced in 1942 with
4203 recruits, peaked in 1957 with 450,422 labourers, and was only
formally ended in 1965 (Samora and Simon 1977: 140).

Of all the major capitalist industrial powers, Japan was alone in not
relying on the importation of large numbers of foreign labourers to fuel
its postwar economy. This was not because of some general rule of
Japanese exceptionalism, but because, unlike in the other industrial
powers, there was still a large indigenous rural population that could be
detached from the land, and a significant proportion of women who
could be enjoined to enter employment for the first time. For instance,
the number of Japanese women 'gainfully employed' increased from
three million in 1950 to twelve million in 1970 (Mandel 1978: 171).

The end of the migrant labour boom

The authorized importation of labourers to the industrial economies
mentioned above lasted roughly until the mid-1970s in Europe, when
sharp restrictions were imposed. The US figures do not show similar
absolute declines in legal immigration, but there were significant
qualitative changes in the occupational and legal categories admitted –
from immigrants to refugees and from agricultural and mass production
workers to the professional, technical and independent proprietor
categories (Keely and Elwell 1981: 192–3).

It is now no longer necessary to mount an elaborate argument listing
the advantages conferred by the deployment of migrant labour by the

host countries and employers in the postwar period, and there is now a remarkable unanimity of views between liberal (see Böhning 1972; Kindleberger 1967), Marxist (see Castells 1979; Castles and Kosack 1973) and official accounts. Perhaps one, remarkably frank, paper the West German government prepared for a conference on 'The Future of Migration' organized by the Organization for Economic Cooperation and Development in May 1986 is sufficient to make the point. The paper (cited in Cross 1988) accepted that the German economy had gained considerable benefits with negligible costs, and continued:

> Until far into the 1960s, the employment of foreigners helped to satisfy the rising demand for labour ... at a time when the labour volume was getting scarcer and scarcer. ... Their considerable flexibility in the economic cycle helped to offset negative employment effects in times of recession and to avoid inflationary shortages in times of upswing. The costs which followed from the employment of foreigners were almost insignificant because of the short periods of stay of the individual foreigners and the low numbers of family members who entered in the course of family reunion.

If the benefits of migration labour were so apparent, why did the import of labour throttle off so dramatically in the mid-1970s? On this question there is no final agreement, but a number of mutually reinforcing explanations or contingent factors may be advanced. I will briefly discuss six factors, specified below in no particular order.

The oil crisis

There is an obvious coincidence of dates in the early 1970s that may lead to a simple association between the dramatic increase in the price of oil and the end of the migrant labour boom. Certainly, the immediate wave of redundancies that followed in energy-intensive industries led to a political situation that would have made the importation of large numbers of 'alien' labourers untenable for most European governments. But, while the oil crisis can partly explain the timing of particular measures, any explanation of the end of labour migration must also be concerned with other deeper, underlying factors.

The rise of xenophobia

One of the key variables, often underestimated by scholars (who frequently assumed the hegemony of 'rational' capital) and governments (who assumed their own hegemony) alike, was the rise of a virulent indigenous xenophobia, often among the working class. This is not to argue, of course, that anti-alien sentiments were exclusive to one class. But the opposite possibility, the belief that patterns of international class solidarity would obviate ethnic and racial allegiances, proved hopelessly idealistic.

In Britain, old protective practices, like closed shops and demarcation agreements, were used to freeze out migrant labour (Duffield 1981), while in France, a municipal Communist Party bulldozed the hostels erected for migrant workers in response to the demands of its constituents. In short, both employers and the state were unable to continue to deploy migrant workers without being cognizant to the countervailing racist sentiments such a policy provoked.

The organization of migrant workers

Much Marxist theory, particularly of the 'capital logic' tendency, depicted migrants as hopeless chaff blown about by fierce economic storms – unable to respond organizationally to the market forces arraigned against them. This picture is partly correct at the earliest stages of migration, among those migrants with a particularly individualist ethic and in circumstances where it was difficult to affect a bond of sociality between coreligionists, those from a similar ethnic group or those who saw a link with workers of all backgrounds.

Whatever the variation in activity across the different cases, there is no doubt that community associations, religious groups and political support groups were sufficiently and increasingly active – precisely at the time when issues such as repatriation, return migration, immigration restrictions and deportations were proposed by politicians, anxious to limit what were perceived as the socially divisive consequences of the untrammelled immigration period. Migrant groups were insufficiently influential to prevent all these measures, but they were, on the whole, powerful enough to resist the pressures to mass repatriation and to press instead for the principle of family reunification to be recognized.

The rise in the cost of reproduction

The increased assertiveness of migrants not only applied to matters of immigration policy and family reunion, but immigrant associations also became increasingly concerned with the full range of social and employment benefits. One should not fall into the trap of believing that immigrant families are disproportionate benefit claimants – the evidence indeed inclines to a contrary assertion (Rex and Tomlinson 1979: 62). However, given the demographic profile and the special language needs of many migrant communities, increased costs arose in respect of childcare, language training and education. Even if we assume only a broadly converging cost of reproduction between indigenous and migrant communities, the crucial advantage accruing to the host country and employer – a minimal or wholly displaced cost of reproduction – no longer obtained as migrant communities gradually reconstituted their family life and became permanent minorities.

Economic restructuring

One way of understanding economic restructuring since the mid-1970s is to argue in terms of new technology impelling a different industrial logic – away from mass production to small-batch production, away from mass production into independent proprietorship, away from manufacturing into services (Piore and Sabel 1984). The same processes also impelled a greater comparative advantage accruing to certain newly industrializing countries (for example, Hong Kong, Korea, Taiwan, Singapore and now the manufacturing monolith, China), particularly in respect of low-bulk and high-value goods where the value added by the labour component was significant.

In *The new helots* (1987: 220–53) I explored the so-called 'new international division of labour' thesis in detail, so here, by way of summary, I simply suggest that many such theories are overly technologically determinist, and can easily confuse cause and consequence. Thus, it is at least plausible to argue that increased levels of class composition and migrant organization made mass production methods less attractive as to assume some exogenous new technology acted as an independent force. But whatever the exact reasons for the movement to independent proprietorship and small-batch and Third World production, this development obviated the need to continue to employ factory hands imported from abroad.

The 'inefficiency' of unskilled labour

In opening this chapter I allude to a remarkable uniformity of opinion between official accounts and liberal and Marxist writers on the benefits conferred by the use of migrant labour. The orthodoxy is, in my view, largely correct, but at an early date Ezra Misham (1970) recorded some dissent by arguing that importing unskilled workers was no substitute for serious investment in skilled production, research and development.

His argument was exaggerated and based on unfulfilled projections of large inflows of migrant labour leading to a rise in the labour–capital ratio and a consequent fall in production. While the broad thesis made unrealistic net migration assumptions, in some sectors, for example the textile industry, it is likely that working cheap migrant labour on a 24-hour shift pattern was used as a way of holding the line against low-cost Asian textiles, thereby avoiding the inevitable day when old machinery and tracks had to be discarded. Misham's views gained a greater resonance as Reaganomics and Thatcherism began to gain ground. As unemployment levels began to rise, arguments that importing migrants was essentially an inefficient way of reducing industrial costs became more widely heard.

Labour flows since the mid-1970s

I have given an indicative, though not an exhaustive account of the explanations for the immigration restrictions of the mid-1970s. But incomplete as this picture is, it may give the false impression that international labour migration had effectively ceased. In fact it continued largely unabated – though with significant differences in the destination areas and the kinds of migrants involved.

In Europe, family reunification, refugees and, to a small degree, illegal entrants, largely account for the post-1970s' migration. In the USA, undocumented workers also accounted for a much greater proportion of migrants after this period. Agribusiness in the south, the sweated trades in the northeast and the service sector more generally continued to deploy imported labour, both legal and illegal. But there was also a clear movement away from employees destined for the mass occupations in the auto and steel industries, towards an acceptance of political refugees (Vietnamese, Cuban and east European) and to those who could be classed as entrepreneurs or proprietors (for example, the Koreans and Hong Kong Chinese).

Outside the USA and Europe, officially-sanctioned labour migration went to the Middle East and other oil-producing countries. But even in these areas important qualitative differences appear. These differences emerge in my more detailed remarks below on migration flows to the oil-rich countries, illegal migrants, refugees and project-tied contract migrants.

Migration to the oil-rich countries

While the quadrupling of oil prices in the 1970s deepened the economic crisis and uncertainty in Europe and the USA (and to a lesser extent, Japan), the same factor allowed for the massive expansion of infrastructural development programmes in the oil-rich countries. What many oil-exporting countries in the Middle East lacked was labour – professional, skilled or manual. Migrant labour was recruited primarily from other Arab countries (Egypt, Jordan, Morocco, Oman and the two Yemens in declining numerical order) and from the Indian subcontinent (India and Pakistan). Other significant contingents to the Middle East came from Afghanistan, Bangladesh, Somalia, Turkey, Korea, the Philippines and the Sudan. So great and so sudden was this migration that by 1975 migrant labour formed 89 per cent of the total labour force in the United Arab Emirates, 83 per cent in Qatar, 71 per cent in Kuwait and 39 per cent in Oman and Saudi Arabia (Ecevit 1981: 260). By 1980, the International Labour Organization (ILO 1984: 102) calculated there were 2,821,720 migrant workers in the oil-producing Middle Eastern countries. Although the overwhelming majority of the workers were of Muslim background, this link did not prove decisive in granting citizenship of the country of employment and many were either sent back to their countries of origin or remained without access to a new citizenship.

Other oil-rich countries, such as Venezuela and Nigeria, manifested similar inward shifts of population, though of proportionately lower size than those of the Middle East. Like France in the immediate postwar period, the Venezuelan authorities, particularly the Council for Human

Resources, determined on a pro-immigration stance. This encouraged a flow of about half a million undocumented migrants, the import of another half million foreign workers between 1976 and 1980 and a strong internal migration flow towards the capital, Caracas (Sassen-Koob 1979: 455–64).

Illegals

Restrictions on immigration in Europe and North America have also failed to impede illegal, or as the ILO terms it, 'irregular'[1] flows of international migrants. Within Europe, the illegal population was estimated in the 1980s to be about 10 per cent of the foreign population as a whole (OECD 1987: 55) and was characterized by Marie (1983) as follows:

> Illegal migration has above all been a strategy adapted to a new institutional context … [offsetting] the stringent restriction on the entry of low-skilled manpower by supplying workers willing to accept low-status jobs with poor working conditions and pay. … Recourse to illegal migrant workers may be interpreted as a movement towards replacing one category of foreigners by another contingent in a less secure position, with a view to more flexible management of the labour force.

The International Labour Organization (ILO 1984: 113–14) argued forcibly that irregular migration should not be conceived as solely comprising those who cross the border fully intending to circumvent unequivocal immigration or employment law. Rather, 'irregular' migrants also include those who are permitted through administrative inefficiency or convenience to enter a country, with regularization taking place later. Other subsets comprise those who enter countries (South America is cited) where few explicit immigration policies exist, or those who enter countries where laws provide contradictory signals to the intending migrant.

The last case is of particular salience to the large numbers of 'undocumented' workers entering the USA from Mexico. Whereas immigration law clearly states that it is illegal to enter the USA outside the procedures established in the Immigration and Nationality Act of 1952, the agribusiness lobby forced through an amendment that permitted the employment of an undocumented worker. This led to a peculiar legalism of economic interest, which lasted until it changed under the Reagan administration, namely that it was acceptable to employ an illegal but unacceptable to be one.

The ILO's attempt to widen the category of 'illegal' to cover the cases of other 'irregular' and 'undocumented' workers is a useful reminder to the authorities to avoid premature assumptions or unjustified stigmatization. But the illegal status attaching to irregular migrants of all kinds has undoubtedly generated a fearful, wary segment of the population that is largely cut off from the protection of the police and the courts and excluded from the political life and social benefits of the society in which they now live. As argued later, they form part of a 'helot' class.

Refugees and asylum-seekers

Who is a refugee? The legal definitions derive from the 1951 international convention that defined refugees as 'persons who are outside their country because of a well-founded fear of persecution for reasons of race, religion, nationality, membership of a particular social group or political opinion'. The 1951 convention was drafted with the needs of the postwar displaced people of Europe firmly in mind. The modified 1967 Protocol sought to take account of events elsewhere in the world and was endorsed by nearly 100 countries.

Though the legal provisions appeared generous, in fact they still bore the mark of their original place of drafting. Moreover, European governments have been less than generous in applying the existing provisions to those demanding entry as a result of the mass displacements occurring in the Third World. As a report for the Independent Commission on International Humanitarian Issues (ICIHI 1986: 33) puts it:

> In the 1970s a new phenomenon emerged. Refugees from the crisis areas of Africa, Asia and Latin America began to move in increasing numbers to the industrialized countries. ... The arrival of many refugees from geographically and culturally distant areas constituted an unprecedented challenge to the legal machinery and conscience of the receiving countries. The refugee problem, previously regarded as a factor in East–West relations, now had a North–South dimension added to it.

This analysis can be elaborated in three respects. First, the volume and effects of the refugee crises were amplified as they coincided with the reduction of aid and social investment programmes to the Third World in response to nationalist and protectionist pressures in the industrialized countries. These pressures became politically effective precisely at the moment when many poor countries had their economic and environmental resources stretched to the limit. Increased energy costs, more expensive imports, political instability and lower commodity prices all placed a number of Third World countries in a position where they were unable to respond effectively to the devastations wrought by famine, war and drought.

Second, the shift from a crisis of East–West relations to one defined in North–South terms can be vividly illustrated in the case of the USA. Prior to 1980, when the USA passed legislation paralleling the agreed international conventions, the official US definition of a refugee referred, *inter alia*, to people 'fleeing communist countries or communist-dominated countries'. The paradoxes and problems of US refugee admissions were highlighted in the summer of 1980, when two streams of refugees – the 'freedom flotilla' from Cuba and those escaping from the Duvalier regime – converged. President Carter was forced to endorse the 20-year-old policy of welcoming refugees from communist regimes, even though many of the Cubans appeared to be less interested in the iniquities of Castro's regime than in the opportunity for some quick pickings in Miami. At the same time the Immigration and Naturalization Service had, increasingly implausibly, to hold the line maintaining that the Haitian boat people were economic and not political migrants, even though it was apparent that many were fleeing from the violence and depredations of the US-supported regime and its armed thugs, the Tonton Macoutes. (For more on this period, see Bach et al. 1981–82; and Cohen 1987: 145–56.)

Third, the volume of refugee migration, and potential migration, expanded to such an extent that many states began to argue that refugees were in effect disguised economic migrants. Zucker and Zucker (1987: xiv) seek to contradict the commonly held official view and to develop a clear distinction between the three categories, immigrant, refugee and illegal, in the following passage:

Refugees are neither immigrants nor illegal migrants, although, like immigrants, they have forsaken their homelands for new countries and, like illegal migrants, they may enter those new countries without permission. But a refugee is, in the end, unlike either. Both the immigrant and the illegal migrant are drawn to a country. The refugee is not drawn but driven; he seeks not to better his life but to rebuild it, to gain some part of what he has lost. The immigrant and the migrant are propelled by hope; for the refugee whatever hope there may be must arise from the ruins of tragedy. The refugee, unlike other migrants, has lost or been denied a basic human need – the legal and political protection of a government. Accompanying that loss has been the loss, as well, of culture, community, employment, shelter – all the elements that contribute to a sense of self-worth. Refugees, whatever their origins, are in need of protection.

However, such definitions depend greatly on politicians, policy-makers or immigration officials sharing liberal and humanist values. The overall figures and the pattern of admissions do not indicate wide acceptance of such views.

In Europe, the number of refugees recognized under the 1951 and 1967 Conventions is very limited, though such individuals do gain the full protection of the host state and can be considered as holding equivalent rights to an indigenous citizen.

In the USA, as Zucker and Zucker (1987) showed, refugee policy and asylum decisions were governed not by the recognition of need or the volume of applications, but by whether the country of origin was currently a recognized enemy of the US government. Between 1980 and 1986 asylum was granted in 29,926 cases, but 76 per cent of these came from just three countries – Iran, Poland and Nicaragua (Zucker and Zucker 1987: 142–3). Admissions of refugees are regulated by quota and numbers exceed quotas only when an unexpected flow from a communist country occurs or – until this no longer became fashionable – when the cold war drum could be beaten. Even then, the exasperation of the Immigration and Naturalization Service and many members of the public was evident in the internment procedures effected and the lack of substantive help given in respect of settlement and employment. Many refugees or asylum-seekers remain unrecognized by the state authorities or are denied entry in the first place.

Project-tied contract workers

Foreign contract workers can be of two major kinds. Either an individual employment contract is drafted, often with an employee's existing multi-national employer, or a host government or employer advertises for foreign workers in permitted categories and signs individual contracts with foreign employees. Such individually-contracted workers, often known as 'expatriates', are likely to be in the skilled, managerial or professional category, to live in subsidized company housing, to have annual leave, child travel and education allowances, a pension arrangement and a generous salary. In short, expatriates provide a good example of privileged aliens – a group I include under the category of 'denizens'.[2]

The second case is much more interesting both because it is less well known and because it has the potential of being deployed on a wide scale by governments anxious to avoid the possibilities of settlement and ethnic group formation, seen even in the case of the guest workers to West Germany. Instead of individual contracts being issued, block visas are provided to the project contractor, who is then held legally responsible for the behaviour of the labour force and its discharge outside the country of work. Of course, there are many historical examples of this type of labour recruitment, but it has become a much more popular mode in recent years. Source countries often include eastern European countries anxious for the foreign exchange brought back by discharged workers. In 1982, for example, 11,335 Yugoslav, 6914 Polish and 1648 Hungarian project-tied workers were employed in West Germany (ILO 1984: 108).

The main practitioners of project-tied workers seem to be concentrated in the Republic of Korea, where construction companies have won extensive contracts in the Middle East, Africa and Asia. In 1981, the value of such contracts was estimated as US\$ 13,000 million. According to the ILO (1984: 112–13), in the case of the Korean contractors, 'virtually every aspect of the migrant workers' daily life is under the protection and control of their employers'. Work camps are set up in remote spots; contact with the locals is minimal; workers are forbidden to form unions; health, accommodation and safety standards are poor;

medical and recreational facilities are equally impoverished; and work-related deaths and injuries are 'high and rising'. Workers so recruited are totally under the thumbs of their employers and the host government has no interest in offering protection or succour in the event of human rights abuses or high levels of exploitation.

What's in a name?

Immigrants, guest workers, illegals, refugees, asylum-seekers, expatriates and settlers – do these labels signify anything of importance? My argument here turns on a belief that although there are considerable similarities between international migrants of all types, the modern state has sought to differentiate the various people under its sway by including some in the body politic and according them full civic and social rights, while seeking to exclude others from entering this charmed circle.

Marshall (1950) first explicitly recognized the important role of citizenship as a means of integrating discontented members of the lower orders and including them in the core society. For him, access to citizenship allowed everyone so favoured to be given some stake in the society, at least in respect of periodic elections, protection and access to some social benefits. With the rise of welfare and distributive states in the postwar world, the social wage – unemployment benefits, social security, housing allowances, tax credits, pensions, subsidized health care – has become a much more important symbolic and economic good. By the same token, states have sought to restrict access to the social wage by deploying workers with limited entitlements. The different statuses reflected in immigrant or guest-worker categories reflect the differential access of such groups to the social wage and to the protection afforded by the agencies of law and order.

If we consider the various categories mentioned, three broad groupings appear – citizens whose rights are extensive, an intermediate group (the denizens) and a group that remains a subject population akin to the ancient helots who hewed wood and toiled for the Spartans without access to democratic rights, property or protection.

Some of the typical subgroups within the different status groups mentioned are listed below (Figure 6.1).

Citizens
Nationals by birth or naturalization
Established immigrants
Convention refugees

Denizens
Holders of one or more citizenship
Recognized asylum applicants
Special entrants

Helots
Illegal entrants
Undocumented workers
Asylum-seekers
Overstayers
Project-tied unskilled workers

Figure 6.1: Subgroups of citizens, denizens and helots

A few remarks on each of the three major categories will perhaps help to lend greater specificity to the labels.

Citizens

This group appears as an increasingly privileged one. Many states have moved from inclusive to exclusive definitions of citizenship, abandoning the principle of *jus soli* (citizenship by being born in a territory) to *jus sanguinis* (citizenship according to the parents' nationality). In the case of the European countries that once had empires (Belgium, France, Britain and the Netherlands), subsequent legislation has frequently ignored or circumvented binding guarantees of citizenship to colonial subjects. While the Dutch on the whole respected the citizenship conferred on subjects of the Netherlands, the French maintained recognition only for a small number of people in the *départements* (French Guiana, Réunion, Guadeloupe and Martinique). The British, for their part, in the Nationality Act of 1982 stripped away the rights of residents of the colony of Hong Kong (and a few other places) and created a new citizenship of 'dependent territories', which conferred no right to live or work in the UK. Under the impact of the destabilizing events in Hong

Kong, Britain has been forced to guarantee the admission of up to 50,000 Hong Kong families. The intention of this guarantee was to stabilize the last years of British rule in the colony (it reverted to Chinese rule in 1997) by buying the loyalty of key officials and entrepreneurs with the offer of settlement and full citizenship in Britain.

Denizens

I conceive of this group as comprising privileged aliens often holding multiple citizenships, but not having the citizenship or the right to vote in the country of their residence or domicile. Tomas Hammar (1990) calculated that resident non-citizens living and working in European countries include 180,000 in Belgium, 2,800,000 in France, 2,620,000 in West Germany, 400,000 in the Netherlands, 390,000 in Sweden and 700,000 in Switzerland. Many of these alien residents may be well-paid expatriates (see above) who are not particularly concerned with exercising the franchise and have compensating employment benefits – a group, in short, that can be seen as transcending the limits of the nation-state. However, the numbers involved in Hammar's calculations suggest that many residents have been systematically excluded from citizenship and its accompanying rights without any compensating benefits deriving from their employment. These form part of the helot category.

Helots

I have used the category 'helots' in a somewhat more inclusive way in Cohen (1987). Here I refer more narrowly to people who have illegally entered the country, people who have overstayed the period granted on their entry visas, asylum-seekers who have not been recognized under the international conventions, those who are working illegally and those who have been granted only limited rights. A good example (cited in Castles et al. 1984: 77) appears in a statement given to officials as to how to operate the 1965 West German Foreigners Law, which stated: 'Foreigners enjoy all basic rights, except the basic rights of freedom of assembly, freedom of association, freedom of movement and free choice of occupation, place of work and place of education and protection from extradition abroad.'

Statements such as this reveal the powerful attempt to try to exclude, detain or deport foreigners who are regarded as disposable units of labour power to whom the advantages of citizenship, the franchise and social welfare are denied.

Conclusion

As Marshall (1950) argued, conferring citizenship is the key indicator of integration and acceptance within a nation-state. The right to elect periodically a new government signifies this basic symbol of inclusion. But the exercise of the vote has become of rather lesser significance than the other attendant benefits of citizenship – access to national insurance systems, unemployment benefits, housing support, health care and social security. In addition to these undoubted advantages, by 2005 citizens of the European nations within the European Union have untrammelled rights to live, work, own property and travel within 25 European countries.

Helots and denizens are, by the same token, symbolically excluded and practically denied all the advantages just listed. In the case of the denizens, this may not be particularly burdensome – a denizen may be an employee of a multinational company with access to private medical insurance. But for a helot, the denial of citizenship is usually a traumatic and life-threatening decision. Given their vulnerability, the helots have become the key means of inducing labour flexibility and provide a target for nationalist and racist outrages.

Our trichotomy leads one to speculate that a new form of stratification has emerged that in origin has little to do with income, occupation, racial or ethnic background, gender, or a particular relationship to the means of production. Of course, there are likely to be coincidences between the different patterns of stratification. A helot is likely to be a migrant from a poor country, a member of a stigmatized minority, with low income, holding an unskilled occupation and having limited access to housing, education and other social benefits. Similarly, a professionally educated, urban, middle-class salary-earner, who happens to be a foreigner, is likely to be a denizen.

Migration after the 1970s to a new country will not necessarily carry the optimistic possibilities characteristic of migration at the turn of the previous century. Then the 'huddled masses', that time from Europe as well as from Asia, threw off their poverty and feudal bondage to enter the American dream as equal citizens. Equally, it was perfectly possible for English and Irish convicts to become landowners and gentlemen farmers in Australia. Nowadays, one's legal or national status – whether, in my terms, a citizen, helot or denizen – will increasingly operate as indelible stigmata, determining a set of life chances, access to a particular kind of employment or any employment and other indicators of privilege and good fortune.

Notes

1. Perhaps a brief terminological note might be helpful here. 'Undocumented', 'irregular', 'unauthorized' and 'illegal' are terms that have all been deployed to describe migrants who have crossed international borders without official sanction. 'Undocumented' is certainly a preferred term in contexts like West Africa or the Spanish–French border where historical cross border traffic has taken place without attempts to regulate this movement. Of course Spanish–French crossings no longer are salient as there is virtually free movement permitted between the 25 countries of the EU. The term 'illegal' is often resisted by pro-migrant groups in that it is taken to imply that states are the final moral arbiters of what is illegal and what is not. I simply use the term 'illegal' in recognition of attempts by states to regulate and their practical role in the enforcement of entry and deportation.

2. The term 'denizens' is derived from Hammar (1990). However, he uses it to refer to all alien residents. In origin, the term referred to an alien admitted to citizenship by royal letters patent by the English crown in the sixteenth century. I have reserved the term 'denizen' for the more privileged alien and used the term 'helots' (cf. Cohen 1987) to refer to those non-citizens whose rights are far less extensive.

Chapter 7

Migration and the new international/transnational division of labour

In this chapter, I will summarize a critique of theories of the new international division of labour (NIDL), which I originally developed elsewhere (Cohen 1987) before turning directly to the current transnational phase in the division of labour. It is perhaps important to emphasize that my critique of NIDL was not meant as a total refutation of the pioneering work of Ernst (1980), or of Fröbel and his colleagues (1980). Their work was crucial in recognizing that global shifts in production facilities, particularly to Southeast Asia, had fundamentally altered the shape and contours of the contemporary world economy.[1] Indeed, the casual traveller to the 'golden economies' of Asia – Hong Kong, Taiwan, Singapore, Korea, Malaysia and now China – cannot fail to be impressed by the sudden evidence of modernity and industrialization. Even using the appellation 'Third World' of such places sounds absurd, particularly when one is conscious of the transformation of great sections of the old industrial boom cities – like Cleveland, Detroit, Birmingham or Liverpool – into depressed slums and economic wastelands. Clearly, an economic transformation of enormous magnitude is taking place, as investment patterns alter and industrial plant and manufacturing employment becomes spatially redistributed.[2]

The NIDL thesis

Taking over the vocabulary of world systems analysis, the NIDL theorists argued that industrial capital from the core was moving to the periphery as 'world-market factories' were established producing manufactured goods destined *for export*. The strategy of export-oriented manufacturing from newly industrializing countries (NICs) was also adopted as an alternative to import-substitution strategies of development, which were held to have failed poor countries. The movement of capital away from the core industrial countries was, in turn, necessitated by the difficulties in securing and realizing high profits as industrial conflict, increased reproduction costs and the growing organization of migrant communities prevented the attainment of high levels of exploitation. These difficulties were particularly evident in European countries, where, at the beginning of the 1970s, the initial economic advantages that accrued to employers by importing large numbers of migrant workers rapidly began to erode. On the one hand, many poor countries had large supplies of cheap, unorganized labour. With the commoditization of agriculture (which technological innovations like the 'green revolution' accelerated) and the displacement of rural people due to dam building and other state activities, their labour became increasingly underutilized. As the rural poor were pushed off the land, unemployment, underemployment and, for some, the process of full proletarianization resulted.

The NIDL theorists further observed that technical and managerial developments in the labour process now allowed the effective use of labour located in the periphery. An increasingly minute division of labour permitted the reorganization of unskilled and semi-skilled tasks. With minimal training, levels of productivity soon matched or exceeded those in metropolitan areas. An investment climate made more attractive by government policies also accelerated the movement of manufacturing capital to parts of the periphery. A number of governments (particularly in Asia) passed laws restricting the organization and bargaining power of the unions. They provided freedom from planning and environmental controls, cheap (and therefore ineffective) health and safety standards, permission to repatriate profits without restriction, tax holidays and, in some cases like Singapore, a powerful paternal state that held out the promise of political stability. At the level of transport and communications, international facilities had dramatically improved in the form of containerized shipping and cheap air cargo, as well as computer, telex and satellite links. Especially in the case of low-bulk, high-value goods, with a high value added at the point of production, it was often no longer necessary for the site of production to be near the end market. Examples of goods of this kind include electrical or electronic goods, toys, shoes and clothes. Finally, young women, who were particularly prone to exploitation given the difficulties of organizing a group characteristically under patriarchal dominance and with a limited commitment to lifetime wage labour, could predominantly staff the world market factories (see Elson and Pearson 1981; Fröbel et al. 1980; Henderson 1985; Henderson and Cohen 1982).

In short, it looked as if metropolitan employers, with their attempts to exploit imported migrant labour to the full having been frustrated in their own countries, had alighted on another strategy. The export of capital could replace the import of cheap labour. Some convincing data from Federal Germany (Fröbel et al. 1980: 275, 276–90) support the empirical demonstration of the thesis. After 1959, when restrictions on German companies investing abroad were lifted, a steep increase in the amount of direct foreign investment began to be noticed – from 3291 million Deutschmarks in 1961, to 19,932 million Deutschmarks in 1971 and to 47,048 million Deutschmarks in 1976. However, this investment did not, in general, represent a net expansion of German capitalist development on a world scale, but rather the integration of new sites and the relocation of certain manufacturing processes previously reserved for domestic manufacturing. Within Germany, this was bound to have consequences for the number of jobs available. A small rise over the period from 1967 to 1973 was followed by a sudden drop of nearly a million jobs over the next three years. However, the loss of domestic jobs coincided with an *increase* in turnover and profit for key German firms. Simultaneously, an estimate for the number of jobs created abroad by German manufacturing firms by 1976 was 1.5 million. Fröbel and his colleagues (1980: 287) are properly cautious in saying that these figures alone 'do not allow us to deduce the extent to which employment abroad has replaced employment in Germany', but the inference is nonetheless there for all to read. By the pattern of imports of manufactured goods, by the statements of the companies themselves and through an examination of the free production zones in low-wage countries, we are led ineluctably to the conclusion that capital has migrated in search of its own comparative advantage, especially in respect of the cost of labour, and at the expense of domestic and imported workers, whose job chances have been correspondingly diminished.

The picture the NIDL theorists drew seems to confirm observable reality in the NICs and also presents a powerful explanation for industrial decline in the other old centres. Part of the work Henderson and I (1982) undertook on international restructuring was a replication study of the German findings using British data. The basic contours of the German experience were evident, the ratio of overseas investment by British capital compared with the rate of investment within Britain (as measured by net domestic fixed capital formation) moving from 3:1 in 1969 to 4:1 by 1980. Again, although it is difficult to separate out the many factors producing unemployment (including government policy, automation, the loss of international competitiveness and under-investment), there is evidence to suggest that in Britain, as in Germany, key firms added to their payroll overseas while cutting their workforce in Britain. Thus, an ILO report (1981: 82) surveying the operations of 118 major British firms over the period from 1971 to 1975 showed that they had added 250,000 employees to their payrolls abroad compared with only 80,000 in the UK. As the study concluded, 'employment-wise they were clearly growing much faster abroad than at home, both in absolute and relative terms'. The USA also revealed a similar picture. Bluestone and Harrison (1982) found that between 1968 and 1976 there was a loss of approximately 15 million jobs as a result of plant closures. The closures partly resulted from technological changes, but managers also saw the transfer of production abroad as an attractive alternative to production at home, as risk was diversified, greater control over labour was achieved and they could take advantage of large international wage differentials (Nash and Fernandez-Kelly 1983: ix).

Critique of the NIDL thesis

While accepting that NIDL theory provides a major key to under-standing some of the processes of capital accumulation in the modern world order, there are nonetheless some major limitations and omissions that inhere in the theory. In this abbreviated account I will concentrate my critique of NIDL theory on two aspects:

- First, *conceptual problems* – where I shall argue that the variety of meanings attaching to the phrase 'division of labour' makes it difficult to understand what precise phenomena are under investigation.
- Second, *historical gaps* – where I maintain that NIDL theorists have

ignored or misconceived the historical evolution and successive phases of the international division of labour. This comment will serve to introduce my discussion on the current phase I describe as 'the transnational division of labour' and its implications for migration.

Conceptual critique

When trying to understand the phrase, 'the new international division of labour', it is necessary first to unscramble the good deal of conceptual ambiguity arising in the prior expression, 'the division of labour'. The notion has been used very differently to explain different phenomena. In its earliest usage, it often was pressed into service to distinguish what are now described as sectoral divisions in the economy – divisions, for example, between industry, agriculture and services. It was used also to define the occupational and skill structure of the labour force and the differences between skilled and unskilled labourers, masters and apprentices, craftsmen and production workers. Additionally, the division of labour referred to the organization of tasks the management characteristically dictated. Who is in the workplace, who is on the production line, who is in the office, who minds the machines and who sweeps the floors? Though related to skill and occupational structure, the detailed specification of tasks is by no means coincidental with skill as Harry Braverman's (1974) contribution on the process of 'deskilling' testifies.

To these three original meanings of 'the division of labour' are others of more recent vintage. First, gender or racial divisions of labour indicate the new sensitivity to the ethnic composition of the labour force and to the role of women in production and reproduction (Pahl 1984: 254–76). Second, there is a spatial division of production and product (an aspect of the division of labour that it may be argued is far from 'new'). And third, perhaps the latest meaning attaching to the notion, the contracting out of some elements of the production processes to well outside the factory gates – into domestic, peasant or household units.

The changing definitions and meanings of the phrase 'division of labour' impel different discussions and have different implications of a more practical and political nature. For example, if it is argued that the putting out system has now revived on an international scale and constitutes an important new feature of capitalist production, feminists who argue for a politics of the home and of reproduction would have a strong case against those who argue for a politics of the factory – from which production would be putatively or potentially disappearing. Equally, if the manufacturing sector in NICs is as significant a feature of contemporary capitalism as the NIDL theorists argue, the whole structure of workers' resistance to capital will have to undergo a massive lateral shift if it is to succeed, particularly when the question of international solidarity is considered. Two diametrically opposed strategies confront metropolitan workers. On the one hand, a more nationalist posture would argue for the preservation of jobs at home by the erection of high tariff walls and import duties designed to keep out manufacturers in the NICs. On the other hand, an internationalist position would dictate that bonds of solidarity should be affected between metropolitan workers and workers in the periphery already employed in branch plants so as to restrict the manoeuvrability of multinational capital and spread the benefits of employment equally between the participant partners.

In short, even only taking two possible meanings of 'the division of labour' we end up with strongly differing pictures of the changing battle lines between the old contestants, 'capital' and 'labour'. There is, of course, no need logically to admit only one meaning of the division of labour as valid, but even if one accepts that a variety of meanings has now legitimately accrued to a particular label, this raises the posterior question of the relative weight, or significance, of the different phenomena grouped under this particular label. The last question is superficially one that is amenable to empirical enquiry, but behind the empirical question lies a paradox that inheres in the measurements so far characteristically deployed to evaluate changes in the international division of labour. The NIDL theorists use as their predominant data aggregate trade and investment figures – in other words they use measures of the migration of *capital* to measure changes in the division of *labour*. This method can lead to some very misleading impressions. For example, it is likely that changes in the location of manufacturing enterprises are far less important in terms of employment (and in terms of profit) than changes between sectors (in particular the movement from industry and agriculture to services and information) within the metropolitan economies. The possibilities for the deployment of subordinate and migrant sections of the labour force in the service sector would thereby easily and misleadingly be missed. There does seems to be a case, on empirical as well as theoretical grounds, for using measurements in the movement of *labour* to indicate changes in the division of *labour*. In my discussion of migration below I point to additional sectors (in the oil-rich countries and in the service and sweatshop sectors of 'world cities') where significant employment of subordinate and professional labour has taken place and which NIDL theory does not easily explain.

Not only is the use of movements of capital a limited means of understanding divisions of labour, but by limiting their conceptual progenitors to nineteenth-century political economists the NIDL theorists have also imposed a self denying ordinance. Thus, they list as their mentors Adam Smith, Charles Babbage and Andrew Ure (Fröbel et al. 1980: 37–44). In addition to these three figures, NIDL theorists depend on another classical theory to underpin their argument namely, Ricardo's basic law of comparative advantage. Ricardo's law can be simply stated as follows: the pattern of international trade is dependent on the said law, 'which states that if two countries, A and B, entered into trade relations, each capable of producing commodities X and Y, A would sell the commodity in which its relative (rather than absolute) cost was lower and correspondingly B would sell the commodity in which its own comparative cost is low' (Bagchi 1982: 16).

This conceptual dependence on classical political economy unfortunately brings in its baggage train the limits of this tradition. In the nineteenth century the state was an insignificant actor on the industrial scene and again, in NIDL theory, it virtually disappears except in Africa and Asia where it appears only as a *bourgeoisie manqué* having to kowtow to the overwhelming power of metropolitan capital. In the nineteenth century, with the major exception of Marx, the rising power of the working class was largely ignored in economic theory. Again, this feature of the classical tradition reproduces itself in NIDL theory, with the social and political relations that surround the production process being almost wholly neglected in favour of discussion of aggregate trade and investment transactions, which reflect the power of capital. All that happens can, in such a view, be explained by the logic of capital without seriously taking into account independent institutional forces, the contradictions between merchants, national capitalists, transnational corporations and governments, or the political and social protests by those who fall victim to the logic of capital. Inter- and intra-class conflict within and between metropolitan, semi-peripheral and peripheral societies hardly make an appearance.

Historical critique

A second critique of NIDL theory lies in its historical insensitivity. Proponents of the theory make a rather curious conceptual leap from nineteenth-century classical political economy to the late twentieth century – almost as if nothing of any great moment had happened over the intervening 100 years. It appears that NIDL theorists boarded a time-machine in the mid-nineteenth century to arrive at Hong Kong and Singapore in the 1970s without bothering to land at any of the intermediate airports – notably those marked on the historical maps as 'Imperialism' and 'Colonialism'. On prima facie grounds it would seem appropriate to assume that imperialism and colonialism had something to do with the evolution of the present-day international division of labour. Indeed, as I have argued before (Cohen 1987: 220–53), the historical patterns established by prior international divisions of labour are so much part of our contemporary reality that the distinction between the 'new' and 'old' international division of labour is not a very useful one. For this reason it is preferable to use the expression 'the changing international division of labour'.

Within this changing division of labour, from the point of view of the form of capital hegemonic in each phase, four sequential phases can be identified – the mercantile, industrial, imperial and transnational divisions of labour. The features of these phases are specified in detail in my earlier work already referred to. Here, five points can simply be noted by way of summary:

- First, the supposedly novel features of the contemporary division of labour to which the NIDL theorists draw attention are not really so novel. Even in the mercantile period, production sites were located abroad and elements of a global labour market were created and reproduced.
- Second, the appellation 'new' is further misleading in that it fails to recognize the indelible heritage of the past. Thus, it is more than plausible to argue that the mercantile, industrial and imperial phases

have left deep scars on the face of the global population and production facilities. That there are Africans in the Caribbean and the
USA, Italians in Brazil and Indians in South Africa is a more salient
and determinant datum informing migration in the period of modern
capitalism than that NICs have begun to employ local labourers (see
Chapter 1 in this book).

- Third, there is a sense of a logical succession between the phases
  mentioned. Just as conventional Marxism adduces a logical end to
  successive modes of production as antagonistic contradictions emerge
  that make a prior mode obsolete, so an analogous sequence can be
  found in the case of the historical phases of the international division
  of labour.
- Fourth, and again the analogy with Marxist theory holds true, there is
  a good deal of overlap between the sequential phases. This is
  obviously because once populations are displaced for reasons appropriate to one phase in the international division of labour, it is near
  impossible to return them (like the legendary genie) to the bottles
  from whence they came. The forms of labour deployed in an earlier
  phase thus continue to operate into the next phase or phases.
- Fifth, the current phase of the division of labour (what I deem 'the
  transnational phase') should be conceived as embracing a number of
  different forms of labour utilization not adequately depicted in NIDL
  theory. These all have implications for the patterning of migration
  flows.

The transnational division of labour: implications for migration

The phrase 'transnational division of labour' is used here to include the
so-called NIDL, but it is meant also to capture wider and subsequent
developments. Essentially, this is the phase of the changing international
division of labour initiated by the collapse of the European colonial
empires in the wake of the Second World War, the rise of transnational
capital, the boom in oil-producing countries and the relocation of a
considerable manufacturing capacity to Asia, especially China. The
European powers' humiliating defeat in Asia, the strength of the anti-
colonial movements and the growth of competitive capital centred in the
USA, and later in Japan, hastened the end of the imperial order. The
transnational phase left in place some neo-colonial relationships (which

the French held onto notably better and the Portuguese notably longer than the other European powers), but also led to a major restructuring of industrial production in the metropoles (allied to the import of migrant labour) and the further internationalization of leading fractions of capital, particularly the oil giants, car companies and firms producing consumer durables, electrical goods and electronic components.

While much manufacturing production shifted to Asia (in accordance with the NIDL thesis) by following the movements of labour, we see that there are continuing demands for labour in the old metropoles, particularly in the services, and certain shifts in the character and direction of migrant labour. I want to highlight here four important shifts in migratory patterns. First, unskilled but also managerial and professional labour was attracted to the oil-rich countries to work in the large-scale development projects initiated because of the newfound wealth of these countries. Second, a large and continuing demand for employment in the services in the old metropolitan countries grew up, particularly in what is now designated the 'global cities'. This demand is often linked to changes in the internal labour market and to illegal migration. Third, certain labour-exporting countries, notably the Philippines, abandoned their attempt to restrict the export of their labour and have sought, sometimes spectacularly, to make a virtue out of necessity. Fourth, because of its enormous statistical and potential importance I will discuss the case of China, which is showing a likely propensity to move from a massive internal movement of rural–urban migration to become a significant player in the global migrant labour force. I will discuss these developments in turn.

Migration to the oil-rich countries

In a number of places in the Arab region and in other OPEC countries oil revenues accelerated in the period after 1973 for about a decade, allowing the initiation of ambitious development plans. In Venezuela, for example, following the oil-price boom that contributed 70 per cent of national revenue, governmental policy switched to a pro-immigration stance, which legitimized and enhanced a flow of perhaps half a million undocumented foreign migrants flowing into Caracas in addition to the vast numbers of internal migrants. The Venezuelan Council for Human Resources planned to import another half million workers during the period 1976–80. The migrants arrived from Colombia, Argentina, Chile and Ecuador (among the Latin American countries) and from Spain, Italy and Portugal (among the European countries) (Sassen-Koob 1979: 455–64). In the Arab region, oil-producing countries showed dramatic increases in imported labour. Workers from India, Bangladesh, Pakistan and Afghanistan poured into the oil-rich countries of the region, with the authorities regarding their Muslim religion as an important reason for permitting their import. In the mid-1970s an estimated 748,000 workers from these countries arrived in Saudi Arabia, with other large numbers going to the United Arab Emirates, Qatar and Kuwait (Birks and Sinclair 1980; Halliday 1977; Kidron and Segal 1981: 38). Some of the large flows of migration were recorded in Arab countries (for example, Egyptians in Libya, and North Yemenis, Jordanians and Palestinians in Saudi Arabia). In other cases, the bulk of the labour force came from outside the immediate area. For example, Sudan alone provided as many as 800,000 workers to the Arab OPEC countries (*Le Monde*, 3 February 1982).

Before the Gulf War in some countries the proportion of foreign to home workers reached almost absurd levels: 50 per cent in Saudi Arabia, 80 per cent in Kuwait and no less than 85 per cent of the total population in the United Arab Emirates (*The Times*, 'Special Report', 23 February 1981). War and politics intervened to reverse significantly some of these trends. As Castles and Miller (2003: 130–1) indicate, the Iraqi invasion of Kuwait in August 1990 led to the displacement of as many as five million foreign workers. Many were simply fleeing the threat or the consequences of war; others were expelled by nervous conservative governments that saw certain groups as the harbingers of terrorism and subversion. In the wake of a radical Islamicist movement (which the notorious al-Queda network symbolized) it was no longer enough to be a coreligionist: indeed, some states in the regions reversed their prior preference for Muslim workers in favour of non-Muslims.

Political reactions to migrant workers were also evident in West Africa. Perhaps a million migrants from Upper Volta, Togo and other nearby countries entered Ghana during the period of its greatest prosperity in the 1950s and 1960s, though the adverse economic climate thereafter produced a strong reaction against 'the aliens' (Peil 1971). As the Ghanaian economy collapsed, workers and petty traders from that country streamed into oil rich and development crazy Nigeria, only in turn to become the subjects of mass expulsion orders in 1983 and 1985, harshly enforced by the Nigerian authorities.

An interesting pattern of skilled migration can also be observed as transnational companies expand their operations abroad to OPEC countries. Although the numbers involved are not that high, Findlay and White (1986) have shown how, in the case of Britain, there was a fundamental shift away from old Commonwealth (Australia, New Zealand and Canada) emigration compared with other destinations. In 1984 only 22 per cent of those leaving the UK went to old Commonwealth destinations compared with 45 per cent in 1973. Moreover, the form of migration was for a fixed-term contract rather than for settlement overseas. This is reflected in the figure of 64 per cent of the 79,000 British citizens returning to the UK in 1984 having been abroad for three or fewer years. These returnees came back not as 'failed migrants' but primarily as skilled, professional and managerial workers having successfully completed their assignments abroad.

In the Gulf States there remained a continued demand for highly skilled expatriate staff even when unskilled labour contracts were being cancelled. In a sample survey, Findlay (1986) drew attention to the case of a British construction company with about 200 staff in the UK and a staff of 110 employees in the Middle East alone (other overseas staff meant the company had far more on its overseas payroll than in its British base). Its Gulf employees included 25 per cent who were professional, 10 per cent managerial, 30 per cent technical and 35 per cent supervisory or foremen. The average length of residence in the Gulf was 20 months. Findlay remarked that 'British regions form a convenient village of return for the new nomads of the world economy'.

Service employment in 'world cities'

The metropolitan economy is marked by the switch of employment from manufacturing to the (broadly defined) service and information sectors. NIDL theory concentrated on the loss in employment in the manufacturing (or industrial) sector and the switch in these jobs from industrialized countries to the NICs. However, even if all the jobs the transnationals created can be said to be net losses for the industrialized countries and net gains for the NICs we are only talking of perhaps four to six million jobs. If, on the other hand, we look at switches between different sectors within industrial economies, since 1950 the share of industrial country employment represented by 'information occupations' alone increased by nearly 3 per cent in each five-year period. By 1975, these occupations accounted for more than one-third of the total labour force. If we examine employment across the four sectors – agriculture, industry, services and information – we can see an anticipated shrinkage in agriculture over the period 1950 to the mid-1970s to a half or a third fewer people employed in France, Japan, Sweden, the United Kingdom, the United States and West Germany. With respect to industry, some shrinkage also occurred in these countries over the period mentioned (as NIDL theory recognizes). But the most significant change is a spectacular growth in the service sector (ILO 1984: 179–80).

The growth of employment demand in the service sector is a feature of a contemporary division of labour particularly highlighted in the work of Sassen-Koob (1983 and 1984). She advances a theory, which in important respects should be laid side by side with NIDL, arguing that the 'technological transformation of the work process, the decentralization of manufacturing and of office work, in part made possible by the technological transformation of the work process, and the transnationalization of the economy generally, have all contributed to the consolidation of a new kind of economic center from where the world is managed and serviced' (Sassen-Koob 1984: 140). Her analysis is concentrated on New York City and Los Angeles, where she shows that there has been a pronounced increase in the domestic and international demand for services, which she identifies as legal, managerial, financial, technical, engineering, accounting, consulting and 'a large array of other such services'. She argues that the expansion of these advanced services is the fastest growing sector of the US economy in terms of 'its share of GNP, employment and exports'. The employment pattern and social structure characterizing Los Angeles and New York City, despite the superficial differences, are moving in a similar direction – a notable expansion in the supply of very high income jobs, a shrinking of the traditional middle income blue and white collar jobs and an *expansion* of the low wage jobs available.

It is this last characteristic that provides a surprising and important finding in that conventional wisdom and other assumptions about restructuring and industrial decline had led many observers to assume that there would be a permanent shrinkage in the number of jobs available for the more dispossessed segments of the labour force (women, blacks and migrants). In fact, Sassen-Koob argues just the opposite: 'The rate of growth of various earnings categories in the service industries from 1960 to 1975 shows a 35 per cent increase in jobs in the highest two earnings classes, an 11.3 per cent increase in jobs in the medium earnings class, and a 54 per cent increase in jobs in the two lowest earnings classes.' As she points out, both New York and Los Angeles contain the largest concentration of ethnic minorities – Hispanic and Asians in Los Angeles and Caribbean peoples in the case of New York City. Although migration from, for example, the Caribbean and Mexico has often been explained by push factors from the recipient countries, Sassen-Koob considers that demand factors in cities like New York provide an equally salient explanation for migration.

What Sassen-Koob's data as yet do not provide is some sort of global indication of this trend and it is therefore only somewhat speculative to argue that one could suggest a similar tendency occurring in other 'world cities'. These, according to some of Friedman's (1985) hypotheses, are cities that integrate the world economy, provide 'base points' for production and marketing, offer sites for the accumulation and concentration of capital, supply points of destination for internal and international migrants, and reveal precisely the occupational profile Sassen-Koob found in Los Angeles and New York. Such cities are arranged in a complex spatial hierarchy and include London, Paris, Rotterdam, Frankfurt, Zurich, Chicago and Tokyo in addition to the two that Sassen-Koob examined fortuitously (in the sense of the world city hypothesis). Though the world city hypothesis still needs much greater empirical anchorage for its validation, the notion that there are such critical nodes in the world economy has great impressionistic appeal. These cities are where the professional and managerial classes meet, where the Intercontinental, Sheraton and Hilton hotels are established, and from where international airlines operate frequent connecting flights. The cities contain stock exchanges, theatres, sophisticated entertainment, town houses and international schools.

If it is right to suggest that Sassen-Koob's findings for New York and Los Angeles can be transposed to a world city context, we should also find a similar growth in the service industries that she describes. To generalize her argument it may be important to extend her list away from what she calls 'advanced services' into the more prosaic activities that service the needs of the world's managers, professionals, financiers and consultants. She partly hints at a wider notion in her own work, but I think it is as well to be explicit that we are talking not only about the expansion of low-wage activities directly related to advanced services, but also about the growth of ancillary occupations – the cleaners and porters in the world's airports, the waiters in the French restaurants, the prostitutes in the night clubs, the chambermaids in the hotels, and the seamstresses manufacturing *haute couture* clothes in the back streets of Paris, New York or London.

What seems difficult at the moment to establish is what proportion of the new service sector jobs is being filled by transfers from internal areas of declining significance in the metropolitan countries (for example, the metal-bashing industries), and what proportion is being filled by new members of the workforce (for example, women entering part-time employment for the first time) or from external migrants, arriving either illegally or on a contractual basis. This lack of precision is frustrating in that it would help address the question of whether labour, often from ethnic minorities previously drawn into the expanding factory employ-ment of the 1950s and 1960s, can profit from the more recent forms of economic restructuring.

If we turn to the USA first, a sophisticated analysis of trends in racial occupational inequality over the four decades 1940–80 provides a basis for advancing an answer to this question. Using an updated index of inequality, Fosset et al. (1986) find that while racial inequality between black and white males between the ages of 25 and 64 of similar educational attainment increased in the 1940s, inequality decreased in the three subsequent decades. When, however, the authors move from the national to the regional level they find that, despite the large increase in economic opportunity in the South during the 1950s, the South also saw a sharp *increase* in the degree of racial inequality for matched black and white males. They demonstrate that public intervention in the labour market and in the educational system through social policies aimed at eliminating discrimination and enhancing equality of oppor-tunity importantly explained the gains that blacks made. The conclusion

I derive from these data is that despite the currently fashionable proposition that 'leaving it to the market' will solve all problems, the shift in labour market opportunities will not in itself produce employment for ethnic minority workers discarded from the manufacturing sector. Some sort of enabling public policy must be put in place to structure and create employment and transfer opportunities.

This observation applies equally well to the case of London where it is apparent that ethnic minority workers are unable to take advantage of what changes in employment possibilities have occurred as a result of the shift from manufacturing to financial services. Massey (1986) reported that between 1966 and 1983 jobs in manufacturing in London fell by 700,000, whereas employment in the financial services sector grew by 100,000 between 1973 and 1984. However, workers within London discarded from manufacturing seem to be victims of a 'skills gap', combined sometimes with difficulties in meeting transport costs. Workers outside London, say from the embattled Midlands, no more than 150 miles from London, are faced with an additional obstacle. The cost of housing in London is often twice the price of the Midlands equivalent. Workers have no or little equity and 'swaps' between public housing tenants in London and the Midlands are virtually impossible to arrange – few council tenants in the south wish to make such a move. What the United States and London examples suggest is that the transfer of ethnic minority labourers from the old public sector or manufacturing labour market will be a very limited phenomenon, at least if left to market forces. The growth of the service sector in 'world cities', therefore, seems to have been accomplished largely by fresh international migration (in the USA we can surmise much of it illegal) and by part-time, perhaps normally female, employment.

Labour-exporting countries: the case of the Philippines[3]

By 1990, the Philippines had become the largest source of permanent migrants from Asia. Between 1980 and 1990 the net international emigration from the country was roughly 540,000, compared with 524,000 from China, 500,000 from India, and 469,000 from Pakistan. Migrants planning to settle abroad went predominantly to the traditional countries of immigration, namely the USA, Canada, Australia and New Zealand. By the early 1990s Abella (1993) estimated that net settler emigration from the Philippines would reach another 580,000 by 2000. These estimates proved too conservative, with official estimates showing a stock in excess of 2.8 million permanent emigrants (Table 7.1).

Table 7.1: Stock estimate of overseas Filipinos by region, December 2003

Region/country	Permanent	Temporary	Irregular	Total
Africa	318	53,706	16,955	70,979
Americas/trust territories	2,386,036	286,103	709,676	3,381,815
Asia, East and South	85,570	944,129	503,173	1,532,872
Europe	165,030	459,042	143,810	767,882
Middle East	2,290	1,361,409	108,150	1,471,849
Oceania	226,168	55,814	31,001	312,983
Region unspecified		8,767		8,767
Seabased workers		216,031		216,031
WORLD TOTAL	2,865,412	3,385,001	1,512,765	7,763,178

Source: Prepared by the Commission on Filipinos Overseas using sources covering 192 countries/territories. See www.poea.gov.ph

Definitions: (a) 'Permanent': immigrants or legal permanent residents abroad whose stay does not depend on work contracts. (b) 'Temporary': persons whose stay overseas is employment related, and who are expected to return at the end of their work contracts. (c) 'Irregular': Those not properly documented or without valid residence or work permits, or who are overstaying in a foreign country.

A far larger number of Filipinos is engaged in other forms of migration. Beginning with the waves of contract labour migration to the Persian Gulf in the mid-1970s, the larger flows have consisted of temporary or 'circular migrants' who are not included in the 'settler' estimates. Temporary migrant departures from the Philippines greatly outnumber emigrants who leave each year to settle permanently abroad (Table 7.1). In this 'circular flow' of temporary migrants, which has become a global phenomenon, Filipinos are also the largest national group of all the Asian countries.

Pressures to emigrate are apparent across the social structure in the Philippines. In 1986, during the depths of the economic crisis, 277,000 college graduates were unemployed, together with another 284,000 who had some college education. Real wages had been deteriorating in all sectors of the Philippine economy since 1980. Average earnings of employed persons in all industries rose in nominal terms from 1193 pesos in 1980 to 2243 pesos in 1986, but when expressed in constant prices wages actually declined by 27 per cent during the period. Real earnings in agriculture dropped by about one-fifth of the already low levels in 1980: the deterioration was slightly less severe in the services sector (Abella 1993).

While real family earnings declined in the Philippines, those in the more dynamic countries of East Asia rose dramatically, creating the kinds of income differentials that help to propel migration. Per capita incomes in the Asian NICs (Hong Kong, Taiwan, Korea and Singapore) rose by 6 to 7 per cent a year between 1965 and 1988 and by over 4 per cent a year in Malaysia and Thailand over the same period. Average wages in Japan and Taiwan are now over ten times and seven times respectively those in the Philippines. For most Filipino families, Abella (1993) continues, emigration is therefore a rational response to the state's inability to generate growth and employment within the country. The Filipino family has become 'transnational' in an effort to protect itself from declining real incomes and standards of living. Emigration is associated with the family's plans for investment in education and the acquisition of land and housing. Increased international mobility imparted a global dimension to what would otherwise be an internal reallocation of family labour to minimize risks. Since opportunities for complete relocation of a family in the more affluent countries are limited, many have opted for the only avenue possible by sending one or more family members abroad. Remittances of the migrants are evidently an important element of this adjustment mechanism since the family is still attempting to maximize the welfare (or minimize the risk) of the core household at home through migration.

Agostinelli (1991) draws attention to another feature of migratory flows from the Philippines, namely the proliferation of contract recruitment agencies suggesting that: 'It is the omnipresent intermediation of recruitment agencies that feeds the growing "commercialization of migration" from the Philippines and other South Asian countries to the Middle East' (Agostinelli 1991: 19). While in the early 1970s recruiters for overseas employment were virtually unknown, the share of labour migration accounted for by recruitment agencies in the Philippines was 72.4 per cent in 1977, 82.2 per cent in 1980 and 96.6 per cent in 1985. The number of legally operating private recruitment agencies rose from four in 1976, to 650 in 1980 and 964 in 1985.

Family strategies and the activities of recruiters were reinforced in the Philippines by an inward-looking industrialization policy based on import substitution. As a consequence there was a bias against exporting commodities. A host of instruments, including tariff and non-tariff barriers to trade, fiscal incentives, state rationing of subsidized credit, and an overvalued exchange rate, all served to protect inefficient domestic enterprises. It may now be too late to switch to a commodity-export strategy in that the liberalized economies of South Asia like China and India (and other smaller countries like Vietnam) have the comparative advantage of cheaper labour and have establish global dominance in many niches.

In summary, a number of complementary factors have reinforced the path of labour export:

- the government supports and promotes labour export;
- remittance income continues to represent an important source of national revenue (in 2004 remittances from overseas workers amounted to US$ 8.5 billion);
- organized labour recruitment is a big business with an effective lobby;
- households have adopted emigration as one means of survival and risk minimization;
- a 'culture of emigration' has developed in which family members are commonly expected to go abroad either temporarily or permanently; and
- alternative strategies of creating labour intensive export manufacturing are limited by competitor nations.

From internal to international migration: China

The history of rural–urban movements of population is well known. As cash-cropping and commercial agriculture took grip in Europe, Asia,

Africa and Latin America, economies of scale and more technological forms of agricultural production pushed workers off the land to swell the teeming cities. The drift to the towns and cities was a response both to changes in the countryside and to the establishment of industrial enterprises in the urban areas.

One difference between earlier periods and the contemporary transnational division of labour is that in the former agrarian countries industrialization was driven by the force of external investment or by an attempt to sell to the world market. The border towns of northern Mexico, for example, where US corporations had established a strip of 800 assembly plants by the 1970s, became swollen with more and more Mexican migrants from central and northern states in the Mexican hinterland. US government officials who had hoped that the establishment of the Border Industrialization Program (as it was called) would staunch the flow of illegal Mexican workers to the USA were confounded. Not only did the programme attract more migrants than could possibly be employed but the plants also normally employed young females, who were entering the labour force for the first time, thus doing nothing to mop up the demand for male employment.

Another contrast with the 'first' industrial revolution is that to enclosures and land consolidation must nowadays be added the demand for energy (especially hydroelectric power), the green revolution and GM crops, the provision of wildlife parks and conservation areas and the commercialization of planting, logging, cropping and packing ('field factories'). All of this has led to massive displacement of rural populations. India and China, where one-third of the world's inhabitants are found, are the key countries involved, but others include Nigeria, Brazil, Indonesia, South Africa and Mexico.

Given the scale of the moment and its potential implications for global migration, I want to focus particularly on the Chinese case. The commercialization of agriculture has shifted millions off the land each year. The Three Gorges dam on the Yangtze River will alone displace 1.2 million people. China's 'floating population' is reckoned to be between 80 and 120 million, a significant figure when compared with the usual estimates of total global immigration (measured by the number of foreign residents) of 175 million. The 'floating population', which has appeared particularly since the modification of the *hukuo* (registration) system, is defined as the number of people who changed residence in any one year. On the same measure, the rate of change of residence may be less than in the USA, but the sheer magnitude is greater and their rate of absorption into urban employment is lower. To be sure, there is a thriving, supercharged manufacturing base in China that absorbs many migrants and, according to one scenario (Harris 2004: 5), might even run out of labour or expand abroad:

> [China] ... is now the third largest trader in the world and has overtaken Japan. This has happened in the space of twenty years, and particularly in two regions – the Pearl River Delta (PRD) and the Yangtze Delta. The PRD is already running out of labour and has a shortfall of two million workers. To compete with the Yangtze Delta region the PRD will have to look eastwards for its workers, first to other Chinese provinces and then perhaps to Sub-Saharan Africa. The end of the Multi-Fibre Agreement in 2005 may encourage Chinese manufacturers to move abroad rather than pay higher wages at home.

Table 7.2: Chinese workers abroad (selected countries)

Japan	1986	75,275	1999	327,005
Russian Far East	1911	36,241	1996	200,000–300,000
Russia	1989	5,200	2002	2–2.5 million
France	1990	200,000	2001	300,000
Thailand			1996	120,000 illegals
Hungary	1988	0	2002	10,000–15,000

Sources: Edwards (2002: 272); Friman (2002: 12); Gelbras (2002: 100); Nyíri (2002: 291, 307); Shkurkin (2002: 85).

Though this scenario may currently seem fanciful – to the casual observer China seems to have inexhaustible supplies of rural labour – there are some indications that internal migration is 'coiled', ready to spring into a global role. The industrial (including rural industrial) labour force in China is often composed of semi-free workers, unorganized and exploited. The Party actually runs compulsory labour camps, subordinating workers partly in order to produce cheap goods for the international market (see Chapter 1). The army too is a major employer. Organization of this workforce and its exposure to cultural alternatives will drive up wages and possibly result in unemployment, thus creating the basis for an emigration flow. This will be further fuelled by the estimate that 300 million people are expected to move from rural to urban areas by 2025. The signs of external movement are already unmistakable (Table 7.2).

Conclusion

In developing a critique of NIDL theory, I laid emphasis on the lack of conceptual clarity in the German theorists, the historical gaps apparent in their neglect of a century marked by colonialism and imperialism, and some empirical omissions in the current transnational phase. The question of empirical omissions has been the one to tax me most in this chapter. In its current form, NIDL theory is too constrained by its nineteenth-century origins in classical political economy, and by its current reliance on radical trade theory and the logic of capital.

As soon as one widens 'the new international division of labour' into a discussion of the transnational division of labour, and accords labour flows as important a place as capital flows, some of the limitations of NIDL theory become apparent. The theory accounts well for the limited movement of workers in the NICs into the export-processing zones. It also implicitly deals with the end of the long migrant labour boom after the Second World War in Europe and the USA (though not with its origins). What it fails to pick up is the statistically significant phenomenon of service employment migration to the old metropolitan cities. Though the data are inconclusive, they suggest that transfers of redundant migrant workers from the growth industries of the 1950s and 1960s has stalled in the face of cheaper and more flexible migrants from abroad. Another important destination was to the oil-rich countries, which activated massive flows of unskilled, semi-skilled and professional migrants, though war and the fear of subversion modified these flows. Finally, telling the story from the point of view of labour, particularly in the labour exporting countries, has generated new insights that are not dependent merely on 'the logic of capital'. Though the data on China are patchy and remain somewhat speculative, I have surmised that considerable emigration from the PRC will arise in the next decades.

Notes

1. While Fröbel et al. (1980) referred to this transformation as 'the new international division of labour', their theory drew implicitly or explicitly on Warren's (1980) attack on dependency theory, on Wallerstein's (1979 and elsewhere) world systems analysis and, to a lesser degree, on the depiction of 'peripheral capitalism' suggested by Amin (1974).
2. I write, in April 2005, as Rover, the last British volume car production company in Birmingham, UK has gone bankrupt and, despite the company going down on bended knees to the Shanghai Automative Industry Corporation, the Chinese company has failed to come to its rescue. The switch from old to new manufacturing locations could hardly be more dramatic. Five to six thousand workers in Birmingham will lose their jobs, while perhaps 15,000 workers in supplier industries in the West Midlands could also be negatively affected.
3. Although the Philippines is the most prominent example of a government-led and supported labour export strategy, other countries, including Turkey, South Korea, India, Pakistan, Bangladesh, Sri Lanka, Jamaica, Cuba, Barbados, Mexico, El Salvador and Nicaragua have all promoted labour exporting policies.

Chapter 8

Globalization, international migration and everyday cosmopolitanism

G lobalization, international migration and cosmopolitanism all require explanation. However, the expression 'globalization' needs particular exposition, for it is used in a contested and popular sense that is not conceptually rigorous.[1] Migration, especially international migration, is both cause and consequence of globalization. I focus here on eight recent forms of migration. My remarks on 'everyday cosmopolitanism' are partly drawn from my work with Vertovec (Vertovec and Cohen 2002). I provide four vignettes to illustrate the connections between the three themes before providing a conclusion.

Globalization

There are at least six aspects of globalization that need mention here:

- changing concepts of space and time;
- an increasing volume of cultural interactions;
- the commonality of problems facing all the world's inhabitants;
- growing interconnections and interdependencies;
- ever more comprehensive networks of transnational actors and organizations; and
- the synchronization of all the dimensions involved in globalization.

Changing concepts of space and time

As shared forces and exchanges powerfully structure our lives, so the world is becoming one place and one system. With all this comes a radical shift in our understanding of space and time. Harvey (1989: 240–54) is especially helpful in explaining this characteristic of globalization. He argues that in pre-modern societies, space was understood in terms of concrete localities. Movement was dangerous and difficult while war, pestilence and famine often made social life unpredictable. For most individuals it was safer to remain in those places where they and their families enjoyed fixed and unchanging rights and obligations. Similarly, the memory of past disasters, the passing of the seasons and the cycle of agricultural work determined understandings of time.

Step by step, often through quite sudden bursts in technical knowledge linked to economic changes, it became possible to measure, divide and so map the physical and temporal dimensions of the world into universal, standardized and predictable units. For example, without the geographical coordinates of longitude and latitude, travel by ship or aeroplane would be considerably more difficult. Harvey (1989: 240) calls the outcome of these ideas and discoveries 'time–space compression'.

What are the implications of this shift? Time and distance have dwindled in significance as forces shaping human actions. Less bound by ties to specific places and events, both space and time have become available for us to manipulate and control. Another implication of the idea of space–time compression is that our social horizons are indefinitely extended. We are less dependent on particular people and fixed social relationships. Moreover, since the 1950s, mass television ownership, coupled more recently with satellite communications, 'makes it possible to experience a rush of images from different spaces almost simultaneously, collapsing the world's spaces into a series of images on a television screen' (Harvey 1989: 293).

We must remember that the world's inhabitants experience these changes unequally. Imagine, for example, people living in two villages located 30 miles apart in a poor region of West Africa. Here, the only telephone does not work, roads are neglected (and impassable in the rainy season) and no one can afford batteries to keep the few radios going. Such people remain almost as far apart in terms of their ability to interact effectively as they were 100 years ago. In a sense, they are *more* distant from each other than people living in, say, Sydney and Paris.

Increasing cultural interactions

For many social scientists, culture is used very broadly to depict all the modes of thought, behaviour and artefacts that are transmitted from generation to generation by emulation, education or the public record. In an everyday context, however, it refers to specific intellectual, artistic and aesthetic attainments in music, painting, literature, film and other forms of expression. Culture in this sense is particularly rich in imagery, metaphors, signs and symbols. With respect to this second understanding of culture, it is important to note that in Western societies earlier distinctions between 'highbrow' and 'lowbrow' or popular culture – enjoyed by ordinary people – have been challenged during the twentieth century. This is linked especially to the rise of the mass media and the widespread dissemination of consumerist lifestyles. There are at least seven consequences that follow:

- It has become increasingly possible to lift cultural meanings out of their original societal contexts and transplant them to other societies.
- We now have the means to access rapidly far greater quantities of cultural meaning of every kind than ever before and from a multiplicity of sources.
- We can obtain full pictures of other lifestyles, especially through the power of visual images conveyed on television and film.
- It is increasingly possible (and necessary to our very survival) to know about other people's cultures. If we do not, we run the risk of being excluded from many potential benefits.
- The electronic mass media of communication, along with fast transport, have the capacity to affect all those who are exposed to it, and to incorporate them into a single experience. Accordingly, we live in what McLuhan (1962) famously called a 'global village'.
- We are made conscious that we live in a pluralist, multicultural world and are invited to participate in its many different possibilities embodied, for example, in cuisine, music, religious practices and marriage customs. But, notwithstanding this point;
- At present, Western and especially US influences dominate the volume and character of cultural and knowledge flows.

The commonality of problems

Interlaced in the fabric of globalization is the growing commonality of problems facing the world's nations and peoples. Of course, we are entitled to be sceptical about how widely such perceptions are shared –

since the lives of many people are still governed by long-held social customs, exclusive religious beliefs and unquestioned national identities. However, their perception of the world is constantly under assault. The media have long brought the events and crises taking place in near and distant locations into our living rooms on a daily and hourly basis. We can recall, in recent years, the invasion of Kuwait in 1990, the terrorist incident at the Olympic Games in Atlanta in the summer of 1996, the famine in Sudan in 1998, the pitiable refugees pouring out of Kosovo in 1999, the repetitive ghoulish images of aircraft ploughing into the Twin Towers in New York on 11 September 2001, the bombs that devastated the tourist resort of Bali in 2002 and, not least, the dreadful tsunami overwhelming many parts of Asia in December 2004. Such events graphically remind us of our common humanity – our vulnerabilities to accident and misfortune – and the existential truth that we all inhabit the same, small planet.

While startling visual images are experienced as collective shocks, there are more material reasons for our sense of empathy with other human beings. In our compressed and integrated globe our choices not only rebound on our own lives, but they also directly affect the lives of others far away. Often, we are unaware of this and do not intend our actions directly to harm distant strangers. For example, the most prosperous fifth of the world's population living in the advanced economies enjoys 64 per cent of global income (Durning 1992: 278). Because their global economic power is so great, their decisions about what to produce and consume, how to invest their money, their lifestyle preferences and leisure pursuits may, without conscious intent, cause unemployment, falling export prices and loss of livelihood for workers and peasants in distant lands.

Another reason for sharing concerns is that certain global problems require global solutions. Acting alone, governments cannot protect their borders, territories or the lives and well being of their citizens from a number of situations. The 1986 nuclear accident at Chernobyl in the Ukraine and the subsequent fallout of radioactive material across wide areas of Europe vividly demonstrated our vulnerability. The threat to national currencies from speculation on the world's financial markets, international drug trafficking and terrorism are other examples of relative national impotence. Only collaboration between governments and regulation at the global level can provide genuine solutions. Whether or not this will be forthcoming is open to doubt. We are uncertain how far citizens will exercise pressure on governments and agencies at both national and transnational levels.

Interconnections and interdependencies

Fast expanding interconnections and interdependencies bind localities, countries, companies, social movements, professional and other groups, as well as individual citizens, into an ever denser network of trans-national exchanges and affiliations. So important are these networks thought to be that one eminent sociologist (Castells 1996) has suggested that we live in a 'network society'. These networks have burst across territorial borders, rupturing the cultural and economic self-sufficiency that nations once experienced. What drives these networks and empowers those participating in them are knowledge and information? As Castells (1996: 469) graphically put it, the power of knowledge flows 'takes precedence over the flows of power'. The overall cumulative impact of these interconnections has meant that societies, and their cities and regions, have tended to spread outwards so as to merge and become coextensive with other societies. At the same time, the once clear-cut separation between the sphere of national life and the international sphere has largely broken down.

Until quite recently most social scientists, especially political theorists, thought about interactions at the world level almost entirely in terms of interstate dealings and exchanges. Thus, nation-states were considered to be far the most dominant, if not the only, players in world affairs. Burton (1972) used the analogy of a snooker game to describe the interactions between states. However, an ever denser network of ties and connections transcended purely interstate relations as powerful *non-state actors* formed relationships to pursue their own interests. Thus, increasingly the international system consisted of different layers of interactions and connections. As Malcolm Waters observes, Burton's metaphor of a snooker table can be used to point to a different future scenario where 'the entire world is linked together by networks that are as dense as the ones which are available in local contexts'. In this view, 'locality and geography will disappear altogether, the world will genuinely be one place and the nation-state will be redundant' (Waters 1995: 28).

Transnational actors and organizations

Who or what are these leading transnational agents whose actions have done so much to extend and intensify the interconnections across national borders since the Second World War?

- *Transnational corporations (TNCs)*. In many ways these are the most powerful and the most evident of such agents and we need no particular explication here.
- *International governmental organizations (IGOs)*. By the early 1980s, according to Scholte (1993: 44), there were 700 IGOs, which together convened approximately 5000 meetings a year. The variety of functions they perform is barely shown by the following examples: the World Meteorological Organization, the International Postal Union, the United Nations High Commission for Refugees (UNHCR), and the Food and Agricultural Organization (FAO).
- *International non-governmental organizations (INGOs)*. Like their national counterparts, INGOs are autonomous organizations not accountable to governments though they may work with them at times. The numbers of INGOs have grown at a remarkable rate, especially since the 1950s. Today, their range of activities is vast, encompassing religious, business, professional, labour, political, green, women's, sport and leisure interests among many others. Some of the best known INGOs are Greenpeace, the Red Cross, Oxfam and Amnesty International. But there are literally thousands of others operating transnationally, and many more that mainly confine their operations within nation-states. By the mid-1980s there were approximately 17,000 INGOs, though not all were equally global in scope.
- *Diasporas and stateless people*. A number of diasporas (like the Jewish and Parsi ones) predate the nation-state. However, other diasporas arose because of religious, ethnic or political disputes with governments over the demand for full citizen rights, the recognition of semi-autonomy or the granting of independent national status. Their experience of persecution or neglect compelled some to leave voluntarily or seek asylum in other countries, thereby forming global diasporas of linked, displaced peoples. Among such groups are Africans, Kashmiris, Tamils, Sikhs, Armenians and Palestinians.[2]

- *Other transnational actors*. Daily, huge numbers of migrants are engaged in forging transnational connections as they travel, alone or in small informal groups, across national boundaries. At their destinations they may reside as temporary visitors or seek long-term settlement. Whatever their circumstances and motives, they transport their cultures and lifestyles with them while becoming exposed, to various degrees, to the host societies' cultures. Thus, global cultures are juxtaposed and sometimes merged.

Synchronization of all dimensions

We can point to a final aspect of globalization. All the dimensions of globalization – economic, technological, political, social and cultural – appear to be coming together at the same time, each reinforcing and magnifying the impact of the others.

In the economic sphere, governments have lost some of their power to regulate their economies as a host of largely autonomous agents like international banks, TNCs and currency markets have flourished in the ever more integrated world economy. Though they are formed through intergovernmental agreements, bodies like the World Trade Organization (WTO) have taken on a life of their own and often compel recalcitrant governments to adopt trade policies they see acting against their particular national interest. Meanwhile, the lure of the free market has drawn many more countries into its orbit. This has allowed money values to penetrate every corner of the globe and into most facets of social and cultural life.

There is growing mass participation in the market economy by workers, consumers, tourists, listeners and viewers. This, together with the revolutions in the electronic media and information technology, has generated the basis for the enormous expansion of cultural flows across the world. Culture in all its forms – as consumer aspirations, pop or rock music, religious, moral and ethnic values or the political ideologies of democracy and socialism – has become the most recent and perhaps most potent addition to globalization. Transmission takes place through different means – through visual images in the mass media, abstract knowledge, or the social milieux created by more varied interpersonal relationships. The explosive potential for enfeebling national cultures and affiliations and for providing new foci of identity and collaboration between citizens of distant countries has only begun to work its way through the world order.

International migration

Despite attempts to restrict, control, manage and select immigrants on the part of states, seen at a global level migration of all sorts has rapidly increased over the last 30 years. At least eight types are evident:

Legal labour migration

Notwithstanding the Western industrial states' strong controls, this form of migration either continued in less obvious ways or flowed to other areas – it did not end. Dealing with Asia alone, Castles and Miller (1998) estimated that by the mid-1990s there were about three million Asians legally employed outside their own countries within Asia, and another three million employed in other continents, notably in the Gulf States. Though the Gulf War of 1991 led to the dramatic repatriation of millions of Asian workers, this flow has resumed despite, or partly because of, the economic crisis in the Asia-Pacific region in the 1990s.

Illegal or undocumented labour migration

Though impossible to estimate with precision, illegal or undocumented labour migration has more than taken the place of those stopped at the frontier. The Mexican–US frontier has remained leaky while a notable new migration space for illegal workers has opened up in South Africa, where the abolition of post-apartheid controls on internal movement has exposed the incapacity of the state to control inward movements from the surrounding region. The North African route to southern Europe is a third example of a new space for illegal migration. Undocumented labour is now taking *two* predominant forms (a) overstaying and (b) deliberate illegal entry. While the former largely remains a matter of individual entrepreneurship, there is increasing evidence of the organization of illegal entry. Large sums of money change hands, entry certificates and visas are forged and border guards are bribed. Often lorry drivers ('truckers'), and travel and shipping agents are involved. One frequent feature that perpetuates illegal entry is the complicity of employers.

Refugee and displacee migration

The number of refugees is also difficult to estimate because of varying statistical criteria, but the UNHCR's 2003 estimate lists some 17 million 'persons of concern' (see Table 8.1). The expression 'persons of concern' covers asylum seekers, internal displacees and a narrower legal definition of the 'refugee' arising from the 1951 Geneva Convention. In paraphrase, a (Convention) refugee is someone who is fleeing from a real threat of persecution in their country of origin on the grounds of their background or political opinions. The reason why this definition is quite restricted in practice is that the Convention places all the responsibility for judging whether the person is, or is not, a refugee in the hands of the admitting state, which may have reasons to deny that status. The number of 'Convention refugees' is therefore much lower than the general estimates.

Table 8.1: Estimated number of 'persons of concern' who fall under the mandate of UNHCR (by region)*

Date	2001	2002	2003
Asia	8,449,900	8,820,700	6,187,800
Africa	6,060,100	4,173,500	4,285,100
Europe	5,592,400	4,855,400	4,268,000
Northern America	1,051,700	1,086,800	962,000
Latin America and Caribbean	575,500	765,400	1,316,400
Oceania	84,500	81,300	74,100
TOTAL	21,814,200	19,783,100	17,093,400

* 'Persons of concern' include refugees, asylum seekers and displacees.
Source: UNHCR (web site last consulted February 2005).

Displacees are of course also not a new phenomenon. At the end of the Second World War, millions of displaced persons (DPs) were settled by international agreement and by the decidedly uncivil decisions of the Allied military authorities. We now have a new name for an old chilling practice, 'ethnic cleansing', whereby newly emerging polities in the former Soviet Union, like the former Yugoslavia or the broken-backed post-colonial states of Africa, expel people who have nowhere to go.

Independent female migration

Feminists in the 1960s declared that women were 'hidden from history'. This observation is perhaps particularly true in the migration field. Many studies of migration dealt with women as a residual category, as those 'left behind'. Where they crossed a border, women have generally been treated as dependent or family members. Numerically and sociologically we have entered a new phase of female migration. This movement is a response to the demand for women in the global service economy. Some of this is in the sex industry, which is particularly strongly based in East Asia. Hostesses and entertainers are required in very significant numbers in countries like Japan – and they are generally supplied from China and Thailand. A somewhat more respectable version of the trade is in the 'mail order bride' trade dominated by the Philippines. The Philippines also is market leader for domestic labour and exports tens of thousands of female domestic workers each year. To the brides and the domestics add waitresses, casual staff in fast food outlets, cleaners, and nurses (particularly geriatric nurses), secretaries, hotel reception staff or stewardesses, many of whom are supplied from outside the country of work. By the mid-1990s 1.5 million Asian women were working abroad.

Skilled transients

Also 'hidden from history', but in a very different way, are a large group of highly-skilled international transients like accountants, computer experts, lawyers, academics, doctors, business managers, construction engineers and consultants. Some are freelance consultants, but most work for international companies trying to complete contracts, initiate business deals or develop branch plants in the country of destination. The crucial element here is that migrants are not leaving a place of origin forever. In recent papers this group of migrants has variously been called 'skilled transients', 'sojourners' or 'denizens' (in the sense of a privileged foreigner). They do not have extensive civic rights in the new countries in which they work. They do not, for example, have the vote, cannot draw on social security systems and do not have rights of permanent residence. On the other hand, they do not really need these facilities and privileges. If they want to vote they can exercise their vote by post. Their companies insure them, often pay for privileged education for their children, provide generous pensions and subsidize family visits. Others operate in the cracks between tourism, self-employment and agency work.

Skilled long-term migrants

Unlike the earlier group, there is also a significant group of skilled workers who are offered permanent settlement and access to citizenship by admitting states. There is now no country that unreservedly welcomes immigrants of all sorts. Indeed, for the last century there have been formal and informal restrictions on immigration. However, a number of countries institutionalized a more rational system of bidding for particular migrants. The two countries that have perfected the system of 'immigration shopping' are Canada and Australia. They have linked their economic development, manpower and immigration departments structurally and are intent on finding selected migrants to fill slots in the labour market. If dentists are needed in Manitoba an immigration vacancy will be created, just as radiographers going to Tasmania are welcomed. (Without going into the points systems in detail, what they are after is skills, youth, good health, education and lack of dependants.) Equally welcomed are permanent 'business' or 'entrepreneurial' migrants who bring investments and often jobs with them. Often, as in the case of the so-called non-resident Indians in the USA, the admitting state sees the group as permanent, while the country of origin still tries to claim the loyalty of its erstwhile countrymen and women. (This dual or split loyalty to the place of origin and place of settlement is something I will discuss more generally below.)

Large-scale internal movements

While in keeping with the subject matter of international politics I have concentrated on international migration, it is worth remembering that internal migration is very much greater in volume though generally less contentious. (It is also worth noting in parenthesis that sometimes, when states and empires are breaking up or where post-colonial boundaries are artificial, it is difficult to tell the difference between internal and international migration.) However, there is at least one case of internal migration (in China) that has global implications. In China up to 120 million people are currently on the move[3] following the abolition of an internal registration system that acted as a constraint on movement. Step migration from rural area, to small town and then on to big city also tends ultimately to result in international migration.

Tourism

Tourists are not normally considered as migrants. However, there is considerable leakage into other forms of migration and tourists have important cultural effects. The movement of tourists involves 'the largest scale movement of goods, services and people that humanity has ever seen' other than during wartime (Greenwood 1989: 17). From 1950 to 1990 the volume of tourist arrivals increased by 17 times. Recent years are shown in Table 8.2.

Table 8.2: International tourism (1996–2004)

Year	Arrivals (millions)	Absolute increase (millions)
1996	586	34
1997	610	24
1998	629	19
1999	652	23
2000	697	45
2001	692	−5
2002	702	10
2003	694	−8
2004*	764	70

* The year 2004 is projected. Absolute numbers are rounded figures.
Source: World Tourism Organization (web site last consulted February 2005).

The fall shown in 2001 arose as a consequence of a fear of flying that followed the terrorist attacks in New York on 11 September 2001 and growth was somewhat erratic until 2004. It is uncertain what the effects of the tsunami and increased security checks in the USA will be. While it is important to look at numbers, the increasing exoticism of tourist destinations, particularly to the tropical world, has major cultural and social effects. More and more people are drawn into the web of tourism as participants, service agents or objects of a tourist gaze.

Everyday cosmopolitanism

As I have suggested, globalization and international migration can generate enormous shifts at the subjective and cultural levels. Many people in many countries (though by no means all) are now willing and eager to think about themselves collectively, as part of a common humanity. While cultural flows are still overwhelmingly sourced from a limited number of countries, flows can go both ways, indeed in multiple directions, as diversity is enhanced, as social actors become self-aware and as identities become broader. At a social or more intimate personal level many individuals now seem to be more than ever prone to articulate complex affiliations, meaningful attachments and multiple allegiances to issues, people, places and traditions that lie beyond the boundaries of their resident nation-state. This holds especially for migrants, members of ethnic diasporas and other transnational communities (Vertovec and Cohen 1999). People active in global social movements also orient their politics and identities toward agendas outside, as well as within, their resident nation-states.

This process of the enlargement of social, cultural and personal agendas can usefully be described as cosmopolitanism. Since it has been around for a long time the term 'cosmopolitanism' has attracted many understandings and uses over the years. Recently such mixed meanings have been elaborated and extended in a burgeoning body of literature in political philosophy and sociology (Vertovec and Cohen 2002). One reason why cosmopolitanism has acquired fresh appeal is because the term seems to represent a confluence of progressive ideas and new perspectives relevant to our culturally crisscrossed, media bombarded, information rich, capitalist dominated, politically plural times. Cosmopolitanism suggests something that simultaneously: (a) transcends the seemingly exhausted nation-state model; (b) is able to mediate actions and ideals oriented both to the universal and the particular, the global and the local; (c) is culturally anti-essentialist; and (d) is capable of representing variously complex repertoires of allegiance, identity and interest. In these ways, cosmopolitanism seems to offer a mode of managing cultural and political multiplicities.

A frequent attack on cosmopolitanism is that this option is only available to the elite – those who have the resources to travel, learn other languages and absorb other cultures. This, historically, has often been true. For the majority of the population, living their lives within the cultural space of their own locality, nationality or ethnicity, cosmopolitanism has not been a possibility. However, in the contemporary world, cultural and linguistic diversity is omnipresent, and the capacity to communicate with others and to understand their cultures is available, at least potentially, to many. Travel and immigration have led to the need for cheek-by-jowl relationships between diverse peoples at work or on street corners, and in markets, neighbourhoods, schools and recreational areas. Some of the most fascinating social research in the field is now generating countless examples of so-called 'everyday' or 'ordinary' cosmopolitanism where, as Hiebert (2002: 212) puts it, 'men and women from different origins create a society where diversity is accepted and is rendered ordinary'.

Such everyday cosmopolitanism might be regarded as a newly recognized form of behaviour. However, in more commonly described settings, cosmopolites have been seen as deviant – refusing to define themselves by location, ancestry, citizenship or language. 'Cosmopolite or cosmopolitan in mid-nineteenth century America', for example, meant 'a well-travelled character probably lacking in substance' (Hollinger 1995: 89). Here 'substance' likely referred to readily identifiable provenance, an integrated and predictable pattern of behavioural practice, including loyalty to a single nation-state or cultural identity. In situations of extreme nationalism or totalitarianism, such as those of the Soviet Union, Nazi Germany or Fascist Italy, cosmopolites were seen as treacherous enemies of the state. It is not coincidental that the Jews and Romanies – 'rootless' peoples without an attachment to a particular land – were the first to be shunted to the charnel houses of the Holocaust and the bleak camps of the Gulag.

Even where the reactions were not so extreme, the common stereotype of cosmopolitans suggested privileged, bourgeois, politically uncommitted elites. They have been associated with wealthy jet setters, corporate managers, intergovernmental bureaucrats, artists, tax dodgers, academics and intellectuals, all of whom maintained their condition by virtue of their wealth, often inherited wealth, and snobbish and superior attitudes. However, with globalization, mass migration and the awareness of inequality, developing a functional cosmopolitanism is now becoming a matter of everyday survival for many workers, labour migrants and refugees who are in no sense 'elite'. Such non-elite cosmopolites need to know how to provide services (as nurses, builders, entertainers, waiters or prostitutes, for example) to foreign sojourners and visitors. If they seek work outside their countries of origin, they need to develop foreign language skills, knowledge of migration policies and routes, and the conversion value of currencies.

Four vignettes

Often simple examples tell a tale that can illustrate wider conceptual arguments. Here are four vignettes that link the themes of globalization, international migration and mundane cosmopolitanism:

The South African dentist

This author (RC) lived in Cape Town, South Africa, over the period from 2001 to 2004. He went to his dentist, a white South African of Afrikaner origin. It was bad news. He needed extensive periodontal work and was required to see the dentist several times. They compared diaries. The fourth week in every month was impossible. The dentist travelled routinely each month to London where he had a practice. He loved living in South Africa, where he enjoyed the climate, sports and the countryside, but he was annoyed at the black government for not managing the economy better. The local currency, the Rand, was at that time losing ground against the strong international currencies. By flying to London each month, he earned hard currency and retained his privileged lifestyle. Under the old apartheid regime, South Africans were excluded from the Commonwealth so he would have been unable to work temporarily in the United Kingdom. He saw the irony of the situation and accepted that by making South Africa more globally respectable, the black government had allowed him to travel and work abroad in a way that was much more difficult before 1994.

The London taxi driver

The British have been collecting census data every ten years for over 150 years, so they are experienced enough not to expect too many surprises. However, when the results of the previous decennial census were reported in October 2002, demographers were astonished find that their expectations of counting nearly 60 million people were overturned. The tally was about one million short. A London taxi driver had his own explanation. He was a typical East Ender, a Cockney with a sense of humour, who had decided that he could earn enough in two months of hard work (at the wheel for 12 to 14 hours a day) to fund his relaxed life style in the Portuguese Algarve for most of the year. He rented his cab to his Bengali neighbour, 'who is a good bloke', for ten months each year. Of course, he was not counted in the census. He was not there at the time. 'There are lots like us – we go in and out of the country as we like,' he said.

The Argentinean academic

RC's brother has a friend in Argentina from a middle-class Jewish family – an academic professionally. The country's economy had collapsed in a spectacular fashion during 2002 and the family decided to leave Argentina, despite being there for five generations. Some went to Israel, braving the security situation there, as they could evoke 'the Law of Return', allowing Jews freely to enter Israel for settlement. Others decided to go Poland where a relevant academic opening had been found. They had had no prior contact with Poland and knew of the history of widespread anti-Semitism in that country. But they also knew that Poland would be in the next group of countries to join the European Union and that would facilitate them entering the more favoured parts of the 'Euro zone' one day.

The Filipina nurse

In October 2002, the British newspapers reported that Filipina nurses were going to be recruited in significant numbers to staff the hospitals in the north of England. There was (and remains) a desperate shortage of staff and the traditional supplies from the Commonwealth, Ireland and southern Europe had dried up. The Filipina nurses spoke English, but *American* English. How could they possibly understand the needs of their patients? The decision was made to subject them to many hours of the TV soap *Coronation Street,* the TV soap depicting working-class life in the English North. There they could learn that when a patient said they wanted 'to spend a penny', they wanted to go to the lavatory.[4]

Connections and conclusion

I have suggested in this chapter that many people are adapting to two important characteristics of the contemporary form of globalization – its pervasiveness and its unevenness. Pervasiveness includes popular knowledge about many culturally diverse lifestyles as well as more practical issues like immigration policies, comparative wage rates, levels of unemployment and currency movements. Those who are mobile are able to use this knowledge to mediate the uneven impact of global development.

Of course I do not pretend that a South African dentist, a London taxi driver, an Argentinean academic or a Filipina nurse are representative of the global population. However, what they signify is that many people from many countries have been touched by the forces of globalization and can see migration as a possibility. We also need to remember that there is a whole gamut of interlocutors – travel agents, former migrants, people smugglers and labour recruiters – who are bringing news of opportunities, some real and some exaggerated, to the far-flung corners of the globe. As people migrate, they need to connect and acquire the tools of functional communication. They become more and more cosmopolitan, not in the sense of a *louche* playboy, a *rentier*, or a debonair, rootless, stateless member of the elite, but in a more prosaic sense. Cosmopolites can also be of working-class origin. They acquire an international language (often English, or a passable version of it). They are 'streetwise' in knowing who is likely to exploit them or turn them away from a frontier. They learn the cultural 'manners' of their hosts – their gestures, greetings, and preferred sports and leisure activities.

The growth of this mundane or everyday cosmopolitanism has profound implications, though we should be cautious of exaggerating its political significance. The new army of global migrants is not the conscious, politicized international working class that Marx imagined in the 1848 *Communist manifesto*. Nonetheless, there is a sense in which 'globalization from above', driven by powerful countries and transnational corporations, is now being paralleled and to a degree subverted by 'globalization from below', driven by the enhanced mobility of labour. Relationships between international migrants and national workers ('blue' and 'white' collar) remain problematic and there is a great deal of differentiation within the migrant groups. Some are looking for settle-

ment and cultural integration; others wish to use international opportunities to buttress traditional lifestyles that are under threat. What is
certain is that the ambiguities and complexities of improved mobility
and mundane cultural interaction will transform social scientific discussion of labour markets, cultural politics, migration studies and ethnic
relations.

Notes

1. My observations on globalization are drawn mainly from Cohen and
   Kennedy (2001).
2. See Cohen (1997) for a typology and an analysis.
3. The figure is an estimate of the 'floating population', which the Chinese
   government measures by the number living outside their place of normal
   residence in any one year.
4. This may need explanation. Years ago access to public lavatories was effected
   by putting a penny in the door – thus the euphemism.

Chapter 9

The free movement of money and people: debates before and after '9/11'

W ith the collapse of communism in the Soviet Union and the other countries of the Warsaw Pact, *emigration* control effectively ended in all but one or two of the world's 191 UN-recognized states. By contrast, *immigration* control has been strengthened everywhere in response both to security concerns arising from the terrorist outrages of recent years and to public concern about the level of immigration. Security issues have also led to some attempts to regulate the flows of money. But how comprehensive and effective are such measures? Increased global mobility, regional free movement zones, dual citizenship, the growth of student and tourist mobility, the demographic and economic needs of rich countries, weak state structures in some developing countries and irregular migration (to name just the major factors) have compromised the effectiveness of policing national frontiers. Likewise, politicians have found it difficult to reverse the neo-liberal measures for free currency movements that were adopted in the last three decades and were designed to 'unfetter' the market. How these contradictory pressures will be resolved remains uncertain. In this chapter I focus on the theoretical, ethical and rhetorical basis for state regulation of the flows of people and, to a lesser extent, on money. I also, more cursorily, compare the two flows.

In the wake of 9/11 and 911 (the atrocities in New York and Madrid respectively) the ethical case for the free migration of money and people was effectively silenced. As money was being used to buy bombs and detonators for mass murder, and certain migrants were establishing terrorist networks, their free movement, it was conventionally assumed, had to be carefully controlled and scrutinized. And who, effectively, could undertake this task if not cooperating state agencies such as Interpol, or state fiscal, immigration and security departments? Precisely because the case for control seems self-evident it is timely to review the ethical and practical cases made for the free movement of people and money, their own self-limiting conditions and the extent to which the contemporary political pressures for further restrictions can be justified by reference to general concepts of social justice and the public good.[1]

The free movement of migrants: Kant and Carens

The longstanding ethical argument for the free movement of migrants is often traced back to Kant's (1795) essay, *Perpetual peace*, in which he claimed that rulers had become too powerful: they ordered people to 'immolate themselves' in the name of the state without any legal restraint and without putting themselves into danger. States perpetrated a 'savage and lawless freedom' and instead needed to submit themselves to 'public coercive laws', embracing all the peoples of the earth (Fine and Cohen 2002: 141). This is a powerful plea for cosmopolitan law. It is based on the premise that the peoples of the earth (*not* rulers or states) own the earth and therefore they must be free to travel anywhere on its surface. It is unjustifiable, therefore, for states to section off this or that bit of the planet. However, as Bauböck (1994: 321–2) argues, Kant is effectively maintaining that anybody should be free to *travel* both in respect of conducting peaceful trade and 'to *offer* themselves for social contact with established inhabitants of any territory' (emphasis added). To be sure, the host society, in Kant's view, is bound to proffer hospitality.

Even in this generous formulation of free mobility, there are clear limitations imposed by Kant and some we may infer. Migration for the purposes of colonization can be undertaken only to 'bring culture to uncivilized peoples' (Kant betrays his 'Occidental' attitudes here), and only in a way that avoids the plunder, subjugation and extermination of conquered peoples (Fine and Cohen 2002: 143). As to the limits we might infer, note that free migration for *peaceful trade* is defended – not a trade in arms, biological agents or drugs. The restriction if there is a likelihood of 'harm' is implied, if not stated. Equally, there seems to be a necessary moment of *consent* by the current residents if travellers have to 'offer' themselves for social acceptance. Proffering hospitality is prior to and not the same thing as conferring social membership.

If we now turn to twentieth-century political philosophers, Joseph Carens (1987: 251–73) probably initiated the most widely cited discussion of the ethics of immigration. Drawing on Rawlsian ideas (Rawls 1971), which were predicated on a single society with a bounded social membership, Carens suggested that the principles of 'fair opportunity' and 'equal liberty' could be extended across societies (not merely within one) to cover such issues as trade (by analogy also money) and migration. With respect to migration, a Rawlsian principle that all people within a society are equal moral persons could not, by extension, be denied to people of other origins. If we hold it right that people should be free to migrate within a country to better themselves, find a loved one, join their coreligionists or extend their cultural horizons, a similar principle could be applied across borders (Carens 1987: 258). Carens derived from Nozick (1974) the argument that the state has no basis on which to compel somebody to treat an alien or a citizen either differently or similarly. In one example he uses, an American employer has the right to offer a job to a Mexican or a native-born Californian without the state's interference. Indeed, I may add, it is clear that many employers feel totally unconstrained about offering 'American jobs' to workers abroad, for example in China or the border zone in northern Mexico. With the exception of a few labour unions, this 'right' by the employer has been unchallenged, certainly in the post-Reagan neo-liberal state.

To use the language of market economics, Carens proposed that there is a good philosophical basis for unimpeded human mobility both on the supply side and the demand side of the equation. Again, however, Carens (1987: 251) allowed a crucial limitation to his own case by distinguishing, in effect, between 'good' and 'bad' migrants. The former were cast in somewhat journalistic terms – Haitians in leaky boats, Salvadorians dying from heat in the Arizonian desert and Guatemalans crawling through rat-infested sewer pipes from Mexico to California ('ordinary peaceful people, seeking only the opportunity to build secure lives for themselves and their families'). The latter were 'criminals, subversives or armed invaders'. The bad migrants clearly could not have rights of free entry.

Carens also reviewed the extent to which Walzer (1983) successfully challenged his, that is Carens's, own case for 'relatively' open borders. He examined, in particular, the validity of Walzer's claim that too many migrants might threaten a society's achievements in the arts, science and culture or, perhaps more plausibly, might compromise a stable public order. He concedes much of Walzer's case. Though Carens was generally resolute in his defence of 'relative' free movement in 1987, in a later publication five years on (Carens 1992: 45) he is noticeably back-pedalling. Even if liberal egalitarians are committed to the idea of free movement of people, 'that idea is not politically feasible today and so it mainly serves to provide a critical standard by which to assess existing restrictive practices and policies'. While all restrictions are wrong in an ideal world, he concludes, some restrictions are worse than others. By 1996 'realistic' and 'idealistic' approaches to the ethics of migration are given equal status. The former 'informs most actual discussions of public policy' and is 'a morally serious approach worthy of more attention than it has received in academic discussions of the ethics of public policy' (Carens 1996: 157). However much the idealistic approach is 'congenial' to philosophers, the realistic position has 'certain characteristic strengths that reveal the limitations and weaknesses' of his preferred position (Carens 1996: 157).

The free movement of migrants: discussion after '9/11'

In some ways it was surprising to find that the philosophical proponents of the free movement of migrants were as self-limiting and as timid in their claims as they were. This weak advocacy opened them to at least three countermoves that were given additional impetus in the period after '9/11'. First, border controls were naturalized so that opposition to excessive (and, as we see later, expensive and ineffective) enforcement measures was deemed incredible or even treasonous. The expressed need for 'homeland security' has been invoked to the point that the historical rights and liberties of the settled populations are being undermined with little political resistance. Second, while in the wake of '9/11' liberal political theorists have articulated a modest defence of migrant rights; these have remained firmly constrained by acceptance of national sovereignty and the need for 'realism'. Finally, checks on immigration have provided the occasion for a reaffirmation of singular national, monochromatic identities and an attack on multiculturalism, diversity and immigration 'of the wrong sort'.

Border controls and the erosion of domestic rights

As was established in Chapter 3 of this book, passport controls are a much later manifestation of state power than has sometimes been supposed. They were also imposed much more patchily than might be imagined. The frontiers between many countries were arbitrary (in the case of Africa most were invented in a conference room in Berlin in 1895 with scant regard to topography and ethnography) or were determined by mountains and oceans that were not regularly policed. In the period of vast migrations of Europeans to the USA between 1870 and 1914, border controls were class based. Those in the upper decks landed without inspection, while only the passengers in steerage met the beady-eyed Ellis Island immigration officials. It is also a useful corrective to remember that even by 2005 only 20 per cent of US citizens had passports, a percentage that is barely exceeded by members of the US Congress.

Despite the need to recognize that many people never travel outside their countries of origin and that passport regimes are not universal, for the bulk of conventional travellers, whose numbers exceeded 700 million in 2004, enhanced border controls have become a tedious reality. Air travellers have to accept extended check-in times and long lines at arrival gates. The security concerns of the USA have been gradually extended to the rest of the world. Border checks have been enhanced by biometric data (finger printing, digital photographs and iris recognition). Even travellers from countries with visa waiver arrangements with the USA are forced to submit to biometric checks on entry and exit.

Increased surveillance of US borders started immediately after '9/11', but the commission established in its aftermath notably hardened its border controls in its final report, issued in July 2004. In summarizing that report, Cooper (2004) explains that it called for the integration of the border security system with screening networks used in the transport system and in the protection of sensitive facilities like nuclear plants. A standardization of *internal* identity documents, like driving licences and birth certificates, had to parallel a comprehensive screening system at *external* points of entry. Foreign governments, private corporations and all 15 (*sic*) national intelligence agencies had to be encouraged or induced to cooperate and coordinate their security efforts. The commission also recommended drawing citizens of the US itself and adjacent countries (like Canada) into the net with compulsory biometric passports.

In April 2005 the US administration responded by announcing that US nationals will need passports to re-enter the USA from Canada, Mexico, Panama and Bermuda by 2008 in view of the need to protect the USA against a terrorist threat. Similarly, Canadians will also have to present a passport to enter the USA. Asked about these measures in an interview with Associated Press, Secretary of State Condoleezza Rice said the USA had to take every precaution to screen out 'people who want to come in to hurt us', while President Bush (http://www.cnn.com/2005/) said that border controls with Mexico had to be tightened to ensure that terrorists, drug runners, gun runners and smugglers did not enter the USA.

I have already intimated that in many areas internal and external security measures, which have been historically separated, are rapidly converging.[2] At the level of street security, shoppers and residents have long had to accept both visible and covert surveillance of their movements. In shopping centres, cameras are pervasive. So many of them have now been installed that there is said to be, in number, one camera for every street in Britain. Government-authorized phone tapping has been massively enhanced and the many eavesdropping devices that are available on the market are used illegitimately by private security agencies. The interception, scanning and reading of snail mail and email are now routinely undertaken. At airports (and increasingly at railway, underground and bus stations) identity and luggage checks are becoming more frequent and pervasive. Body searches, X-rays and invasive cameras are either current or planned. Biometric data are now imbedded in passports, credit cards and other ID documents. These and other measures amount to historically unprecedented intrusions into citizens' private lives.

A defence of migrant rights

In an important contribution to the post-'9/11' debate, Ruhs and Chang (2004: 70) argue that what is distinctive about international labour migration (in contrast to trade and capital flows) is that migrants 'lay claim to certain rights *vis-à-vis* the host state and their fellow residents'. Despite an acceptance of the language of 'rights', they continue, the participants to the debate show a marked inability to discuss the ethical assumptions underpinning their arguments. Inward migration is discussed in terms of skill and utility, rather than the rights that are to be conferred, however minimal, after admission. Rights like job mobility, access to the courts, welfare services, health benefits and the right to vote are rarely made explicit. In some countries temporary workers can become permanent residents – a route that is explicitly prohibited in other countries. As Ruhs and Chang (2004) argue, variations in the conferral of rights like these lead to quite different outcomes. For example, if migrant workers are permitted to change jobs, the preferential access of nationals to the internal labour market is thereby challenged.

Variations in accorded rights also, they argue (Ruhs and Chang 2004: 83–5), depend on the 'moral standing' accorded to the nationals, migrants and citizens of the sending countries who may not be migrants but whom migration may affect. The moral standing of the different participants in turn relates to where the social actors and decision-makers locate themselves on a cosmopolitan–nationalist spectrum. Here Ruhs and Chang (2004: 91 *et seq.*) are drawn back to the realistic–idealistic dyad enunciated by Carens and discussed earlier. International organizations like the ILO and NGOs may hold rights-based and cosmopolitan views of migrants ('idealists'), but it is hardly surprising that national policy-makers have to yield to the pressures that elevate the moral standing of nationals above that of migrants ('realists'). So far, so predictable, but Ruhs and Chang provide an unexpected twist to the argument. Because migrants are more productive, have lower claims on welfare and other benefits and are less likely to be criminals than the longstanding population (despite many myths to the contrary), there may be a material stake in protecting and furthering the interests of migrants.[3] Also, most countries both send and receive migrants, so according a degree of recognition and respect to a migrant may be necessary to advance a moral claim to protect your own nationals abroad.

In combining realistic and idealistic perspectives, Ruhs and Chang (2004) enunciate a balanced set of prescriptions that avoids general declarations of human rights, as applied to all migrants, in favour of more targeted core rights that are carefully monitored, transparent and effectively enforced. Again, they deem programmes for temporary work (and enforced departure) legitimate so long as some pathways for permanent settlement are established in return for a largely unspecified set of positive 'ticks' against the temporary migrant. It is difficult to see what such an evaluation might comprise. Would it be too fanciful to imagine that such tests might include good conduct (denoted by the absence of a criminal record), a valued economic contribution, a high degree of assimilation to the majority's language and way of life, a loyalty test, a limited number of dependants or a clean bill of health?

While I have considerable sympathy for many of the ethical dilemmas Ruhs and Chang raise and some admiration for their detailed reasoning, it is nonetheless clear that a self-denying ordinance arising from past tentativeness and a present atmosphere of immigration restrictions has severely circumscribed liberal political philosophy on the ethics of immigration policy. On the one hand, this line of reasoning recognizes the economic contribution of migrants and the need to protect minimal standards of decency and universality. On the other, the sovereignty of state power is left intact and it is acknowledged that politicians will find it impossible not to elevate the moral standing of the national over the migrant.

The attack on diversity: the question of immigration restriction

The neo-conservative and conservative right in the USA and Europe has seized the political moment afforded by the terrorist threat to question both the extent of migration and the degree of recognition afforded to migrants' home cultures, religions, languages and social practices. The attack on diversity and difference has been particularly fierce in the USA. Perhaps the most powerful academic voice on this question is that of Samuel P. Huntington (2004: 142–3), a professor of politics at Harvard and the director of security planning for the National Security Council in the Carter administration. In his *cri de cœur* titled *Who are we?* he angrily denounces those in the USA who had discarded earlier notions that the USA was a 'melting pot' or 'tomato soup' and proposed instead that it was more like a 'mosaic' or 'salad bowl' of diverse peoples. He insists on the primacy of the English-speaking, Protestant, eastern seaboard and deplores the 'deconstructionists' who sought to 'enhance the status and influence of subnational racial, ethnic and cultural groups', which, he claims, had deleterious effects on democratic values and liberties:

> They downgraded the centrality of English in American life and pushed bilingual education and linguistic diversity. They advo-

cated legal recognition of group rights and racial preferences over the individual rights central to the American Creed. They justified their actions by theories of multiculturalism and the idea that diversity rather than unity or community should be America's overriding value. The combined effect of these efforts was to promote the deconstruction of the American identity that had been gradually created over three centuries.

(Huntington 2004: 142)

The main implication of this argument for the free movement of migration is that freedom can be curtailed for the sake of freedom. This Rawlsian principle[4] could be used to discountenance both 'unlimited immigration' and the immigration of 'dangerous' people. Let us immediately concede the second example. It is generally not a good idea to roll out the red carpet for psychopaths, gangsters, drug dealers or terrorists. The first is more ambiguous. Does large-scale immigration really pose a threat to public order, economic prosperity, social well-being or cultural cohesion? This is by no means an invariable outcome. In circumstances of underpopulation and demoralization, a large, culturally cognate cohort of immigrants with skills and capital will generally be welcomed. In circumstances where the settled population is under threat or perceives a threat (of job loss, housing shortage or welfare rationing) the arrival of a large, culturally dissimilar group may well be resisted even if the long-term effects may be benign. It is certainly more than possible that an ambitious politician will fan the flames of xenophobia.

Is it justifiable to reduce the risk of this last negative reaction, thereby generating a moral purpose for immigration restriction? I would argue that defending a settled population's rights must mean there is something worth defending – for example, hard-fought civil liberties, a tradition of toleration for unpopular minorities, the production of imaginative works of art and literature or a broad-minded education system. For immigration restrictions to have an ethical rationale it should be clear which freedom or freedoms are being protected, which are being threatened, why such a threat is real and how a restriction will help to retain a particular freedom. Perhaps it is easier to construe this argument in the opposite direction. Restricting inward migration (or appearing to advocate this position) to win an election, while pretending a more noble purpose is at stake, is clearly reprehensible.

In this respect it could be instructive to contrast the immigration policies of recent Canadian and Australian governments with the immigration practices of France and the UK. Whereas the former pair has entered into an open dialogue with its settled population on appropriate numbers and criteria for exclusion, governments in France and the UK have on the whole remained secretive and patrician in the implementation of their policies, now recognizing the claims of the gang masters for cheap agricultural labour, later throwing sops to the right-wing newspapers and political parties. If they are to be legitimate at all, restrictions have to be open, consensual and clearly used to defend an existing freedom that would otherwise be in jeopardy. Restrictions, in this moral universe we are constructing, cannot be used for a concealed purpose, especially if that purpose is unworthy.

The case for free movement of money

Advocacy of the case for the free movement of money might conveniently begin with Adam Smith's views in *The wealth of nations* (cited Jordan and Düvell 2002: 242). As Smith, a man with his feet on the ground, pointed out in 1776:

> A merchant, it has been said very properly, is not necessarily the citizen of any particular country. It is in great measure indifferent to him from what place he carries on his trade; and a very trifling disgust will make him remove his capital, and together with it all the industry which it supports, from one country to another. No part of it can be said to belong to any particular country, either in buildings, or in the lasting improvement of lands.

This is an interesting counterpoint to Marx's now discredited declaration that 'workers have no country'; it was clear in this respect that Smith was the more prescient political economist. Smith's comment also has the virtue of showing that, unlike his epigones, 'the invisible hand of the market' did not blind him. Here the agency that drives the market is all too visible. Whereas Smith (in this quote at least) overtly recognizes the power of *capitalists* as autonomous and international economic actors, twentieth century neo-liberals like Hayek (1986) and Friedman (1962) first anthropomorphized the market, then virtually turned it into a god. Any restraint on capital was regarded as violating their primary conviction that economic power should not be subordinated to political power. With the benefit of perhaps 30 years of the partial implementation of this doctrine, it has to be conceded that freeing the market has exposed the limits of ill-informed and glacially slow growth by state planning, which often served the interests of the bureaucracy rather than the people in whose interests the planners nominally held power. But the doctrine has become too indiscriminate and all embracing – encompassing constraints on politicians' capacity to tax and spend, to impose tariffs and quotas, to regulate prices, wages, safety or environmental standards, or to set minimum standards of entry for skilled occupations and the professions.

Also central to the neo-liberal world-view was the removal of any limit on the movement of money. Perhaps in order to damn by association, Friedman claimed that exchange controls were 'to the best of my knowledge invented by Hjalmar Schaat in the early years of the Nazi regime'.[5] He continued (cited in Lal 1992: 99):

> There is much experience to suggest that the most effective way to convert a market economy into an authoritarian economic society is to start by imposing direct controls on foreign exchange. This one step leads inevitably to the rationing of imports, to control over domestic production that uses imported products or that produces substitutes for imports, and so on in a never-ending spiral.

While even Friedman acknowledges that the state should act as an umpire to prevent economic actors coercing one another, this role remains a residual afterthought. Markets for wages, prices, finance and investment capital should be freed, he thought. While neo-liberal doctrine remains dominant in most countries, the minimalist restrictions on the movement of money were undermined in the wake of the terrorist attacks on the World Trade Center and Pentagon in 2001. Just 17 days after the attacks the UN passed a unanimous and wide-ranging Security Council resolution (Resolution 1373/2001) that demanded surveillance and major restrictions on the movement of finances. It is worth quoting these provisions at some length from the official press release:

All States should prevent and suppress the financing of terrorism, as well as criminalize the wilful provision or collection of funds for such acts. The funds, financial assets and economic resources of those who commit or attempt to commit terrorist acts or participate in or facilitate the commission of terrorist acts and of persons and entities acting on behalf of terrorists should also be frozen without delay. ...

The Council also decided that States should prohibit their nationals or persons or entities in their territories from making funds, financial assets, economic resources, financial or other related services available to persons who commit or attempt to commit, facilitate or participate in the commission of terrorist acts. States should also refrain from providing any form of support to entities or persons involved in terrorist acts; take the necessary steps to prevent the commission of terrorist acts; deny safe haven to those who finance, plan, support, commit terrorist acts and provide safe havens as well. ...

The Council noted with concern the close connection between international terrorism and transnational organized crime, illicit drugs, money laundering and illegal movement of nuclear, chemical, biological and other deadly materials. In that regard, it emphasized the need to enhance the coordination of national, subregional, regional and international efforts to strengthen a global response to that threat to international security.

The effect of this international concern has been to strengthen greatly the hands of those national authorities that, for other reasons, were also concerned about the largely unregulated movement of money. Those laundering drugs money, or involved in corrupt transactions (perhaps bribing state officials to award contracts) or simply evading tax could conveniently be swept up in the discourse of 'security' and 'terrorism'. Ordinary citizens wishing to open bank accounts, effect cash payments or transfer assets find that the level of intrusion by banks, estate agents and lawyers violates any historical protections for the privacy of trans-actions. In the name of security, investigators are even managing to prise open offshore accounts, and accounts in countries like Switzerland and Bermuda. In Luxemburg, Russian entrepreneurs are simply and routinely told that the cost and nuisance value of carrying out checks on them make it impossible to open a bank account.[6]

Without wishing to support such intrusions on personal liberty and privacy, the harm principle (the obligation not to injure or damage others) can be evoked to suggest at least some obligations to restrict the unfettered movement of capital. The following might provide a shopping list for beneficial restrictions:

- Regulating the operations of speculative finance, particularly in preventing massive fluctuations in the value of a country's currency.
- Preventing 'dumping' and 'swamping' by external capital, which kills off local enterprise and initiative.
- Reducing the effects of capital flight by insisting on local labour and capital participation and a phased exit of profits and investment capital.
- Ensuring that capital movements are not the result or the means to conceal profits derived from drugs or people trafficking, illegal weapons, or illicit gambling profits.
- In line with the UN's Security Resolution 1373 discussed earlier, monitoring the movement of money that might provide vital leads to criminal or terrorist activities.

In short, given its disruptive effects, some now proven by bitter experience, the unconditional movement of money is no longer morally credible, even if powerful intellectual and political supporters continue to sustain the idea.

Putting the movement of people and money together

If we are to synthesize the two sides to this argument, no convincing cases have been made for unconstrained movement by either people or money, a view that the advocates of each position partly concede, though more in the case of people than money. There remains, of course, a question about why the two propositions should be considered together. One proposition may be compelling and the other not, while the comparison between the two may be analytically useful without demonstrating a causal or reciprocal connection.

The argument that there is a connection is perhaps made most forcibly by Marxist scholars (for example Harris 1996) and by extreme libertarians. The former see the movement of workers as a scant but necessary form of balance against the power of capitalists to shift their money more or less at will (the point Adam Smith made). Although workers may be forced to sell their labour power, international mobility, so it is argued, at least gives them the opportunity to strike a better bargain. Or will it? The libertarian position is that all the factors of production (in Smith's day *land, labour* and *capital* – but we would nowadays have to add *knowledge*) should be equally mobile or 'free'. At least in the short and medium run, if this were to happen, capitalists (not workers) may be able to benefit from an international race to the bottom. The likelihood that workers would be able to level up depends on the assumption that their international mobility will lead to greater solidarity and cohesion of purpose with workers in other lands – an outcome that is by no means certain.

There is also a connection, though a more indirect one, between free money and free movement of people in the way that states have positioned themselves on each issue. Whereas all (let's say nearly all) states encourage the inward movement of capital, some continue to regulate the exit of money, though to an increasingly more limited degree. Again, whereas all (again, nearly all) states have since the collapse of the Warsaw Pact permitted free exit, all states have increased their controls on the entry of people. The reciprocal connection is that it is sometimes possible to effect a 'trade-off' between the two movements. To take but one example: using the power of digital technology a cyber-proletariat can be created in call centres in Bangalore by the export of capital rather than by the import of labour. It is perhaps not too fanciful to describe this as 'virtual migration'.

The practical and political limits of restriction

Even if the connection between, and the constraints on, the free movement of money and people are recognized, there remains the important task of justifying the extent of the limits on each and considering what consequences, intended and unintended, might arise from such constraints. Here I consider three questions:

- Can 'good' migrants be separated from 'bad' migrants?

- Are restrictive measures likely to be affordable and effective?
- Are politicians in a strong position to judge the potential threat posed by free movement?

Can 'good' migrants be separated from 'bad' migrants?

I have already alluded to Carens's somewhat cardboard characterizations of migrants. However, immigrants do not arrive at Heathrow or Charles de Gaulle airports sporting devils' tails or angels' wings. Many immigrants are young or bring impressionable young families. It would be absurd to demand an oath of loyalty of a four-year-old or to interrogate such a child about ritual slaughter, nude sculptures, alcohol abuse, religious education or the wearing of veils. Perhaps it would not be so absurd to ask his or her parents about these things. What, however, would be the purpose of such an interrogation? It seems to imply a non-questionable view that indigenous practices are not subject to comment or criticism.

Let me provide two examples. Family values are strongly articulated and defended by Indian and Chinese immigrants who characteristically show low rates of teenage pregnancy, single-headed households, juvenile delinquency and neglect of old people. Again, abstinence or restraint in the consumption of alcohol (which results in so many needless deaths and injuries) might also be a lesson usefully learnt from some immigrants. I appreciate that many normative considerations are introduced by these examples, which require further defence. However, my primary argument is that it is not apparent on *prima facie* grounds that an imported culture is inferior to a host culture or will not offer positive alternatives to local social practices.

Let us consider a related question. There is nothing to stop migrants deceiving immigration authorities about their ideological convictions or preferred social attitudes, especially if these are not illegal. (By contrast, concealing an illegal source of money would be a criminal offence punishable by law.) Despite this, it seems to be a reasonable expectation on the part of the host society that immigrants should not be deceitful and should intend to obey the laws of the country they are entering. Likewise, in principle there is nothing offensive about a loyalty ceremony associated with citizenship (long held in Canada and recently initiated in Britain). The principle is not unlike that first enunciated by

Kant – a (legal) immigrant may *offer* herself or himself for social membership; a citizenship ceremony would confer it in a public arena.

This argument differs from the one Walzer (1983: 61) made, namely that states are like (private) clubs in which the membership is free to exclude whomsoever it pleases subject to the rules of the club. Carens's (1987: 265–70) rebuttal of Walzer's conflation of a club and a state is persuasive on a number of grounds, the most obvious being that there is a legal and moral distinction between a private and public act of exclusion. In the former setting freedom of association is a paramount virtue; in the latter equal treatment between all is the major ethical consideration. To repeat, it may be legitimate to ask intending adult immigrants (of sound mind) whether they intend to obey the laws of the land and are not harbouring a sinister intent directed against the life, liberty and well-being of the inhabitants of the country from which they aspire to acquire citizenship. This creates a moral equivalence between a politician's demand for exclusion and an immigrant's claim for inclusion. And lest this appears too naïve, it may be useful to note that current immigration laws permit deportation on the grounds that an immigrant's statements to a responsible authority were shown to be intentionally misleading.

Are control measures affordable and effective?

In a 2003 IOM report (cited by Pécoud and Guchteneire 2005: 4), it is claimed that the annual cost of enforcing immigration restrictions is between 25 and 30 billion US dollars. This covers not only border controls, but also issuing visas and passports, apprehending, detaining, prosecuting and deporting unwanted migrants, inspecting labour conditions, processing asylum-seekers' claims and resettling refugees. To get some sense of comparison, this sum is only about one-sixteenth of the US defence budget. However, it would pay for three years of clean water for all the world's 6.1 billion people.

At any event, since the costs of policing frontiers are considerable, it is legitimate to ask whether the measures undertaken are effective. There is a considerable weight of evidence now to suggest that sophisticated control measures are met with more sophisticated methods of evasion. The trafficking of people is now highly profitable and professionally organized. Moreover, once a culture of emigration is established in a labour-exporting zone and networks of migrants are in place, it is extremely difficult to stop the movement of determined migrants (see Pécoud and Guchteneire 2005: 4).

Those who believe that extensive use of digital technology and a more determined and costly regime can finally control unwanted movement have of course contradicted these general observations. Koslowski (2004 and 2005), however, who has studied the implementation of the current policies, casts considerable doubt on their effectiveness. The magnitude of the task is considerable. Take the USA in the year after '9/11', remembering that there are 326 legitimate ports of entry, 2000 miles along the Rio Grande and 5500 miles separating Canada and the USA. Recorded entries for 2002 were 440 million (down from 500 million in 2001) and exits were not effectively recorded. As Koslowski (2004: 9) argues, lost forms, incomplete data entry and exit from a lightly policed land frontier meant that there was no way that over-stayers could be detected and deported with certainty. Indeed, several of the '9/11' terrorists had overstayed their visas.

The two land borders with the USA (Canada and Mexico) presented special problems. The Ambassador Bridge, linking Windsor to Detroit, carried motorcar parts for 'just-in-time' production to the three major automobile manufacturers in Michigan. Up to ten million vehicles crossed the Ambassador Bridge each year – inspecting them on the basis of current infrastructure and technology would be impossible without halting production in a key manufacturing state.

Nor should one forget that if the stakes are high enough, identity theft and the forging of passports will become more commonplace. According to Koslowski (2005) in 2004 there were 12,404 fraudulent claims to US citizenship detected and 79,273 fraudulent passports intercepted at all ports of entry. One can reasonably surmise that the number detected and intercepted was only a fraction of the total.

There is one other element to this story that needs mention. Much of the data capture and process hundreds of millions of records that are needed to operate the US–VISIT system, which has been subcontracted to companies that have inadequate security measures and sometimes are located in countries with strong links to terrorism. A major security breach was reported in April 2005 (*Guardian*, 13 April 2005: 21) when Reed Elsevier allowed access to the personal details of as many as

310,000 US citizens. Information that might have been accessed (and that could now be on the market for sale) includes names, addresses, social security and drivers' licence numbers, the precise building blocks for identity theft and illegal documentation. What is even more damaging is that those who operate the system are often victims of 'the technological fallacy'. Believing that the system is secure when it is not leads to more serious errors in control systems (just as believing that wars can be won by guided missiles alone leads to more 'Vietnams' and 'Iraqs').

Can politicians effectively assess a potential threat?

In public discussions about the legitimacy of the war in Iraq we have all been saturated with talk about 'the precautionary principle'. It was said that even if Saddam Hussain had not possessed weapons of mass destruction, he had *programmes* to produce them and the stated intention to use them. It is worth noting that had Bush and Blair believed Saddam Hussain's proclamations, they would have had a higher estimation of the candour of politicians than most of the rest of us share. If, however, they were relying on intelligence reports (whether erroneous or not), they could validly argue that the precautionary principle dictated that they act decisively and overwhelmingly to disarm Saddam Hussain or overthrow his regime.

The burden of proof demanded is of course much lower than that demanded in a criminal court, where both the intention to act and the act itself must be attributed to the perpetrator without reasonable doubt. In the US constitutional tradition the president can act on a less severe burden of proof – namely if there is 'a clear and present danger' to the country. But how clear and how present was it? Supposing an armed secret agent of the Spanish government observed a known member of a terrorist network about to push the keys on his mobile telephone that would trigger a bomb that would certainly kill many civilians: in such a circumstance that agent would, without doubt, seek to kill the terrorist and would, again without doubt, be supported in this act by the majority of public opinion.

Now let us consider money launderers and migrants. If they present a threat at all, it would be a far more diffuse, uncertain and long-term threat. The profits from illegal business activities might be used to further illicit activities, to invest in 'green equities' or to buy a life of affluence in the sun. To echo Carens's (1987) argument, most migrants will be seeking a peaceful and secure life. What they bring with them (in terms of skills, cultural practices and financial capital) and what they contribute may be wholly benign. There will be room for disagreement in making any cost/benefit assessment. Two equally experienced police officers might disagree about how particular money launderers are most likely to use their illicit gains. There might be short-term tensions but long-term gains in the admission of a particular cohort of migrants.

In short, assessing a potential threat that might arise from movements of money or migrants is a matter of human judgement and, therefore, of human error. Unfortunately, the political leaders of many countries are unlikely to exercise wise judgements either because they are ill equipped to engage in philosophical reasoning or have limited knowledge of the social sciences; they are often in the hands of narrow ideologues or special interest groups; or they are sometimes untrustworthy and often thought to be so. What we saw on the streets on Spain after 911 was a populace angry that it was compelled to place life-and-death decisions in the hands of people not fully capable of making them without considering their own political advantage.

Conclusion

Attempts to ascertain proponents' views about free movements of capital and people invariably reveal considerable self-doubt and a number of limiting conditions. When one adds to these old arguments the pressures derived from contemporary security concerns it is clear that the restrictionists have won the argument. But, as I have suggested, the debate about free movement cannot stop there. In imposing restrictions one has to bear in mind the justification for such limits and the dangers to our own liberty if we abnegate too much or too many of our hard-won freedoms.

The common thread underlying these measures is fear and politicians' manipulation of fear. The public has accepted a level of surveillance that has escalated with the rising level of public concern for safety and security. The connection to the movement of money and migrants is that there are either proven or alleged causal links between unregulated mobility, and security and criminal concerns. Those who have worked in

the field of ethnic relations are long used to the tendency of local populations to blame immigrants for anything that goes wrong – but in
particular for street violence, criminal activity and drugs dealing. The
nihilist terrorist, who sadly is not merely a phantom of the imagination,
simply adds to the cast of folk devils. There are at least three grounds for
concern:

- The first is that the more affluent sections of the population will
  become so preoccupied with personal security that they will retreat to
  gated communities, leaving the streets and public spaces to a condition previously depicted only in science fiction.
- The second is that the mesh that is used to filter out dangerous aliens
  and ill-gotten gains will become finer and finer. In this respect there
  will be an intractable escalator as the 'bad guys' (Bush's term) get
  smarter and the 'good guys' have to try harder and harder to catch
  them.
- The third is that there are simply no serious mechanisms in place to
  restrain the security agencies from undertaking further and more far-
  reaching forms of surveillance. Particular measures may either be
  ineffective, inappropriate or disproportionate, yet we (the public)
  have no means to stop the escalator. People who have questioned
  security measures on grounds of civil liberties are largely ignored or
  derided.

Fear, it is rightly said, is contagious and with this primordial response
irrationality and poorly considered responses become common. Investors who oil the wheels of the economy and migrants who generate jobs,
wealth and creative cultural and social options make an important
contribution towards preventing economic stagnation, dulling cultural
stasis and social decay. However, it is extremely difficult to tell the
difference between benign and malign mobility. Consequentially, imple-
menting a system of control, restriction, sorting and surveillance
necessarily raises difficult questions.

What values and freedoms do we wish to defend? Can we explicitly
define them? Who is challenging our cherished freedoms and how are
they doing so? Can we act in advance of a clear and present danger and
how long in advance, at what level of threat and on what grounds? Have

we honestly assessed the values and norms brought by migrants in an informed and open-minded way? Who is permitted to operate our systems of surveillance and restriction? Are they adequately trained and informed? Are their motives pure and untainted by personal interest or undisclosed influences? Are the measures we effect proportionate, appropriate, effective and legal? Who will police our police? These questions are unanswered here, but despite the current climate of fear and anger we need at least to ask them.

Notes

1. My thanks go to my colleague James Brassnet for sight of his illuminating co-written paper (Parker and Brassnet 2005) that has not yet been integrated into my argument.
2. An innovative online journal called *Surveillance and Society* (see www.surveillance-and-society.org) can usefully be consulted to extend this discussion.
3. The data on Britain are reproduced in the *Financial Times* Lex Column. They are as follows: Home Office figures for 1999/2000 show that those born outside the UK contributed £31.2 billion in taxes and claimed £28.8 billion in benefits and services. A study by the Institute for Public Policy Research using 2004 data shows an *increasing* net contribution by immigrants. Each immigrant contributed £7203 to government revenues, £342 more than each UK-born person, while costing £476 less (*Financial Times*, 3 May 2005: 20).
4. Rawls uses 'liberty' not 'freedom'. I appreciate that much can be made of the distinction, but that debate is not salient here.
5. One hesitates to correct a Nobel laureate in economics, but it is well established that the belligerents in the First World War used exchange controls 'in order to pursue expansionary financial policies and still maintain their parities' (Bordo 2000: 17). The reference to Germany is also erroneous. Exchange controls were imposed in that country on 20 July 1931 'in the face of a speculative attack' on the mark (Bordo 2000: 39). This was 16 months before the Nazis came to power in November 1932.
6. My thanks to my colleague Eleni Tsingou for this information.

References

Abella, Manolo A. (1993) 'Labor mobility, trade and structural change: the Philippine experience', *Asian and Pacific Migration Journal*, 2 (3) 249–68

—— (1994) 'Introduction' to special issue on 'Turning points in labor migration', *Asian and Pacific Migration Journal*, 3 (1) 1–8

Adamson, A. (1972) *Sugar without slaves: the political economy of British Guyana, 1834–1964*, New Haven, CT: Yale University Press

Adorno, Theodor W., Else Frenkel-Brunswik, Daniel J. Levinson and R. Nevitt Sanford (1950) *The authoritarian personality*, New York: Harper & Row

Agostinelli, Gianni (1991) *Migration–development interrelationships: the case of the Philippines*, New York: Centre for Migration Studies

Alburo, Florian A. (1994) 'Trade and turning points in labor migration', *Asian and Pacific Migration Journal*, 3 (1) 49–80

Amin, Samir (1974) *Accumulation on a world scale*, 2 vols, New York: Monthly Review Press

Amor, M. B. Hadj (1994) *International aid to reduce the need for migration: the Tunisian case*, World Employment Progamme Research Working Paper, Migration Series No. 66, Geneva: International Labour Organization

Anderson, Benedict (1983) *Imagined communities: reflections on the origins and spread of nationalism*, London: Verso

Anderson, Bridget (2000) *Doing the dirty work: the global politics of domestic labour*, London: Zed Books

Anker, Richard (2000) *Conceptual and research frameworks for the economics of child labour and its elimination*, ILO/IPEC working paper, Geneva: ILO

Anthias, Floya and Nina Yuval-Davis (1993) *Racialized boundaries: race, nation, gender, colour and class and the anti-racist struggle*, London: Routledge

Anti-Slavery International (www.anti-slavery.org)

Applebaum, Anne (2004) *Gulag: the history of the Soviet labour camps*, London: Penguin

Bach, R. L., Jennifer B. Bach and Timothy Triplett (1981–82) 'The "Flotilla Entrants": latest and most controversial', *Cuban Studies*, 11 (2) July 1981 and 12 (1) January 1982, 30–48

Bagchi, A. K. (1982) *The political economy of underdevelopment*, Cambridge: Cambridge University Press

Bales, Kevin (1999) *Disposable people: new slavery in the global economy*, Berkeley: University of California Press

Banton, Michael and Robert Miles (1988) 'Racism', in E. Ellis Cashmore (ed.) *Dictionary of race and ethnic relations*, London: Routledge, 247–51

Baldwin, Roger (ed.) (1953) *A new slavery: forced labor, the communist betrayal of human rights*, New York: Oceana Publications

Barry, Brian and Robert E. Goodin (eds) (1992) *Free movement: ethical issues in the transnational migration of people and money*, New York: Harvester Wheatsheaf

Barth, Frederick (1969) *Ethnic groups and boundaries*, Bergen: Universitetsforlaget

Bauböck, Rainer (1994) *Transnational citizenship: membership and rights in international migration*, Cheltenham, UK: Edward Elgar

Bauman, Zigmunt (1991) *Modernity and the holocaust*, Cambridge: Polity

Bindoff, S. T. (1961) *Tudor England*, Harmondsworth: Pelican

Birks, J. S. and C. A. Sinclair (1980) *International migration and development in the Arab region*, Geneva: International Labour Organization

Bluestone, B. and B. Harrison (1982) *The deindustrialization of America*, New York: Basic Books

Böhning, W. R. (1972) *The migration of workers in the United Kingdom and the European Community*, London: Oxford University Press

Böhning, W. R. and M.-L. Schloeter-Paredes (eds) (1994) *Aid in place of migration: selected contributions to an ILO–UNHCR meeting*, Geneva: International Labour Office

Bordo, Michael D. (2000) 'The globalization of financial markets: what can history teach us?' Paper to a conference on International Financial Markets: The Challenge of Globalization, Texas A&M University, 31 March

Borkin, J. (1978) *The crime and punishment of I. G. Farben*, Glencoe, The Free Press

Brantlinger, Patrick (1986) 'Victorians and Africans: the genealogy of the myth of the dark continent', in Henry Louis Gates Jr (ed.) *'Race', writing and difference*, Chicago: University of Chicago Press, 185–222

Braverman, Harry (1974) *Labor and monopoly capital*, New York: Monthly Review Press

Bruni, M. and A. Venturi (1995) 'Pressure to migrate and propensity to emigrate: the case of the Mediterranean Basin', *International Labour Review*, 134 (3) 377–400

Burton, J. (1972) *World society*, Cambridge: Cambridge University Press

Cadbury, W. A. (1910) *Labour in Portuguese West Africa*, London: Routledge

Carens, Joseph (1987) 'Aliens and citizens: the case for open borders', *Review of Politics*, 49 (2) 251–73

   (1992) 'Migration and morality: a liberal egalitarian perspective', in Brian Barry and Robert E. Goodin (eds) *Free movement: ethical issues in the transnational migration of people and money*, New York: Harvester Wheatsheaf, 25–47

   (1996) 'Realistic and idealistic approaches to the study of migration', *International Migration Review*, 30 (1) 156–70

Cashmore, E. Ellis (1988) 'Prejudice', in E. Ellis Cashmore (ed) *Dictionary of race and ethnic relations*, London: Routledge, 227–30

Castells, Manuel (1979) 'Immigrant workers and class struggles in advanced capitalism: the western European experience', in Robin Cohen, Peter C. W. Gutkind and Phyllis Brazier (eds) *Proletarians and peasants: the struggles of Third World workers*, New York: Monthly Review Press, 353–79

   (1996) *The rise of the network society* (vol. 1 in his *The information age: economy, society and culture*), Oxford: Blackwell

Castles, Stephen and Godula Kosack (1973) *Immigrant workers and class structure in western Europe*, London: Oxford University Press

Castles, Stephen and Mark J. Miller (1998) *The age of migration: international population movements in the modern world*, Basingstoke: Macmillan (second edition)

   (2003) *The age of migration: international population movements in the modern world*, Basingstoke: Palgrave Macmillan (third edition)

Castles, Stephen with Heather Booth and Tina Wallace (1984) *Here for good: western Europe's new ethnic minorities*, London: Pluto Press

Cesarani, David (1987) 'Anti-alienism in England after the First World War', *Immigrants and Minorities*, 6 (1) 5–29

Chesnais, Jean-Claude (1990) 'Migration from eastern to western Europe, past (1946–89) and future, 1990–2000', Paper presented to second meeting of senior officials entrusted with preparing the Conference of Ministers on the Movement of Persons Coming from Central and Eastern European Countries, Council of Europe, Strasbourg, 8/9 November

Chiswick, Barry R. (2005) *Economics of migration*, Cheltenham: Edward Elgar

Cock, Jackie (1989) *Maids and madams: domestic workers under apartheid*, London: The Women's Press

Cohen, D. W. and J. P. Greene (eds) (1972) *Neither slave nor free: the freedmen of African descent in the slave societies of the new world*, Baltimore: Johns Hopkins University Press

Cohen, Robin (1987) *The new helots: migrants in the international division of labour*, Aldershot: Gower

(1994) *Frontiers of identity: the British and the Others*, London: Longman

(1997) *Global diasporas: an introduction*, London: UCL Press

Cohen, Robin and Paul Kennedy (2001) *Global sociology*, London: Palgrave and New York: NYU Press

Cohen, Robin, Peter C. W. Gutkind and Phyllis Brazier (eds) (1979) *Peasants and proletarians: the struggles of Third World workers*, New York: Monthly Review Press

Cohen, Stanley (1972) *Folk devils and moral panics*, London: MacGibben and Kee

Cooper, Betsy (2004) '9/11 commission urges immigration and border reform', Migration Policy Institute, Washington, DC (http://www.migrationinformation.org/feature/display.cfm?ID=243)

Cooper, Frederick (1980) *From slaves to squatters: plantation labour and agriculture in Zanzibar and coastal Kenya, 1890–1925*, New Haven, CT: Yale University Press

Cornelius, Wayne A., M. Philip and H. James (1994) *Controlling immigration: a global perspective*, Stanford, CA: Stanford University Press

Corrigan, Paul (1977) 'Feudal relics or capitalist monuments? Notes in the sociology of unfree labour', *Sociology*, 11, 435–63

Cross, Malcolm (1988) 'Migrants and the new minorities in Europe', unpublished paper, Centre for Research in Ethnic Relations, University of Warwick

Cunningham, W. (1969) *Alien immigrants to England*, New York: Augustus M. Kelley (first published 1897)

Dallin, D. J. and B. I. Nicolaevsky (1948) *Forced labour in Soviet Russia*, London: Hollis & Carter

Dalrymple, William (2003) *White mughals: love and betrayal in eighteenth century India*, London: Flamingo

Dasent, J. R. (1890) *Acts of the Privy Council of England*, new series, vol. VII, AD 1558–1570, London: HMSO

Davies, I. (1966) *African trade unions*, Harmondsworth: Penguin Books

Díaz-Briquets, Sergio and Sidney Weintraub (eds) (1991a) *Determinants of emigration from Mexico, Central America and the Caribbean*, vol. 1, Boulder, CO: Westview Press

   (1991b) *Regional and sectorial development in Mexico as alternatives to migration*, vol. 2, Boulder, CO: Westview Press

Dickstein, Morris (1993) 'After the cold war: culture as politics, politics as culture', *Social Research*, 60 (3) 531–44

Dowty, A. (1987) *Closed borders: the contemporary assault on freedom of movement*, New Haven: Yale University Press

Duffield, Mark R. (1981) 'Racism and counter-revolution in the era of imperialism: a critique', unpublished paper for the annual conference of the Conference of Socialist Economists, Bradford

Dufoix, Stéphane (2003) *Les diasporas*, Paris: Presses Universitaires de France

Durning, A. T. (1992) *How much is enough? The consumer society and the future of the earth*, London: Earthscan

Ecevit, Z. H. (1981) 'International Labor Migration in the Middle East and North Africa: trends, effects and policies', in M. M. Kritz, C. B. Keely and S. M. Tomasi (eds) *Global trends in migration: theory and research on international population movements*, New York: Center for Migration Studies, 259–75

Echenberg, Myron (1975) 'Paying the blood tax: military conscription in French West Africa', *Canadian Journal of African Studies*, 9, 171–92

Edwards, Penny (2002) 'Time travels: locating *xinyimin* in Sino-Cambodian histories', in Pál Nyíri and Igor Saveliev (eds) *Globalizing Chinese migration: trends in Europe and Asia*, Aldershot: Ashgate

Ehrenreich, Barbara and Arlie Hochschild (eds) (2003) *Global women: nannies, maids and sex workers in the new economy*, London: Granta

Elson, Diane and Ruth Pearson (1981) '"Nimble fingers make cheap workers": an analysis of women's employment in Third World export manufacturing', *Feminist Review*, no. 7

Engerman, S. (1973) 'Some considerations relating to property rights in man', *Journal of Economic History*, 33

Ernst, D. (1980) *The new international division of labour: technology and underdevelopment*, Frankfurt, Campus Verlag

Falchi, Nino (1995) *International migration pressure challenges, policy response and operational measures: an outline of the main features*, Geneva: International Organization for Migration

Ferencz, B. B. (1979) *Less than slaves: Jewish forced labor and the quest for compensation*, Boston: Harvard University Press

Findlay, Allan (1986) 'From brain exchange to brain gain: policy implications for the UK of recent trends in skilled migration from developing countries', *International migration for employment working paper*, no. 43, Geneva: International Labour Organization

Findlay, Allan and Paul White (1986) (eds) *West European population change*, London: Croom Helm

Findley, Sally E. (1993) 'Choosing between African and French destinations: the role of family and community factors in migration from the Senegal River Valley', Working paper no. 5, CERPOD, BP 1530, Bamako, Mali

Fine, Robert and Robin Cohen (2002) 'Four cosmopolitan moments', in Steven Vertovec and Robin Cohen (eds) *Conceiving cosmopolitanism: theory, context and practice*, Oxford: Oxford University Press, 137–62

Finley, Moses I. (1980) *Ancient slavery and modern ideology*, London: Chatto & Windus

(1981) *Economy and society in Ancient Greece*, London: Chatto & Windus

First, Ruth (1983) *Black gold: The Mozambican miner, proletariat and peasant*, Sussex: The Harvester Press

Fossett, M. A, Omer R. Gale and William R. Kelly (1986) 'Racial occupational inequality, 1940–80: national and regional trends', *American Sociological Review*, 51, June, 421–9

Fraginals, M. M. (1976) *The sugar mill: the socio-economic complex of sugar in Cuba, 1760–1860*, New York: Monthly Review Press

Fraser, Peter (1981) 'The fictive peasantry: Caribbean rural groups in the nineteenth century', in Susan Craig (ed.) *Contemporary Caribbean: a sociological reader*, Trinidad: The editor, 319–47

Freeman, Gary P. (1979) *Immigrant labor and racial conflict in industrial societies, 1945–1975*, Princeton: Princeton University Press

Friedman, J. (1985) 'The world city hypothesis', unpublished paper, Conference on the International Division of Labor, Centre of Urban Studies and International Sociological Association, University of Hong Kong, August

Friedman, Milton with the assistance of Rose D. Friedman (1962) *Capitalism and freedom*, Chicago: University of Chicago Press

Friman, H. Richard (2002) 'Evading the divine wind through the side door: the transformation of Chinese migration to Japan', in Pál Nyíri and Igor Saveliev (eds) *Globalizing Chinese migration: trends in Europe and Asia*, Aldershot: Ashgate

Fröbel, F., J. Heinrichs and O. Kreye (1980) *The new international division of labour: structural unemployment in industrialised countries and industrialisation in developing countries*, Cambridge: Cambridge University Press

Frost, E. C., M. C. Meyer and J. Zoraida Vázquez (eds) (1979) *El trabajo y los trabajadores en la historia de México*, Mexico, DF and Tucson: El Colegio de Mexico and University of Arizona Press

Gelbras, Vilya G. (2002) 'Contemporary Chinese migration to Russia', in Pál Nyíri and Igor Saveliev (eds) *Globalizing Chinese migration: trends in Europe and Asia*, Aldershot: Ashgate

Ghosh, B. (1992) 'Migration, trade and international cooperation: do the interlinkages work?' *International Migration*, 30 (3/4)

—— (1995) 'Gains from global linkages: trade in services and movement of persons', unpublished manuscript

Gillman, Peter and Leni Gillman (1980) *'Collar the lot!' How Britain interned and expelled its wartime refugees*, London: Quartet Books

Gilroy, Paul (1987) *'There ain't no black in the Union Jack': the cultural politics of race and nation*, London: Hutchinson

Glazer, Nathan and Daniel P. Moynihan (1983) *Beyond the melting pot: the Negroes, Puerto Ricans, Jews, Italians and Irish of New York City*, Cambridge, MA: Massachusetts Institute of Technology Press

Goldberg, David Theo (1993) *Racist culture: philosophy and the culture of meaning*, Oxford: Blackwell

Goldin, Ian et al. (1993) *Trade liberalization: global economic implications*, Paris and Washington: OECD and World Bank

Goodman, D. and M. Redclift (1981) *From peasant to proletarian: capitalist development and agrarian transitions*, Oxford: Basil Blackwell

Goulbourne, Harry (1991) *Ethnicity and nationalism in post-imperial Britain*, Cambridge: Cambridge University Press

Green, W. (1976) *British slave emancipation: the sugar colonies and the great experiment*, Oxford: Clarendon Press

Greenwood, D. J. (1989) 'Culture by the pound: an anthropological perspective on tourism as cultural commoditization', in V. L. Smith (ed.) *Host and guests: the anthropology of tourism*, Philadelphia, PA: University of Pennsylvania Press

Hall, Catherine (1992) *White, male and middle class: explorations in feminism and history*, Cambridge: Polity

Hall, Stuart (1991) 'Ethnicity: identity and difference', *Radical America*, 23 (4) 9–20

Halliday, Fred (1977) 'Labour migration in the Middle East', *MERIP Reports*, (59) 1–17

Hammar, Tomas (1990) *Democracy and the nation state: aliens, denizens and citizens in a world of international migration*, Aldershot: Avebury

Harris, Nigel (1996) *The new untouchables: immigration and the new world workers*, Harmondsworth: Penguin

(2004) 'What will drive international migration? Response', in Global Commission on International Migration, *Report on the migration futures workshop held at St Antony's College, Oxford*, Geneva: GCIM

Harvey, David (1989) *The condition of post-modernity*, Oxford: Blackwell

Hayek, Friedrich A. von (1986) *The road to serfdom*, London: Ark Paperbacks

Head, Judith (1980) 'State, capital and migrant labour in Zambezia, Mozambique: study of the labour force of Sena Sugar Estates Limited', Ph.D. thesis, University of Durham

Henderson, Jeff (1985) 'The new international division of labour and urban development in the contemporary world-system', in D. Drakakis-Smith (ed.) *Urbanisation in the developing world*, London: Croom Helm

Henderson, Jeff and Robin Cohen (1982) 'On the reproduction of the relations of production', in R. Forrest, Jeff Henderson and Peter Williams (eds) *Urban political economy and social theory*, Aldershot: Gower, 112–43

Hiebert, Daniel (2002) 'Cosmopolitanism at the local level: the development of transnational neighbourhoods', in Steven Vertovec and Robin Cohen (eds) *Conceiving cosmopolitanism*, Oxford: Oxford University Press

Hochschild, Arlie R. (2000) 'Global care chains and emotional surplus value', in Will Hutton and Anthony Giddens (eds) *On the edge: living with global capitalism*, London: Jonathan Cape, 130–46

Hollinger, David A. (1995) *Postethnic America: beyond multiculturalism*, New York: Basic Books

Holmes, Colin (1988) *John Bull's island: immigration and British society, 1871–1971*, Basingstoke: Macmillan

(1991) *A tolerant country: immigrants, refugees and minorities in Britain*, London: Faber & Faber

Homse, E. L. (1967) *Foreign labor in Nazi Germany*, Princeton: Princeton University Press

Huntington, Samuel P. (2004) *Who are we? America's great debate*, London: Simon & Schuster

Husbands, Christopher T. (1994) 'Crises of national identity as the "new moral panics": political agenda-setting about definitions of nationhood', *New Community*, 20 (2) January, 191–206

ICIHI (1986) *Refugees: dynamics of displacement*, London: Zed

ILO (1981) *Employment effects of multinational enterprises in industrialised countries*, Geneva: International Labour Organization

ILO (1984) *World labour report I: employment, incomes, social protection, new information technology*, Geneva: International Labour Organization

Jackson, J. A. (1963) *The Irish in Britain*, London: Routledge & Kegan Paul

Jackson, Peter and Jan Penrose (eds) (1993) *Constructions of race, place and nation*, London: UCL Press

Joly, Danièle and Robin Cohen (eds) (1989) *Reluctant hosts: Europe and its migrants*, Aldershot: Avebury

Jordan, Bill and Franck Düvell (2002) *Irregular migration: the dilemmas of transnational mobility*, Cheltenham, UK: Edward Elgar

Kant, Immanuel (1795) *Perpetual peace*, edited and with an introduction by Lewis White Beck (1957) Indianapolis: Bobbs-Merrill

Kaye, R. and R. Charlton (1990) *United Kingdom refugee admission policy and the politically-active refugee*, Research Papers in Ethnic Relations, No. 13, Coventry: Centre for Research in Ethnic Relations, University of Warwick

Keely, Charles B. and Patricia J. Elwell (1981) 'International migration: Canada and the US', in M. M. Kritz, Charles B. Keely and Silvano M. Tomasi (eds) *Global trends in migration: theory and research on international population movements*, New York: Center for Migration Studies, 181–207

Kempadoo, K. and J. Doezema (eds) (1998) *Global sex workers: rights, resistance and redefinitions*, New York: Routledge

Kidron, Michael and Ronald Segal (1981) *The state of the world atlas*, London: Heinemann Educational Books

Kindleberger, C. P. (1967) *Europe's post-war growth: the role of labor supply*, Cambridge: Harvard University Press

Kloosterboer, W. (1960) *Involuntary labour since the abolition of slavery: a survey of compulsory labour throughout the world*, Leiden: E. J. Brill

Koslowski, Rey (2004) 'Intersections of information technology and human mobility: globalization vs. homeland security', position paper prepared for ESRC/SSRC Money and Migration after Globalization Colloquium, University of Oxford, 25–8 March

(2005) 'Virtual border and e-borders', lecture to the Centre on Migration Policy and Society, University of Oxford, April

Kosmin, Barry (1981) 'Exclusion and opportunity: traditions of work amongst British Jews', in P. Braham et al., *Discrimination and disadvantage in employment: the experience of black workers*, London: Harper and Row in association with the Open University Press

Kotkin, Joel (1993) *Tribes: how race, religion and identity determine success in the new global economy*, New York: Random House

Kundu, Kunal Kumar (2004) 'India sees the value of its NRIs', *Asia Times Online*, 9 July (www.atimes.com)

Laclau, E. (1971) 'Feudalism and capitalism in Latin America', *New Left Review*, no. 67

Lal, Deepak (1992) 'The migration of money from a libertarian viewpoint', in B. Barry and R. E. Goodin (eds) *Free movement: ethical issues in the transnational migration of people and money*, New York: Harvester Wheatsheaf, 95–114

Lal, Victor (1990) *Fiji, coups in paradise*, London: Zed Books

Landa, M. J. (1911) *The alien problem and its remedy*, London: P. S. King & Son

LCHMT (1930) *Acts of the Privy Council of England*, London: HMSO

Louis, W. R. and J. Stengers (1968) *E. D. Morel's history of the Congo movement*, Oxford: Clarendon Press

McLuhan, Marshall (1962) *The Gutenberg gallery: the making of typographical man*, Toronto: University of Toronto Press

Magubane, Bernard (1979) *The political economy of race and class in South Africa*, New York: Monthly Review Press

Mandel, E. (1978) *Late capitalism*, London: Verso

Marie, C. G. (1983) *L'immigration clandestine et travail clandestin*, Paris: Ministère des Affairs Sociales et de la Solidarité Nationale

Marshall, Thomas Humphrey (1950) *Citizenship and social class, and other essays*, Cambridge: Cambridge University Press

Martin, Philip L. (1992) 'Foreign direct investment and migration: the case of Mexican maquiladoras', paper presented at the seminar on Migration and Development, tenth IOM Seminar on Migration, 15–17 September, Geneva

    (1993) 'Trade and migration: the case of NAFTA', *Asian and Pacific Migration Journal*, 2 (3) 329–67 [also consulted was a similar paper with the same title prepared for the Institute for International Economics, Washington, dated 1992]

    (1994) 'Epilogue: reducing emigration pressure: what role can foreign aid play', in W. R. Böhning and M.-L. Schloeter-Paredes (eds) (1994) *Aid in place of migration: selected contributions to an ILO–UNHCR meeting*, Geneva: International Labour Office

Marx, Karl (1976) *Capital*, vol. 1, Harmondsworth: Pelican in association with New Left Review

Massey, Doreen (1986) 'The international division of labour and local economic strategies: thoughts from London and Managua', unpublished paper, ESRC Conference on Localities in an International Economy, Cardiff, September

Massey, Douglas S., J. Arango, G. Hugo, A. Kouaouchi, A. Pellegrino and J. E. Taylor (1993) 'Theories of international migration: a review and appraisal', *Population and Development Review*, 19 (3) 431–66

(1994) 'An evaluation of international migration theory: the North American case', *Population and Development Review*, 20 (4) 699–751

Meissner, Doris M. (1993) *International migration challenges in a new era: policy perspectives and priorities for Europe, Japan, North America and the international community: a report to the Trilateral Commission*, New York: Trilateral Commission

Mintz, Sidney (1974) *Caribbean transformations*, Chicago: Aldine

Misham, E. J. (1970) 'Does immigration confer economic benefits on the host country?', in Institute of Economic Affairs, *Economic issues in immigration*, London: IEA

Molle, W., J de Koning and C. Th. Zandvliet (1992) *Migration for employment: can foreign aid reduce East–West migration in Europe? With special reference to Poland*, World Employment Programme, Working Paper 67, Geneva: ILO

(1994) 'Can foreign aid reduce East–West migration in Europe, with particular reference to Poland?' in W. R. Böhning and M.-L. Schloeter-Paredes (eds) *Aid in place of migration: selected contributions to an ILO–UNHCR meeting*, Geneva: International Labour Office, 39–72

Moore, Barrington (1966) *Social origins of dictatorship and democracy: lord and peasant in the making of the modern world*, Harmondsworth, Penguin

Moore, R. (1977) 'Migrants and the class structure of western Europe', in R. Scase (ed.) *Industrial society: class cleavage and control*, London: Allen & Unwin

Morgado, Cosme (1989) 'The role of members of parliament in immigration cases', *Policy Papers in Ethnic Relations*, No. 14, Coventry: Centre for Research in Ethnic Relations, University of Warwick

Nash, J. and M. P. Fernandez-Kelly (eds) (1983) *Women, men and the international division of labour*, Albany: State University of New York Press

Nayyar, Deepak (1994) 'International labor movements, trade flows and migration transitions: a theoretical perspective', *Asian and Pacific Migration Journal*, 3 (1) 33–48

Nevinson, H. W. (1906) *A modern slavery*, London: Harper

Nicol, Andrew (1981) *Illegal entrants*, London: Runnymede Trust

Nieboer, H. J. (1910) *Slavery as an industrial system: ethnological researches*, The Hague: Nijhoff

Noakes, T. D. (1980) Review of *Less than slaves: Jewish forced labor and the quest for compensation* by B. B. Ferencz (Boston: Harvard University Press, 1979), *Times Higher Educational Supplement*, 18 April

Nozick, Robert (1974) *Anarchy, state and utopia*, New York: Basic Books

Nyíri, Pál (2002) 'Mobility, entrepreneurship and sex: how narratives of modernity help Chinese women in Hungary evade gender constraints', in Pál Nyíri and Igor Saveliev (eds) *Globalizing Chinese migration: trends in Europe and Asia*, Aldershot: Ashgate

Nzula, Albert, I. I. Potekhin and A. Z. Zusmanovich (1979) *Forced labour in colonial Africa*, London: Zed Press

O'Neill, Onara (1993a) 'Permeable boundaries, multiple identities', Paper to the Fabian Society Philosophy Group, London School of Economics, December

  (1993b) 'Justice and boundaries', Paper to the Fabian Society Philosophy Group, London School of Economics, December

OECD (1987) *The future of migration*, Paris: Organization for Economic Cooperation and Development

Pahl, Ray E. (1984) *Divisions of labour*, Oxford: Basil Blackwell

Parker, Owen and James Brassnet (2005) 'Contingent borders, ambiguous ethics: migrants in (international) political theory', *International Studies Quarterly*, 49, 233–53

Passel, Jeff (2005) 'Unauthorised', *Migration News*, 12 (2) April [Available at http://migration.ucdavis.edu]

Pécoud, Antoine and Paul de Guchteneire (2005) *Migration without borders: an investigation into the free movement of people*, Global Migration Perspectives, Working paper, Global Commission on International Migration, No. 276, April, Geneva (www.gcim.org)

Peil, Margaret (1971) 'The expulsion of West African aliens', *Journal of Modern African Studies*, 9 (2) 205–29

Phizacklea, A. (2000) 'The politics of belonging: sex work, domestic work: transnational household strategies', in S. Westwood and A. Phizacklea, *Transnationalism and the politics of belonging*, London: Routledge, 120–45

Pieke, F., P. Nyíri, M. Thunø and A. Ceccagno (2004) *Transnational Chinese: Fujianese migrants in Europe*, Stanford, CA: Stanford University Press

Piore, M. J. and C. F. Sabel (1984) *The second industrial divide: possibilities for prosperity*, New York: Basic Books

Potts, Lynda (1990) *The world labour market*, London: Zed Books

Power, Jonathan (1979) *Migrant workers in Western Europe and the United States*, Oxford: Pergamon Press

Pratt, Mary Louise (1986) 'Scratches on the face of the country; or, what Mr Barrow saw in the land of the Bushman', in Henry Louis Gates Jr (ed.) *'Race', writing and difference*, Chicago: University of Chicago Press, 139–62

Rawls, John (1971) *A theory of justice*, Cambridge, MA: Harvard University Press

Rex, John and Sally Tomlinson (1979) *Colonial immigrants in a British city: a class analysis*, London: Routledge & Kegan Paul

Richardson, Peter (1976) 'Coolies and landlords, the North Randfontein Chinese miners' strike of 1905', *Journal of Southern African Studies*, 2 (2) 151–77

Roche, T. W. E. (1969) *The key in the lock: the history of immigration control in England from 1066 to the day*, London: John Murray

Rodney, Walter (1981) *A history of the Guyanese working people, 1871–1905*, London: Heinemann

Ruhs, Martin and Ha-Joon Chang (2004) 'The ethics of labour immigration policy', *International Organization*, 58, 69–102

Rumbaut, Ruben (1997) 'Assimilation and its discontents: between rhetoric and reality', *International Migration Review*, 31 (4) 923–60

Russell, Sharon Stanton (1992) 'Migrant remittances and development', paper presented at the seminar on Migration and Development, tenth IOM Seminar on Migration, 15–17 September, Geneva

Russell, Sharon Stanton and Michael S. Teitelbaum (1992) *International migration and international trade*, World Bank Discussion Paper No. 160, Washington, DC: World Bank

Russell, Sharon Stanton, Karen Jacobsen and William Deane Stanley (1990a) *Migration and development in sub-Saharan Africa*, vol. 1, *Country analyses*, World Bank discussion papers, 101, African Technical Department Series, Washington, DC: World Bank

(1990b) *International migration and development in sub-Saharan Africa*, vol. 2, *Country analyses*, World Bank Discussion Paper No. 102, African Technical Department Series, Washington, DC: World Bank

Sahlins, Peter (1992) *Boundaries: the making of France and Spain in the Pyrenees*, Berkeley: University of California Press

Said, Edward (1991) *Orientalism: Western conceptions of the Orient*, Harmondsworth: Penguin

Samora, J. and P. V. Simon (1977) *A history of the Mexican-American people*, Notre Dame: University of Notre Dame Press

Sampson, Edward E. (1993) *Celebrating the Other: a dialogic account of human nature*, Hemel Hempstead: Harvester Wheatsheaf

Sarup, Madan (1991) *Education and the ideologies of racism*, Stoke-on-Trent: Trentham Books

Sassen-Koob, Saskia (1979) 'Economic growth and immigration in Venezuela', *International Migration Review*, 13 (3) 455–71

(1983) 'Capital mobility and labour migration: their expression in core cities', in R. Timberlake (ed.) *Urbanisation in the world economy*, New York: Academic Press

(1984) 'The new labour demand in global cities', in M. P. Smith (ed.) *Cities in transformation*, Beverly Hills: Sage, 139–71

Schierup, Carl-Ulrick (1990) *Migration: socialism and the international division of labour*, Aldershot: Avebury

Schiller, G. (1994) 'Reducing emigration pressure in Turkey: analysis and suggestions for external aid', in W. R. Böhning and M.-L. Schloeter-Paredes (eds) *Aid in place of migration: selected contributions to an ILO–UNHCR meeting*, Geneva: International Labour Office, 203–40

Scholte, Jan Aart (1993) *International relations of social change*, Buckingham: Open University Press

Seagrave, Sterling (1995) *Lords of the rim: the invisible empire of the overseas Chinese*, New York: G. P. Putnam's Sons

Seeley, Sir John (1883) *The expansion of England*, Cambridge: Cambridge University Press

Sheffer, Gabriel (2003) *Diaspora politics: at home abroad*, Cambridge: Cambridge University Press

Shkurkin, Anatolii M. (2002) 'Chinese in the labour market of the Russian Far East: past, present, future', in Pál Nyíri and Igor Saveliev (eds) *Globalizing Chinese migration: trends in Europe and Asia*, Aldershot: Ashgate

Skeldon, Ron (2000) 'Trafficking: a perspective from Asia', *International Migration*, 38 (1) 7–30

Solzhenitsyn, A. (1979) *The Gulag archipelago, 1918–56*, London: Fontana

Speer, A. (1981) *The slave state: Heinrich Himmler's masterplan for SS supremacy*, London: Weidenfeld & Nicolson

Stark, O. (1991) *The migration of labor*, Cambridge, MA: Basil Blackwell

Starobin, R. (1970) *Industrial slavery in the old South*, New York: Oxford University Press

Sukhre, Astri (1994) 'A comprehensive refugee policy', in W. R. Böhning and M.-L. Schloeter-Paredes (eds) *Aid in place of migration: selected contributions to an ILO–UNHCR meeting*, Geneva: International Labour Office, 13–38

Swianiewicz, S. (1965) *Forced labour and economic development: an enquiry into the experience of Soviet industrialization*, London: Oxford University Press

Teitelbaum, Michael S. and Sharon Stanon Russell (1994) 'International migration, fertility and development', in Robert Cassen (ed.) *Population and development: old debates, new conclusions*, New Brunswick, NJ: Transaction Publishers

Tinker, Hugh (1974) *A new system of slavery: the export of Indian labour overseas, 1830–1920*, London: Oxford University Press
    (1984) 'Into servitude: Indian labour in the sugar industry, 1883–1970' in Shula Marks and Peter Richardson (eds) *International labour migration: historical perspectives*, London: Maurice Temple Smith for the Institute of Commonwealth Studies

Trapido, Stanley (1971) 'South Africa in a comparative study of industrialisation', *Journal of Development Studies*, 7 (3) 309–20

Troup, Edward (1925) *The Home Office*, London: G. P. Putnam & Sons

Turner, John Kenneth (1911) *Barbarous Mexico*, Chicago: Charles H. Kerr & Company van Onselen, Charles (1976) *Chibaro: African mine labour in Southern Rhodesia, 1900–33*, London: Pluto Press

Vertovec, Steven and Robin Cohen (eds) (1999) *Migration, diasporas and transnationalism*, Cheltenham: Edward Elgar

(2002) *Conceiving cosmopolitanism: theory, context and practice*, Oxford: Oxford University Press

Wallerstein, Immanuel (1974) *The modern world system: capitalist agriculture and the origins of the European world economy in the sixteenth century*, New York: Academic Press

(1979) *The capitalist world-economy*, Cambridge: Cambridge University Press

Wallman, Sandra (1986) 'Ethnicity and the boundary process in context', in J. Rex and D. Mason (eds) *Theories of race and ethnic relations*, Cambridge: Cambridge University Press

Walzer, Michael (1983) *Spheres of justice*, Oxford: Blackwell

Warren, B. (1980) *Imperialism: pioneer of capitalism*, London: Verso

Waters, Malcolm (1995) *Globalization*, London and New York: Routledge

Williams, Eric (1964) *Capitalism and slavery*, London: André Deutsch

Watts, Charlotte and Cathy Zimmerman (2002) 'Violence against women: global scope and magnitude', *Lancet*, 359, 1232–7

Womack, John (1979) 'The historiography of Mexican labour', in E. C. Frost, M. C. Meyer and J. Zoraida Vázquez (eds) *El trabajo y los trabajadores en la historia de México*, Mexico, DF and Tucson: El Colegio de Mexico and University of Arizona Press

Wu, Harry (2001) 'The violent machine', *New Internationalist*, 337, August

Yeates, Nicola (2004) 'A dialogue with "global care chain" analysis: nurse migration in the Irish context', *Feminist Review*, 77, 79–95

Zolberg, Aristide (1989) *Escape from violence: conflict and the refugee crisis in the developing world*, New York: Oxford University Press

Zolberg, Aristide et al. (1986) 'International factors in the formation of refugee movements', *International Migration Review*, 20 (2) 151–69

Zucker, N. L. and N. F. Zucker (1987) *The guarded gate: the reality of American refugee policy*, San Diego: Harcourt Brace Jovanivich

Index